JUST BUSINESS

JUST BUSINESS
Multinational Corporations
and Human Rights

John Gerard Ruggie

W. W. NORTON & COMPANY

NEW YORK * LONDON

For information about permission to reproduce selections from this book,
write to Permissions, W. W. Norton & Company, Inc.,
500 Fifth Avenue, New York, NY 10110

For information about special discounts for bulk purchases, please contact
W. W. Norton Special Sales at specialsales@wwnorton.com or 800-233-4830

Manufacturing by Courier Westford
Production manager: Anna Oler

ISBN 978-0-393-93797-8

W. W. Norton & Company, Inc.
500 Fifth Avenue, New York, N.Y. 10110
www.wwnorton.com

W. W. Norton & Company Ltd.
Castle House, 75/76 Wells Street, London W1T 3QT

1 2 3 4 5 6 7 8 9 0

Dedicated to
Kofi A. Annan—
son of Ghana, citizen of the world,
and my favorite boss

CONTENTS

PREFACE

This book is a reflection on an unusual global policy process. In 2005 what was then the United Nations Commission on Human Rights (now Human Rights Council) created a mandate for an individual expert to look anew into the subject of business and human rights, following years of failing to find common ground between opposing sides. The United Kingdom initiated the idea and secured its adoption. To give the position greater visibility, the Council asked the UN Secretary General to appoint the mandate-holder as his Special Representative. Kofi Annan, who was Secretary-General at the time, asked me to take on the assignment. The task I was initially given was largely descriptive: identifying what international human rights standards currently regulate corporate conduct, as opposed to the conduct of states and individuals; and clarifying the respective roles of states and businesses in safeguarding these rights.

In principle, the mandate included all types of businesses, large and small, although in practice it was intended to shed particular light on multinational corporations. Multinationals operate as globally integrated entities but are not subject to any single global regulator, thus creating governance challenges not posed by large national firms let alone corner grocers.

The mandate kept expanding until, six years later, the Human Rights Council unanimously endorsed a set of Guiding Principles on Business and Human Rights that I had developed, with the support of business associations and individual firms as well as civil society and workers organizations. Other international and national standard-setting bodies have incorporated the Guiding Principles, companies have begun to align their practices with them, and advocacy groups use them in their campaigning work. The Guiding Principles have even featured in a crucial case before the United States Supreme Court concerning whether and under what circumstances the 1789 Alien Tort Statute, originally intended to combat piracy among other things, applies to the overseas conduct of corporations irrespective of where their home base may be. My aim in this book is to explain how the mandate got from there to here, what it means for the protection of human rights against corporate-related harm, and what lessons it might hold for responding to ever-mounting global governance challenges.

Once I managed to raise sufficient funds from interested governments, I was able to recruit a superb team of professionals without whom it would have been impossible to construct the building blocks for the Guiding Principles: conducting intensive research and extensive consultations; organizing global networks of volunteers in law firms, universities, NGOs, and businesses; initiating pilot projects; and producing several thousand pages of documentary materials. The eight who crossed the finish line with me are Christine Bader, Rachel Davis, Gerald Pachoud, Caroline Rees, Andrea Shemberg, John Sherman, Lene Wendland, and Vanessa Zimmerman. Although we were physically scattered across time zones we worked together seamlessly as one team, with good humor making us forget insane workloads and travel itineraries. No mere words of thanks can do justice to their immense contributions. The Guiding Principles are as much their achievement as mine. Amy Lehr, Michael Wright, and David Vermijs were with us for parts of the journey and Jonathan Kaufman helped get me started.

The political process of moving the mandate's work through the Human Rights Council, a quasi-legislative body, was managed by five countries: Argentina, India, Nigeria, Norway, and Russia. Each played key roles within their respective regional groups. Norway had the overall lead. Ambassador Bente Angell-Hansen, together with her colleagues in Geneva and Oslo including Foreign Minister Jonas Gahr Støre, made gaining Council endorsement of the Guiding Principles a personal and national priority. On the business side, the mandate benefited greatly from cooperative relationships with the International Chamber of Commerce, the International Organisation of Employers, and the Business and Industry Advisory Committee to the Organisation for Economic Cooperation and Development. Civil society organizations participated in all forty-seven mandate consultations, and several, including Global Witness and Oxfam, worked particularly closely with us. It isn't possible to list all of the other institutions and individuals that became part of our extended team—for example, the more than two dozen law firms around the world that conducted pro bono research for us, on which I draw in subsequent chapters. But I do want to single out three legal analysts who followed the mandate closely and provided real-time big-picture assessments when

I was struggling through the weeds: Larry Catá Backer, Andrew Clapham, and Mark Taylor. I am also grateful to Mary Robinson, former President of Ireland and UN High Commissioner for Human Rights, for sharing her wisdom on human rights and speaking up for me when some questioned mine.

I dedicate this book to Kofi Annan, for whom I had the honor to work in several capacities for more than a decade. He is an inspirational leader, eager to try out-of-the-box approaches to seemingly insoluble problems, and a profoundly humane person, caring deeply about the individuals around him as well as about our common fate on this planet. He has been a great boss, wonderful mentor, and dear friend.

My deepest debt is to my wife, Mary Ruggie, whose human rights these past seven years have not benefited from my endeavors to advance them for others. My next project is to try and make that up to her.

Introduction

WHY BUSINESS AND
HUMAN RIGHTS?

Historians may look back at the 1990s as a "golden age" for the most recent wave of corporate globalization. Multinational firms emerged robustly, in larger numbers and greater scale than ever before. They weaved together integrated spheres of transnational economic activity, subject to a single global strategic vision, operating in real time, connected to and yet also transcending merely "national" economies and their "inter-national" transactions. Soon half of world trade comprised "internal" transactions within networks of related corporate entities, not the traditional arms-length "external" exchange among countries. Multinationals did well, and so, too, did people and countries that were able to take advantage of the opportunities created by this transformative process.

But others were less fortunate. Evidence mounted of sweatshop conditions and even bonded labor in factories supplying prestigious global brands; indigenous peoples' communities displaced without adequate consultation or compensation to make way for oil and gas company installations; foods and beverages firms found with seven-year-old children toiling on their plantations; security forces guarding mining-company operations

accused of shooting and sometimes raping or killing trespass-
ers and demonstrators; and Internet service providers as well
as information technology companies turning over user information to government agencies tracking political dissidents in
order to imprison them, and otherwise helping those governments to practice censorship.

How, in a world of profit-maximizing firms and states jeal-
ously guarding their sovereign prerogatives, can multinational
corporate conduct be regulated to prevent or mitigate such
human costs? How can companies that continue imposing them
be held to account? Globally operating firms are not regulated
globally. Instead, each of their individual component entities is
subject to the jurisdiction in which it operates. Yet even where
national laws exist proscribing abusive conduct, which cannot
always be taken for granted, states in many cases fail to implement them—because they lack the capacity, fear the competitive
consequences of doing so, or because their leaders subordinate
the public good for private gain.

As if by some dialectical force, individuals and communities
adversely affected by corporate globalization began to invoke the
language of human rights to express their grievances, resistance,
and aspirations. Human rights discourse—affirming the intrinsic
worth and dignity of every person, everywhere—became a common ground from which they began to challenge and seek redress
for the human costs of corporate globalization. Of course, such
efforts lack the material power of multinationals or states. What
has emerged, as a result, is a complex and dynamic interplay
between "the power of norms versus the norms of power."[1] But
this raises two further questions: How can human rights norms
most effectively be embedded in state and corporate practice to
change business conduct? More challenging still, how can this be
fostered and achieved in the global sphere where multinational

corporations operate but which lacks a central regulator? On these questions human rights proponents and global businesses have been locked in a stalemate. The main global public arena in which this clash has occurred has been the United Nations, which first attempted, unsuccessfully, to negotiate a code of conduct for multinational corporations as far back as the 1970s.[2]

In the late 1990s, the UN Sub-Commission on the Promotion and Protection of Human Rights began drafting a treaty-like document called "Norms on the Responsibilities of Transnational Corporations and Other Business Enterprises with Regard to Human Rights" ("Norms"). In 2003 it presented the text for approval to the Commission on Human Rights, its intergovernmental parent body (which later became the Human Rights Council). The Norms would have imposed on companies, within their "sphere of influence," the same human rights duties that states have accepted for themselves under treaties they have ratified: "to promote, secure the fulfillment of, respect, ensure respect of and protect human rights."[3] The Norms triggered a deeply divisive debate between human rights advocacy organizations and the business community. Advocates were fervently in favor because the Norms proposed making these obligations binding on companies directly under international law. Business vehemently opposed what it described as "the privatization of human rights," transferring to companies obligations that they believed belonged to states. The proposal found no champions on the Commission, which declined to act on it.

But enough governments from various regions of the world believed that the subject of business and human rights required further attention even if this particular instrument was unacceptable to them. Facing escalating advocacy campaigns and lawsuits, business itself felt a need for greater clarity regarding their human rights responsibilities from some reasonably objective and authoritative source. The governments also realized, however, that an intergovernmental process was unlikely to achieve much progress on so new, complex, and politically charged an issue without first finding some common terrain on which to move forward. Hence the Commission established a special mandate for an individual expert, which was intended to signal its concern but remain modest in scope: mainly to "identify and clarify" existing standards for, and best practices by, businesses, and for the role of states in regulating businesses in relation to human rights; and to research and clarify the meaning of the most hotly contested concepts in the debate, such as "corporate complicity" in the commission of human rights abuses and "corporate spheres of influence" within which companies might be expected to have special responsibilities. To add a degree of visibility to the mandate on the international stage, the Commission requested that the UN Secretary-General appoint the mandate-holder as his "Special Representative on the issue of human rights and transnational corporations and other business enterprises."

And so it came to be that in July 2005 I received a call from then–Secretary-General Kofi Annan, asking me to serve in this post. I had been Annan's Assistant Secretary-General for Strategic Planning during his highly successful first term, from 1997 to 2001. My main role was to help develop initiatives and messaging that advanced his vision of the United Nations in the new century—pushing the UN's concerns beyond the precincts of governments toward *We the Peoples,* the title of his celebrated report to the 2000 Millennium Summit. This included more effective engagement with civil society and the business community; devising the Millennium Development Goals, a global set of poverty reduction benchmarks; a more intense focus on universal rights, including promoting the idea that sovereignty should no longer be permitted to serve as a shield behind which governments feel free to butcher their own people; and several rounds of institutional reforms. In 2001, Annan was awarded the Nobel Peace Prize for, among other achievements, "bringing new life to the organization." I then returned to my previous life as an academic.

The new assignment, Annan explained in his call, required someone with knowledge of business and human rights issues but, in light of their political sensitivity, did not represent any of the major stakeholder groups involved—governments, businesses, and civil society—while being able to work with them all. It would be a two-year, part-time project that I could conduct without leaving Harvard. I would submit a report each year summarizing my work, conduct one or two consultations around the reports, and then recommend next steps. It seemed both interesting and doable, so I accepted. Little did I know then how challenging, how consuming, and how consequential this assignment would become.

I soon found myself at the center of a storm, as *The Economist* magazine later described it.[4] The prior polarized debate continued, barely stopping for a breather, because the main international human rights organizations did not accept that the "Norms" initiative had come to an end, having invested heavily in it. Amnesty International USA, for example, hailed the Norms as "representing a major step toward a global legal framework for corporate accountability."[5] The Amnesty International Secretariat had published a "glossy" (booklet) and lined up its national chapters for a global campaign in support of the Norms' ultimate adoption. The International Federation for Human Rights, comprised of more than 150 organizations in over 100 countries, sent me a letter stating that they "insist on the central role in the current debate of the Norms. . . . The question now is how to build on [them] and how to further implement these Norms; it is not whether to repeat this exercise all over."[6] But on the other side, business insisted on precisely the opposite. In a joint letter the Secretaries-General of the International Chamber of Commerce and the International Organisation of Employers, the largest global business associations, stated that I should "explicitly recognize that there is no need for a new international framework."[7] Instead, they urged me to focus on identifying and promoting good practices and providing companies with tools to enable them to deal voluntarily with the complex cluster of business and human rights challenges. When I asked representatives of governments in an informal Geneva meeting shortly after my appointment what advice they had for me, I got only one direct answer: "Avoid a train wreck." It was an inauspicious beginning.

Now fast-forward to June 2011—after six years, nearly fifty international consultations on five continents, numerous site visits and pilot projects, and several thousand pages of research reports. The UN Human Rights Council unanimously endorsed a set of "Guiding Principles" on business and human rights that I developed, with the support of all stakeholder groups—even though the Council had not requested any such thing. This also marked the first time that either the Council or its predecessor, the Commission, had "endorsed" any normative text that governments did not negotiate themselves. The Guiding Principles lay out in some detail the steps required for states and businesses to implement the "Protect, Respect and Remedy Framework" I had proposed to the Council in 2008 and which it had welcomed. It rests on three pillars:

1. the state duty to protect against human rights abuses by third parties, including business enterprises, through appropriate policies, regulation, and adjudication;

2. an independent corporate responsibility to respect human rights, which means that business enterprises should act with due diligence to avoid infringing on the rights of others and address adverse impacts with which they are involved;
3. the need for greater access by victims to effective remedy, both judicial and nonjudicial.

Simply put: states must protect; companies must respect; and those who are harmed must have redress.

At the conclusion of my mandate, the Council established an interregional working group of experts to oversee the UN's follow-up, focused on disseminating and implementing the Guiding Principles, supporting efforts to assist underresourced countries and smaller firms, and advising the Council on additional steps that may be required. Moreover, core elements of the Guiding Principles have also been adopted by other international standard-setting bodies, including the Organisation for Economic Co-operation and Development, the International Standards Organization, the International Finance Corporation, and the European Union. This has created an unprecedented international alignment coupled with a broad portfolio of means for securing implementation. Numerous companies and industry associations as well as governments have announced plans or have already begun to align their practices with the Guiding Principles. NGOs and workers' organizations are using them as a tool in their advocacy.

Thus, in a relatively short period of time the global business and human rights agenda shifted from a highly polarized and stalemated debate to significant convergence. This hardly means that business and human rights challenges have come to an end. Nor does it mean that everyone was equally happy with the outcome. But as I stated in my final presentation to the

Human Rights Council, it does mark the end of the beginning: by providing a common global platform of normative standards and authoritative policy guidance for states, businesses, and civil society.

This book has two aims. One is to tell the story of how we got from there to here in the case of my particular business and human rights mandate. That story is interesting in itself because success hinged on taking the main protagonists beyond their comfort zones, in which they had failed to achieve progress. Human rights advocates traditionally have favored going the international treaty route—what they call the "mandatory" approach. The business community traditionally has favored the combination of compliance with national laws where companies operate, coupled with the adoption of voluntary measures and promotion of best practices by business, arguing that the market then would drive the process of change. As for states, even when recognizing a need to act, they have also been conflicted. States that host multinationals compete for foreign investments; home states are concerned that their firms might lose out on investment opportunities abroad to less scrupulous competitors; and both are pressured by their respective business communities to favor voluntary over mandatory means.

But binding international standards require an international treaty—or the slow and gradual accretion of customary international law standards. What is more, the leading human rights NGOs were demanding some overarching and comprehensive legal framework, not merely corporate accountability in relation to a specific set of rights, and a framework that would impose duties on companies directly under international, not national, law. Apart from issues of effectiveness and enforcement, which I address in a later chapter, major treaties on complex and controversial human rights subjects require time for the subject to ripen and negotiations to conclude. To cite but one example, in 2007 the UN General Assembly adopted a "soft law" declaration, which is not legally binding, on the rights of indigenous peoples—one of a score of subjects that would have to be included in a business and human rights treaty—and it was twenty-six years in the making. At minimum, then, even the treaty approach would require interim measures to respond to current needs. As for market-based solutions, a pure model of self-regulation for so systemic a challenge as business and human rights lacks prima facie credibility, and it is difficult to imagine how the identification of best practices alone would get markets to a tipping point unless it was coupled with some authoritative way of determining what constitutes "best" as well as some means of dealing with those who act otherwise. Achieving significant progress, I believed, would require moving beyond the mandatory-vs.-voluntary dichotomy to devise a smart mix of reinforcing policy measures that are capable over time of generating cumulative change and achieving large-scale success—including in the law. This book recounts how I developed that heterodox approach and the results it is producing.

My second aim is to tell that story in such a way that broader lessons can be learned from it. Multinational corporations became the central focus of business and human rights concerns because their scope and power expanded beyond the reach of effective public governance systems, thereby creating permissive environments for wrongful acts by companies without adequate sanctions or reparations. Thus, business and human rights is a microcosm of a larger crisis in contemporary governance: the widening gaps between the scope and impact of economic forces and actors, and the capacity of societies to manage their adverse consequences. Yet human rights are not merely the proverbial canary in the coal mine signaling that all is not well; respect for human dignity also can and should be one of the foundations on which to bridge those governance gaps, from the local level to the global, and in the private sector no less than the public. Creating a more *just* business in relation to human rights involves finding ways to make respecting rights an integral part *of* business—that is, just making it standard business practice. However, there is no single Archimedean leverage point from which this can be achieved; success depends on identifying and leveraging a multiplicity of such points, but within the same normative and strategic framing. This is also true, I believe, of bridging other highly complex and controversial instances of global governance gaps, such as climate change, where neither centralized command-and-control regulation nor business as usual offers a viable solution.

This book comprises five chapters. The first summarizes some of the emblematic cases that put business and human rights on the international policy agenda, from the first global campaign against Nike for its overseas labor practices to the scathing criticism the CEO of Yahoo! faced in a U.S. congressional hearing for turning user information over to Chinese authorities. It also outlines more broadly the country and sector attributes in which corporate-related human rights abuses have tended to occur with greatest frequency. Chapter 2 explains why neither mandatory nor voluntary responses to these challenges by themselves provide a fix, and it outlines the contours of the heterodox approach I developed. Chapter 3 presents the Protect, Respect and Remedy Framework and the Guiding Principles for implementing it, which embody that approach. Chapter 4 lays out the strategic paths that led from my mandate's modest beginnings in "identifying and clarifying" things to the widespread endorsement and uptake of the Guiding Principles, which also may help inform similar efforts at closing global governance gaps. Chapter 5 addresses next steps in driving the business and human rights agenda forward. The remainder of this Introduction sketches in the context for the discussion to follow.

I. ECONOMIC TRANSFORMATION

Human rights traditionally have been conceived as a set of norms and practices to protect individuals from threats by the state, attributing to the state the duty to secure the conditions necessary for people to live a life of dignity. The postwar international human rights regime, a remarkable achievement in a world of self-regulating states, was premised on this conception. The idea that business enterprises might have human rights responsibilities independent of legal requirements in their countries of operation is relatively new and still not universally accepted.

Business and human rights became an increasingly prominent feature on the international agenda in the 1990s. The liberalization of trade, domestic deregulation, and privatization throughout the world extended the scope and deepened the impact of markets. The rights of multinational corporations to operate globally increased greatly through, for example, more robust and enforceable rules protecting foreign investors as well as intellectual property. According to one UN study, some 94 percent of all national regulations related to foreign direct investment that were modified in the decade from 1991 to 2001 were intended to further facilitate it.[8] At the same time, innovations in transportation and communication technology made those global operations cost-effective and near-seamless. But standards protecting people and the environment from the adverse effects of these developments did not keep pace. Manufacturing companies in the industrialized world adopted new business models sourcing their products in low-cost and weakly regulated overseas jurisdictions. Extractive companies, such as oil, gas, and mining, have always had to go where the resources were found, but by the 1990s they were pushing into ever-more-remote areas, often inhabited by indigenous peoples who resisted their incursion, or operating in host countries engulfed by the civil wars and other serious forms of social strife that marred that decade, particularly in Africa and parts of Latin America. Financial and professional services followed their clients abroad.

In relation to business and human rights, two features stood out on this transformed economic landscape: it became clear that many governments were unable or unwilling to enforce their domestic laws in relation to business and human rights, where such laws existed at all; and multinational firms were unprepared for the need to manage the risks of their causing or contributing to human rights harm through their own activities and business relationships. Advocacy groups organized campaigns against multinationals. Local communities began to push back, particularly against extractive companies with their large physical and social footprints. The language of human rights became part of the vernacular of affected individuals and groups around the world, emerging as an increasingly prevalent narrative challenging harmful corporate practices.

For their part, some businesses on the frontlines of globalization responded with policies and practices pledging to follow responsible business conduct—what became known as corporate social responsibility, or CSR for short. Companies began to establish CSR units to monitor workplace standards in their global supply chains, whether in consumer electronics or apparel and footwear. So-called fair trade labeling and other certification schemes extended similar promises, ranging from coffee beans to toys and forest products. A number of collaborative initiatives were established with industry partners, sometimes including NGOs and governments as well—the Kimberley Process to stem the flow of conflict diamonds being a notable example.

The political ethos of the era also contributed to the rapid expansion of CSR. To oversimplify only slightly, as governments moved toward greater deregulation and privatization, they promoted CSR initiatives and private-public partnerships in place of more direct governance roles. This was as true of Tony Blair's "Third Way" and Bill Clinton's "New Democrats" as it was of the Chinese government's privatization of state-owned enterprises and whatever obligations they had to workers and communities. A growing number of governments, including in emerging market countries, adopted national policies promoting voluntary CSR practices, such as having companies issue reports describing social and environmental policies though rarely actual performance. At the UN, I was a chief architect of the Global Compact, launched in 2000 and now the world's largest CSR initiative with some 7,000 company participants and national networks in more than 50 countries. It was not conceived as a regulatory instrument, however, for which it had no mandate from governments. It was designed as a learning forum to promote socially responsible practices in the areas of human rights, workplace standards, the environment, and anticorruption; share best practices and develop tools; recruit new actors into the CSR world, ranging from emerging market firms and their governments to investors and business schools; and to disseminate the CSR message to new market segments, such as mainstream investors. The Compact is the archetype of voluntarism, and many governments, including in the so-called BRIC countries (Brazil, Russia, India, and China), encouraged their firms to join.

CSR initiatives evolved rapidly, though less so in human rights than in other social and environmental domains. But they also exhibit built-in limitations: most do not address the role that governments must play in bridging governance gaps; they tend to be weak in terms of accountability provisions and remedy for harm; and by definition they involve only companies that voluntarily adopt such measures, in a form and at a pace of their own choosing. When I began my mandate, of the 80,000 or so multinational corporations in the world, fewer than 100 were known to have any policies or practices in place that addressed the risk of their involvement in human rights harm—beyond whatever specific and highly variable legal requirements might exist in their countries of operation.[9] Hence the drive by advocacy groups, affected individuals and communities, as well as other stakeholders to strengthen the international human rights regime directly by expanding its scope and provisions to encompass business enterprises.

II. THE HUMAN RIGHTS REGIME

The idea of human rights is both simple and powerful. The operation of the global human rights regime is neither. The simplicity and power of human rights reside in the idea that every person is endowed with "inherent dignity" and "equal and inalienable rights." The essence of rights is that they are considered entitlements, not granted by the grace or at the discretion of others. Hence, international human rights instruments speak of "recognizing" rights, not creating them. The international human rights regime was built on this precept, beginning with the Universal Declaration of Human Rights, adopted by the UN General Assembly in 1948 "as a common standard of achievement for all peoples and all nations."[10]

Two United Nations Covenants adopted in 1966, which entered into force a decade later, turned many of the Declaration's aspirational commitments into legal obligations, for states that ratified them, to respect the enumerated rights and ensure their enjoyment by individuals within their territory or jurisdiction. One covenant addresses such civil and political rights as life, liberty, and security of the person; fair trial and equal protection of the law; the right not to be subjected to torture or other forms of cruel, inhuman, or degrading treatment; not to be subjected to slavery, servitude, or forced labor; freedom of movement, thought, and conscience; the right to peaceful assembly, family, and privacy; and the right to participate in the public affairs of one's country.[11] The other covenant addresses economic, social and cultural rights, including the right to work and to just and favorable conditions of work; to form and join trade unions; to social security, adequate standards of living, health, education, rest, and leisure; and to take part in cultural life and creative activity.[12]

The Declaration and the two Covenants together constitute the "International Bill of Human Rights." They have been supplemented by seven additional UN treaties, further elaborating upon prohibitions against racial discrimination, discrimination against women, and torture; affirming the rights of the child, migrant workers, and persons with disabilities; and prescribing national prosecution or extradition for the crime of forced disappearance. The International Labour Organization (ILO) has adopted a series of conventions regarding workplace rights, again with ratifying states as the duty-bearers within their respective jurisdictions. Its Declaration on Fundamental Principles and Rights at Work, representing what might be described as "the core of the core" internationally recognized workplace rights, includes freedom of association and the effective recognition of collective bargaining; elimination of all forms of forced or compulsory labor; effective abolition of child labor; and elimination of discrimination in respect to employment and occupation.[13]

Separate regional human rights regimes exist in Europe, Africa, and the Americas. In 2002 the Rome Statute of the International Criminal Court (ICC) came into force. The Court can prosecute individuals for genocide, crimes against humanity, and war crimes in a number of circumstances: where national courts of states parties are unwilling or unable to investigate and prosecute such crimes; where the accused is a national of a state party, or the alleged crime took place on the territory of a state party irrespective of the nationality of the accused; or where a situation is referred to the Court by the UN Security Council, in which case none of the other criteria need to be met. The Security Council did so, for example, in the case of Sudan's President Omar Hassan Ahmad Al Bashir who was indicted on ten such counts; Saif al-Islam Gaddafi, son of Colonel Muammar Gaddafi, also stands indicted. But the Court lacks the power on its own to bring them to The Hague for trial. The combination of these institutional innovations—the UN and regional human rights systems, coupled with the ILO core conventions and the ICC—constitute what is often referred to as the twentieth-century "human rights revolution."

However, the UN-based human rights regime is neither designed nor is it capable of acting as a centralized legal regulative system. To begin with, states adopt and ratify treaties voluntarily; none can be forced to do so. Not all states have ratified all human rights treaties, and not all implement those they have ratified. Even where legal obligations do exist, the regime lacks adjudicative and enforcement powers. Expert committees (called treaty bodies) are established under each treaty to receive, and make observations on, reports that states parties are required to submit periodically regarding their adherence to treaty obligations, and to offer recommendations and commentaries on treaty provisions in light of evolving circumstances. But most countries do not accept treaty bodies' views as a source of law. In addition, many economic, social, and cultural rights—the rights to adequate standards of living, health, and education, for example—are subject to "progressive realization," that is, achievement to the maximum extent permitted by available resources. This adds to the difficulty of assessing compliance, especially in relation to third parties such as business enterprises. In any case, implementation falls to the individual state—its domestic judicial and political processes—and to such assistance or leverage as other actors, whether states, international agencies, or activist groups, are willing and able to bring to bear on those whose performance falls short.

These challenges are magnified where the conduct of multinational corporations is involved. By multinational corporations I simply mean companies that conduct business in more than one country, whether as vertically integrated firms, joint ventures, corporate groups, cross-border production networks, alliances, trading companies, or through ongoing contractual relationships with off-shore suppliers of goods and services; and whether publicly listed, privately held, or state-owned.

International human rights treaties impose duties on states that ratify them. In turn, companies are subject to whatever standards states apply to them in their home and host countries. For example, the United States has not ratified the economic, social, and cultural rights covenant, nor has China ratified the covenant on civil and political rights. Thus, variations exist as to which international human rights standards apply in different countries, and multinational corporations are likely to be subject to different, sometimes contradictory, standards in their countries of operation. Advocates have urged that companies should simply adhere to international standards where they are more protective of human rights than national laws. But that can be tricky to satisfy when the two are in conflict. An internationally recognized right may be legally prohibited by the host country—the right to form unions, for example, or gender equality. There are no authoritative international means to resolve such conflicts of standards, and requiring divestment in all such cases might do more harm than good and would be resisted by multinationals and states alike.

Only in limited instances has international human rights law reached companies directly—for instance, if they commit or are complicit in the commission of egregious violations, such as genocide, war crimes, torture, extrajudicial killings, forced disappearances, and slavery-like practices. But even then, the law can be enforced only in jurisdictions where such charges can be brought against companies. The most prominent venue has been the United States under the Alien Tort Statute. This was adopted in 1789 to combat piracy, protect ambassadors, and ensure safe conducts. It was discovered by human rights lawyers more than two hundred years later as a means for foreign plaintiffs to bring civil suit in federal courts, first against individuals and then against multinational corporations as "legal persons," for violating "the law of nations or a treaty of the United States." The pathbreaking case against a major corporation was *Doe v. Unocal,* in which Burmese villagers sued the California-based oil company (subsequently bought by Chevron) for complicity in forced labor, rape, and murder allegedly committed by Burmese military units constructing and securing Unocal's pipeline route through that country to Thailand. That case was settled, reportedly for $30 million. Some one hundred such cases have been brought against multinationals in U.S. courts, but the statute's applicability to legal as opposed to natural persons is currently under review by the U.S. Supreme Court.

Furthermore, while the layperson's image of multinational corporations may reflect their actual day-to-day practices, that image does not conform to prevailing legal doctrine. Multinational corporations operate as globally integrated entities or "groups." But legally, the parent company and each subsidiary are construed as a "separate legal personality," subject to the individual jurisdictions in which they are incorporated. Therefore, the parent company is generally not liable for wrongs committed by a subsidiary, even where it is the sole shareholder, unless the subsidiary is under such close day-to-day operational control by the parent that it can be seen as being its mere agent. This makes it extremely difficult for any jurisdiction to regulate the overall activities of multinationals, and it can prevent victims of corporate-related human rights abuses from obtaining adequate remedy.

Yet the global corporate group has numerous ways of influencing governments. It may threaten to withdraw its investment from a host country. It may be able to sue the host government under binding international arbitration if its investment has been negatively affected by legislative or administrative measures. Ad hoc panels of arbitrators may construe such measures as breaching an international investment agreement, even if the host country is merely enacting its international human rights obligations in a nondiscriminatory manner as between domestic and foreign investors. Additionally, the subsidiary has access to its home country as a potential source of political leverage, and through it to the international financial institutions, such as the World Bank, on which the host country may depend for support.[14] Multinationals have also been known to threaten to relocate their home base in order to avoid robust domestic regulation: for example, there are more mining companies listed in Canada than in any other country, and the threat of setting up headquarters somewhere else hung over an ultimately unsuccessful effort through a private member's bill in Parliament to impose regulations on those companies' overseas operations.[15] Thus, under the existing rules of the game, multinational corporations pose regulatory challenges not posed by national firms, while the absence of a global regulator makes those rules hard to change.

Having said all that, multinational corporations are also subject to a variety of pressure points to which states and national companies may be less vulnerable. Each link in the distributed network of a multinational increases the available entry points through which other social actors can seek to leverage the overall company brand, its operations and resources, with the aim of improving the firm's social performance—by investors, consumers, and home country regulatory agencies; local communities and civil society actors, often supported through transnational links; and a company's own personnel concerned about differential treatment of human rights in overseas-vs.-home-country workplaces and communities. In short, the conduct of multinational corporations may be susceptible to a diverse set of economic and social compliance mechanisms that differ from those affecting states and national companies—so that lessons from the experience of the latter may not fully capture the opportunities for driving change through multinationals.

International law must and will continue to evolve in order

to guide and govern aspects of the business and human rights agenda. But the desire to achieve that goal through negotiating an all-encompassing legally binding framework is at best a long-term proposition. Even if one were to start down that road, responding to existing needs requires identifying and undertaking shorter-term measures as well. And great care must be taken when promoting longer-term solutions to avoid having an idealized image of the end point—the perfectly conceived and perfectly enforced international legal regime—trump consideration of effective measures in the here and now. Amartya Sen, philosopher and Nobel laureate in economics, takes to task those who view human rights as mere "proto-legal commands" or "laws in waiting."[16] His view is that human rights are "strong ethical pronouncements as to what should be done. They demand acknowledgement of imperatives and indicate that something needs to be done for [their] realization. . . ."[17] But he does not believe that the very idea of human rights is or should be confined to their role as either laws' antecedents or effects. To do so would unduly constrict—Sen actually uses the term "incarcerate"—the social logics and processes other than law that drive evolving public recognition of rights.[18] I share Sen's view.

In short, this is what I found when I surveyed the global business and human rights picture at the outset of my mandate: a deeply divided arena of discourse and contestation lacking shared knowledge, clear standards and boundaries; fragmentary and often weak governance systems concerning business and human rights in states and companies alike; civil society raising awareness through campaigning against companies, and sometimes also collaborating with the most willing among them to improve their social performance; and occasional lawsuits against companies brought mainly through the innovative use of legal provisions that were originally intended for different purposes. To gain a more granular understanding of these issues in one particularly troubled industry sector, I arranged a visit to the Peruvian highlands in January 2006, where conflicts between mining companies and communities had been in the news—and continue to be to this day.

III. CAJAMARCA

The province of Cajamarca, roughly the size of the U.S. state of Rhode Island, lies in northwestern Peru. It is a region of pastures and peasants, largely indigenous, who farm and graze cattle. One of the most heavily mined areas in Peru, a country where mining accounts for more than 60 percent of export earnings, it is also one of the poorest. Not far from the provincial capital of the same name is South America's largest gold mine, Minera Yanacocha. It is a joint venture between Denver-based Newmont Mining (just over half of the shares) and Compañía de Minas Buenaventura, Peru's largest publicly traded precious metals company. The International Finance Corporation (IFC), the World Bank's private sector arm, holds a 5 percent stake as part of its program to promote economic growth through private investment in the natural resources sector.

In October 2005 the mine was the subject of lengthy investigative journalism coverage in the *New York Times* and a program in the *Frontline* series of the U.S. Public Broadcasting System.[19] Newmont invited me to visit the operation to see firsthand their efforts to respond to their challenges. Through Oxfam America, I also arranged to meet with community leaders and NGOs in Cajamarca and Lima. I make no attempt here to fully assess the situation at that time, but merely provide a brief sketch of the main factors and actors as I saw them, and of how they informed my framing of the UN assignment I had been given.

Yanacocha rises from approximately 10,000 to nearly 14,000 feet, with the operation spread across 600 square miles.[20] Constructing the site involved blasting mountaintops, and mining it consists of progressively carving out a pit roughly 60 square miles in size, carting off boulders and leaching them in a diluted cyanide solution. This process allows small deposits of gold to be separated from the rock and then smelted—30 tons or more of rock and earth for every ounce of gold—while consuming large quantities of water and releasing a variety of minerals and heavy metals, including mercury. The water then needs to be treated and the by-products contained and disposed of safely.

There are few if any issues related to the operation that did not generate some level of community objection and opposition from the start: allegations of inadequate consultation and compensation for the resettlement of people; lack of job opportunities for locals (mining is capital-intensive and many jobs require skills that locals do not have and would need to be trained for); inward migration of people looking for work, bringing overcrowding and rising crime, including prostitution, to the city; large numbers of dead fish floating belly-up in lakes and streams around the mine. In 2000, a company-contracted truck spilled more than 300 pounds of mercury over 25 miles of road, reportedly poisoning 900 people. In 2004, Newmont sought to expand its operation to a nearby mountain, Cerro Quilish, which is said to have spiritual significance for the indigenous population and supplies Cajamarca with water. In response, more than 10,000 people laid siege to the mine. Police and special forces fired tear gas; someone fired bullets. Newmont gave in and halted the project. By the time I arrived in early 2006, the company had identified another site nearby, Minas Conga, where it hoped to apply the lessons learned at Yanacocha to better manage its relations with the community. Newmont did develop far more extensive and sophisticated CSR policies and practices over time. Nevertheless, in November 2011, operations at the Conga site, at $4.8 billion the biggest single investment in Peru's history, had to be suspended when the government imposed a state of emergency, citing public safety concerns raised by massive protests that had become inextricably entwined with national and local political rivalries.[21]

At the time of my visit, Newmont was not alone among mining companies in lacking effective systems to assess its potentially adverse impacts on the environment and community before operations or expansions began; or for engaging stakeholders in ongoing consultations thereafter, addressing grievances about any harm done. In the wake of Cerro Quilish, Yanacocha's general manager told a reporter that he spent 70 to 80 percent of his working hours dealing with social issues—which suggested to me that he, personally, was attempting to be the missing system. During my visits to the mine I saw that Newmont had established water treatment facilities and a lab to sample the outflow, and I was taken to a small and well-stocked fishing pond fed by recycled water. The company also supported the development of local crafts, including textiles and jewelry; helped transport teachers to rural schools; improved some roads; and hooked up a nearby part of the city to its own electrical grid. Its CSR and community relations teams were growing in numbers and expertise. But their approach seemed largely reactive to external pressure and ad hoc in nature. It lacked metrics for measuring the costs of conflicts with the community or the benefits of getting the relationship right. And the company's operations division continued to dictate time lines based on production and cost targets. It was evident that the company did not enjoy a strong "social license to operate"—broad acceptance of the company's operations by the community. And still, as if deliberately to reinforce that vulnerability, Roque Benavides, the CEO of Buenaventura, Newmont's local joint venture partner, famously said in a 2005 television interview: "I hate the term social license. I do not understand what social license means . . . I expect a license from the authorities . . . I don't expect a license from the whole community."[22]

But the authorities in some respects were part of the problem. Peru had ratified numerous UN human rights treaties, but as in many countries then and now, their relevance for business and human rights was poorly understood let alone acted upon. Moreover, a Maoist insurgency and economic mismanagement had driven out foreign investment in the 1980s, so successor governments felt obliged to extend extremely favorable terms for its return. Corruption and crony capitalism were endemic. The prevailing social structure pitted better-off Peruvians of Spanish descent against the far poorer indigenous populations in mining communities. Effective public sector capacity was lacking: I was told that the entire Cajamarca province had only three environmental inspectors, and they worked out of the Ministry of Mines. By the time of my visit a new regulation had been adopted that returned a share of mining revenues to local communities, but I saw little evidence of it. More than 60 percent of the population lived below the poverty line, infrastructure was lacking, housing dilapidated, and schooling scarce. Local authorities (I met with the mayor) seemed content for the company to be the focus of community pressure for better public services. Indeed, as recently as January 2012 the country's Prime Minister complained that much of the resources sent to the Cajamarca region had not been spent on programs benefiting local residents.[23]

Other governmental actors were also connected to the operation. The IFC is a coinvestor and made some efforts to improve relations between the community and the mine. Following the mercury spill in 2000, the Office of the Compliance Advisor/ Ombudsman (CAO), which is empowered to respond to complaints against IFC projects, offered to commission an independent health study, but it could not be carried out, according to an official report, in part "due to lack of cooperation from government authorities."[24] But CAO did facilitate a five-year process intended "to improve dialogue and resolve issues of concern" between the company and community. At the time of my visit the IFC had just adopted social and environmental performance standards that it would require clients to meet, in part triggered by its experience with projects like Yanacocha, but of course they could not be imposed retroactively. For its part, the U.S. government in the 1990s had been deeply involved in persuading the Peruvian authorities to grant Newmont the majority holding in Yanacocha, from high levels in the State Department to the CIA station chief in Lima. But even today the U.S. has no policy to guide or assist American-based multinationals with managing the environmental and human rights risks of their overseas operations, nor to advise or support local governments in coping with the massive impacts of an operation such as Yanacocha.

Community resistance and protests can arise spontaneously. In Cajamarca they have also had a leader, a former Catholic priest by the name of Marco Arana, known as Father Marco to his supporters and "the red priest" to his adversaries. (He was defrocked in 2010 when he became a candidate for electoral office). Arana runs an NGO called GRUFIDES (Group

for Training and Intervention for Sustainable Development). In
a long meeting with him in 2006, I asked Arana how it came to
be that blocking access to the mine was such a routine practice
in Cajamarca. He responded: "They don't listen to us when we
come with small problems, so we have to create big ones." It
was Arana who negotiated with Newmont to halt their plans
to mine the Quilish site after the intense 2004 blockade. He
later reported that his movements were being followed and
his life threatened, alleging that individuals in Forza, Yanacocha's security contractor, were involved.[25] I was introduced to
Arana through Oxfam America, which has a local affiliate in
Lima and at that time also provided funding to GRUFIDES,
as did a German Catholic development NGO, Misereor. Both
organizations have followed UN business and human rights
discussions closely, including my mandate. Thus, in addition
to providing operating support to community groups, these
international NGOs serve as a bridge between the global and
local levels: communicating developments in global debates to
local communities, and in turn making it possible for local civil
society to get its message out and connect with others on the
global stage. For instance, in 2005, Oxfam arranged for Arana
to attend Newmont's annual general meeting in Denver, where
he attracted the attention of shareholders and the press, and
also had a brief exchange with the CEO. Misereor funded the
participation of a number of civil society representatives from
developing countries in several of my mandate consultations.
Through such networks, civil society actors track and seek to
influence the political and corporate spheres.

I have entitled chapter 2 "No Silver Bullet." There is no single
or simple way to resolve enormously complex situations such as
I found in Cajamarca. Besides, a Peruvian mining operation
is not a representative sample of the universe of global busi-

ness and human rights challenges that my mandate was meant to address. However, Yanacocha did bring into relief many of the elements that a systematic global effort to achieve stronger protection against corporate-related human rights harm would have to address: specifying the respective roles and responsibilities of governments and business enterprises, and how those responsibilities should be discharged; the need for greater access to effective remedy for those whose human rights are harmed by corporate conduct; and providing clear benchmarks by means of which other social actors—for example, civil society, workers' organizations, investors, and consumers—can hold both to account. Contrary to the preferences expressed by international business at the outset of my mandate, such an effort would require the development of an authoritative international framework that could serve as a common platform for the different actors. But contrary to the aspirations expressed by the major international human rights organizations, this could not plausibly be achieved through some single overarching international legal instrument.

IV. PRINCIPLED PRAGMATISM

The successful expansion of the international human rights regime to encompass multinational corporations must activate and mobilize all of the rationales and organizational means that can affect corporate conduct. Thus, I made it clear from the outset that I would follow a course I called principled pragmatism: "an unflinching commitment to the principle of strengthening the promotion and protection of human rights as it relates to business, coupled with a pragmatic attachment to what works best in creating change where it matters most—in the daily lives of people."[26] Columbia University historian Samuel Moyn's keen insight, that "human rights are not so much an inheritance to preserve as an invention to remake," is particularly appropriate in the business and human rights context.[27] I envisioned a model of widely distributed efforts and cumulative change. But for such efforts to cohere and become mutually reinforcing, they require an authoritative focal point that the relevant actors can rally around. Providing that focal point became my strategic aim.

Developing the Guiding Principles that were the mandate's final product itself was subject to several guiding principles. I briefly flag them here; they are elaborated throughout subsequent chapters. The most fundamental was to recognize and build on a core feature of the governance of multinational corporations that we saw very clearly in the Cajamarca case. Three distinct governance systems affect their conduct in relation to human rights: the system of public law and policy; a civil governance system involving external stakeholders that are affected by or otherwise have an interest in multinationals; and corporate governance, which internalizes elements of the other two. In the academic literature this institutional feature of the global economy is described as polycentric governance.[28] Each governance system constitutes a complex cluster of its own. The system of public law and policy, stipulating formal rules for corporate conduct, operates at two levels: the individual home and host countries of multinationals, and the international sphere wherein states act collectively and international institutions operate. The system of civil governance, expressing social expectations of corporate conduct, operates locally in host and home countries, and it is increasingly connected transnationally. Corporate governance also comprises two dimensions. One reflects the integrated strategic vision, institutional design, and management systems that these companies require to function as globally operating businesses, including enterprise-wide risk management. The other reflects the separate legal personality of corporate parents and their affiliates, by which they partition their assets and limit their liabilities. In order to achieve better protection for individuals and communities against corporate-related human rights harm, each of these governance systems needs to be mobilized and pull in compatible directions.

To foster that mobilization the Guiding Principles draw on the different discourses that reflect the respective social roles these governance systems play in regulating corporate conduct. For states the focus is on the legal obligations they have under the international human rights regime as well as policy rationales that are consistent with, and supportive of, those obligations. For businesses, beyond compliance with legal obligations that may vary substantially across countries in their applicability or enforcement, the framing centers on how to manage the risk of involvement in adverse human rights impacts through effective human rights due diligence and alternative dispute resolution mechanisms. For people whose human rights are harmed by corporate conduct and civil society generally, the Guiding Principles constitute a basis of further empowerment through provisions for engagement with business, and by providing authoritative benchmarks by which to judge the conduct of governments and businesses—and also by which governments and business can judge one another. Within the human rights community, this unorthodox formulation initially was the most controversial conceptual move I made because it was not considered to be fully "rights-based." But for reasons that will become clearer as we go along, more than any other step, it accounted for the Guiding Principles' success.

Moreover, human rights advocacy groups and lawyers

have focused their efforts on legal means to hold companies to account for human rights abuses after they have been committed, in the hope and expectation that this would serve as a deterrent to future violations. The Guiding Principles also make recommendations for strengthening judicial remedy. But I sought equally to expand the preventative side of the equation directly: identifying and developing enabling rules for states and companies alike to avoid or at least reduce the incidence of corporate-related human rights abuses. I did so for two reasons. For one, as Father Arana noted and my subsequent research confirmed, many instances of what turned out to be major corporate-related human rights crises began as lesser grievances that companies ignored and which then escalated. Better to catch those early. For another, preventative measures can be implemented more readily—in terms of time, resource requirements, and overcoming political resistance—than judicial systems can be built or reformed.

Finally, I wanted at all cost to avoid having my mandate become entrapped in or sidetracked by lengthy intergovernmental negotiations over a legal text, which I judged would be inconclusive at best and possibly even counterproductive. It was too important to get the parameters and perimeters of business and human rights locked down in authoritative policy terms, which could be acted on immediately and on which future progress could be built. Therefore, I took great care to base the mandatory elements of the Guiding Principles on the implications of existing legal standards for states and businesses; to supplement those with policy rationales intended to speak to the interests and values of both sets of actors; and in addition to Human Rights Council endorsement, I also sought to have core elements of the Guiding Principles adopted as policy requirements by other entities with the authority and responsibility to do that. In short, I aimed for a formula that was politically authoritative, not a legally binding instrument. In a 2007 law journal article summarizing mandate work to date, I stated my expectation that legal developments would follow from such an effort, but as "precision tools" on specific matters that already enjoyed a degree of international consensus.[29] As we shall see, this has begun to happen.

V. THE UN MANDATE

One additional set of introductory remarks is necessary to explain the institutional and procedural conditions under which my mandate operated. To put it very simply: I had no power but persuasion, and virtually no material resources to conduct the mandate other than those I was able to raise myself. To borrow my Kennedy School colleague Joseph Nye's celebrated term, this was "soft power" in its softest form.[30]

"Special Procedures" is the name given to independent experts appointed by the UN Human Rights Council to examine either specific country situations or thematic issues. My mandate fell into the latter category. According to the official description, thematic mandates address "major phenomena of human rights violations worldwide." It continues: "The Mandate-holders of the special procedures serve in their personal capacity, and do not receive salaries or any other financial compensation for their work." What it does not say is that, beyond limited staff support and minimal allowances for travel, these mandates are provided with no resources for their implementation. I began with the part-time assistance of a professional in the Office of the High Commissioner for Human Rights and three round-trip tickets between Boston, my home base, and Geneva, where the Human Rights Council meets and the High Commissioner is located. I then assembled a team of outstanding professionals who conducted research and managed the process—lawyers, policy analysts, an M.B.A., and two diplomats on leave from their foreign ministries. We worked with networks of volunteers in numerous countries, benefited from pro bono research provided by more than two dozen law firms, and convened extensive consultations around the world. I viewed the mandate not merely as a research and drafting exercise, but as a global campaign of sorts, to reframe a stalemated policy debate and establish global standards and authoritative policy guidance. Funding for these activities came in the form of voluntary contributions from governments structured as research grants to Harvard's Kennedy School of Government, which administered the entire project. Chapter 4 explains how I deployed and amplified this soft-power resource base to achieve the mandate's aim.

Such mandates are created by a Human Rights Council resolution (previously by the Commission). The Council comprises forty-seven UN member states elected on a regional basis for three-year terms; all other states may participate fully as observers but cannot vote. Resolutions require a lead sponsor from among Council members. The United Kingdom led the creation of the initial mandate, working with four other core sponsors: Argentina, India, Nigeria, and the Russian Federation. This cross-regional grouping—one core sponsor from each of the five regional groups (African, Asian, Eastern European, Latin American and Caribbean, Western European and "Others")— reflected the importance of working across north-south and east-west political divides, which is essential to achieving progress in this field. Norway took over the lead in 2006, when the Council replaced the Commission.

My formal role was to submit annual reports to the Council for its consideration, and to the UN General Assembly for informational purposes. Reports are submitted in written form and then presented in a brief oral statement to the respective bodies. This is followed by an "interactive dialogue" in which delegations make statements and ask questions, and the mandate-holder is given a brief opportunity to respond. At Human Rights Council sessions, accredited nonstate observers, including international organizations, NGOs, and business associations, also have the opportunity to speak. The Council's formal response to recommendations proposed by a mandate-holder also comes in the form of a resolution, negotiated by delegations.

My mandate evolved in three phases. Neither of the latter two was foreordained; each required specific Council renewal. The first, from 2005 to 2007, was the "identifying and clarifying" phase. The Council commended that work for providing a better understanding of the issues at stake and invited me to take another year to develop recommendations on how best to advance the agenda. I returned in 2008 with only one recommendation: that the Council respond favorably to the Protect, Respect and Remedy Framework I elaborated in that year's report, on the premise that the most urgent need was not for a shopping list of items but for a foundation on which thinking and action could build. The Council unanimously "welcomed" the Framework and extended my mandate another three years, asking me to "operationalize" it: to provide concrete and practical guidance for its implementation. That is how I came to present the Guiding Principles in 2011—comprising thirty-one principles, each with a Commentary elaborating its meaning and implications. The Council endorsed the Guiding Principles, again unanimously. At that point I had reached the six-year maximum term limit for any mandate-holder, and an expert working group was appointed to oversee the next phase.

The reader may be forgiven for thinking that this is an unusual way to advance the global protection of human rights. But that is how governments in their wisdom have structured the process. And it can have advantages. When I formally presented the Guiding Principles to the Human Rights Council and asked for its endorsement, the Algerian ambassador took the floor to say that governments could not endorse a normative text that they did not negotiate themselves. Instead, he proposed submitting the Guiding Principles to an intergovernmental process for "further examination and enrichment"—diplomat-speak for killing the initiative. I responded, with uncharacteristic passion, that I was old enough to have witnessed the collapse of repeated efforts by governments to negotiate UN codes of conduct for multinational corporations going back to the 1970s, some of which I knew the ambassador had been involved in earlier in his career. All had failed, I reminded the Council, because governments could not reach consensus. Here, I said, you have an instrument that you could never have negotiated yourselves, given the diverse and conflicting interests at stake. All stakeholder groups support it. So seize the opportunity, I urged. Endorse it, and then move on. They did.

Subsequent chapters elaborate on how and why this happened, beginning with a more detailed look at specific instances and overall patterns of business and human rights challenges that put this issue onto the international agenda in the first place.

I end this Introduction on a confessional note. The most difficult puzzle I faced at the outset of this project was existential. My task was to identify ways for getting business enterprises to address their adverse human rights impacts, especially in countries that lack the capacity or sometimes the will to stand up to large multinational firms. But who was I to be? Was I advocate or diplomat? The independent scholar I had been before or a mediator between companies and people with grievances against them? Who were my allies, and who might the adversaries be? By what means could I overcome the predictable obstacles and perhaps even turn one or two into an advantage? There was no road map or user's manual to guide me.

One of the early consultations I convened brought together leaders of indigenous peoples groups from across Latin America. I asked them to brief me about the issues that mattered most to them. Then I shared my tentative plans for how I intended to pursue my assignment. At the end one of the participants, dressed in traditional attire, pulled me aside. She thanked me for bringing the group together and listening to their concerns. Then she added: "But you speak too much from your head, and not enough from your heart. If you want to succeed, you have to let your heart speak." It took me a few seconds to come up with a response. But when I did, my existential crisis was resolved. I said words to this effect: "I will let my heart drive my commitment to human rights. But I'll need my head to steer the heart through the very difficult global terrain on which we are traveling." That is also the spirit in which this book is written.

JUST BUSINESS

Chapter One

THE CHALLENGE

In mid-2010, the *New York Times* reported a rash of suicides by workers at Foxconn Technology in Shenzhen, China.[1] The article included allegations of abusive workplace conditions and practices, underage workers on assembly lines, severe health and safety risks that turned into deadly industrial accidents, falsification of overtime records, and improper disposal of toxic wastes. Foxconn is the world's largest contract electronics supplier. Among other products, it manufactures iPhones and iPads for Apple. The reports were shocking to lovers of Apple products. But what was most surprising was how long Apple had managed to avoid close international scrutiny and criticism, not only for its apparent failure to address these problems in a major supplier, but contributing to some of them through its own practices as a buyer—such as when CEO Steve Jobs suddenly decided to revamp the screen on a new iPhone model a little more than a month before it was due in stores, thereby imposing an assembly-line overhaul and production schedule on the supplier that simply could not be met without violating already weak workplace standards.[2] Not until February 2012 did Apple announce that it would permit a third party, the Fair Labor Association (FLA), to audit its supplier facilities in China. The FLA, a Washington-based nonprofit, has been conducting factory monitoring for upscale brands since 1999.

There is no comprehensive and authoritative global repository of information on the involvement of multinational corporations in human rights abuses. But there are intuitive as well as anecdotal grounds for suspecting an actual increase starting in the 1990s. In part, it is a matter of sheer numbers: there are many more companies operating in more countries around the world, increasingly in sociopolitical contexts that pose novel challenges for corporate leadership, especially with regard to human rights. In addition, for many companies, going global has meant adopting network-based operating models involving multiple layers of corporate entities and different forms of corporate relationships spread across numerous countries. Networks, by their very nature, involve divesting a certain degree of control over significant operations, substituting negotiated relationships for hierarchical structures. While this form of extended enterprise may enhance the economic efficiency of the overall enterprise, it also has increased the challenges firms face in managing their global value chains—the full range of activities required to bring a product or service from its conception to end use. As the number of connections in value chains increases, so too do the vulnerabilities for the global enterprise as a whole posed by each link in the chain.

Thus, quite apart from acts of malfeasance or bad judgments by corporate officials, these structural shifts, if left unattended, increase the probability that "the company" in some manifestation or other will run afoul of prevailing social norms, its own corporate principles, and in some cases the law as well. The core business and human rights challenge lies in devising instruments of public, civil, and corporate governance to reduce these tendencies and to provide remedy for harm where it does occur. The first step in this endeavor is to develop a more systematic picture of the problem itself.

In the present chapter, I describe a sampling of cases that became emblematic of the array of business-related human rights challenges, and tease out from them some of the key dimensions they illustrate about globalization and governance in relation to human rights. I also present broader patterns and correlates of alleged corporate abuse, so as to widen and deepen our understanding of the challenges.

I. EMBLEMATIC CASES

Nike

In a 2004 *Harvard Business Review* article, Simon Zadek, then the CEO of AccountAbility, a cutting-edge niche consultancy, described Nike, a premium brand in athletic shoes and sportswear, as being "a leader in progressive practices," exemplifying the successful completion of a five-step progression on "the path to corporate responsibility."[3] It wasn't always so. Only a few years earlier Nike was the poster child for what critics described as a global race to the bottom, of all that was wrong with corporate globalization.

Nike was one of the first manufacturing companies to completely outsource production: starting in Japan in the 1970s, shifting to South Korea and Taiwan in the early 1980s, and, when the cost model there came under pressure, convincing owners of its Korean and Taiwanese supplier factories to set up shop elsewhere in Asia, especially China and Indonesia. By 1990, Nike's overseas sourcing factories employed more than 24,000 workers, supplying more than 6 million pairs of shoes,

among other items.[4] Serious trouble for Nike began in Indonesia
in the early 1990s, when American labor rights activists in part-
nership with local institutions began to interview workers, issue
newsletters, and lay the bases for campaigns. Initially, the issue
was low wages and abusive working conditions—19 cents (U.S.)
an hour, according to workers interviewed on a CBS news
report, while basketball superstar Michael Jordan received $20
million a year for endorsing the product.[5] Workers also claimed
that they could not leave factory premises except on Sundays
and even then needed a permission letter from management.
Child labor was added to the list of particulars when a photo-
graph of a twelve-year-old Pakistani boy stitching Nike soccer
balls appeared in *Life* magazine.[6] Later in the decade Nike suppliers in Vietnam were found to be using an adhesive containing a chemical known to cause respiratory illness, in doses that
exceeded even weak Vietnamese standards.[7]

A perfect storm of bad publicity enveloped Nike throughout the 1990s.[8] It included violent strikes at several Indonesian
factories; union-organized summer internship programs for
American college students on how to campaign against large
corporations, out of which emerged a national coalition to put
on alert campus stores selling, and athletic teams wearing, Nike
and similarly sourced products; an "International Nike Day
of Protest" in twenty-eight U.S. states and twelve countries;
plus highly unflattering feature roles in the acerbic Doones-
bury cartoon strip, a Michael Moore documentary, two CBS
news programs, the "Battle of Seattle," as the demonstrations
that shut down the World Trade Organization 1999 ministerial
meeting came to be known, as well as in Naomi Klein's book,
No Logo, often referred to as the "bible" of the antiglobalization
movement.[9]

With the company and its stock price battered, Phil Knight,

founder and CEO, conceded in a 1998 speech at the National Press Club in Washington, D.C.: "The Nike product has become synonymous with slave wages, forced overtime and arbitrary abuse. I truly believe that the American consumer does not want to buy products made in abusive conditions."[10] Nike became a founding member of the UN Global Compact, a multistakeholder forum for promoting good corporate practices. At the inaugural press conference in 2000, a reporter asked Secretary-General Kofi Annan if being on the same stage as Phil Knight wasn't like supping with the devil. Annan's quick riposte: the angels don't need our help. Still, the activists weren't quite done. After Nike had taken initial steps down the path described by Zadek and begun to issue progress reports on its workplace practices, a California resident brought suit against the company alleging that the reports violated a state statute prohibiting false and misleading advertising. Nike claimed the reports constituted free speech and, therefore, were protected by the First Amendment. But the California Supreme Court ruled them commercial speech and the U.S. Supreme Court remanded the case without ruling. Nike settled.[11]

Like many companies in similar situations, Nike initially had responded to the barrage of criticism by saying, in essence: "We don't own this problem. These are not our factories. We have no equity relationship with them. We simply buy their products." Nike was right in strictly legal terms, but wrong to infer that this answer would suffice. Transnationally connected social actors clustered around Nike's global supply chain, linking abusive conditions in supplier factories to receptive audiences in Nike's home market, and pressuring the brand to accept an ownership share in the problem. Global brands that outsource all production are far more commonplace today than when Nike got started. And well beyond such "virtual companies," far-flung and complex supply chains are now ubiquitous in the global economy, found in every industry, and on every continent. Much has been learned about managing human rights challenges in supply chains, and Nike has been a significant innovator in the process.[12] But the core questions of precisely who is responsible for what, for how much of it, and the most effective ways to respond remained unresolved as a matter of policy and law.

Bhopal

The massive leak of methyl isocyanate gas at Union Carbide's pesticide plant in Bhopal, India, not long after midnight on December 3, 1984, remains the most deadly industrial disaster in history. *Newsweek* described the morning-after scene in these words: "It looked like a neutron bomb had struck. Buildings were undamaged. But humans and animals littered the low ground, turning hilly Bhopal into a city of corpses."[13] Thousands of people living in the shantytowns near the facility died immediately and more succumbed in subsequent weeks, months, and years; tens of thousands were disabled, and children were born with disabilities. More than a quarter-century later, closure still has not been attained. As recently as March 2008, a group of survivors and supporters marched the 800 kilometers (500 miles) from Bhopal to Delhi to stage a sit-in at the Prime Minister's office, others chaining themselves to his official residence's gate, campaigning for promised health care, safe drinking water, and other forms of social and environmental support.[14] Along the way, the tragedy generated scores of lawsuits at state and federal levels in India and the United States, and a $470-million Union Carbide compensation payment approved by the Indian government in 1989 that victims felt was inadequate and represented "surrender before the multinational"[15]—and which it took the government seventeen years fully to disburse.[16]

Unlike the Nike case, there seemed little question about who "owned" this problem: Union Carbide (UC) did. But who, exactly, was Union Carbide? The American parent company owned 50 percent of UCIL (Union Carbide India Limited), with the government of India and private shareholders owning the rest; the stock traded on the Calcutta exchange. UCIL was operated largely as an independent subsidiary. By Indian government policy, management and workers were almost entirely Indian nationals, and Indian courts had jurisdiction over UCIL. Within days of the disaster the government of India filed criminal negligence charges against UCIL and seized its assets.[17]

American lawyers with power-of-attorney forms in hand arrived in Bhopal at roughly the same time, and soon after filed more than 145 suits in U.S. courts against the parent company UC on behalf of Bhopal victims, in amounts up to $20 billion per case.[18] In April 1985, the government of India also sued UC and UCIL in U.S. federal court, for an unspecified amount.[19] Why bring suit against the parent company? One reason is that it might have been at fault, despite the relative independence of its subsidiary. For example, claims were made about defects in the plant's original design, which preceded UCIL's existence, and that safety features were lower than for similar plants in the United States. Another reason is that parent companies have deeper pockets than their subsidiaries; the combined annual revenues of UCIL's fourteen plants in India at the time of the disaster were $200 million. But why bring these cases in U.S. courts? Because of the simple fact that as a rule courts in the host country do not have jurisdiction over parent companies located in other countries, only the locally operating subsidiaries.

All U.S. court cases were consolidated into one, in the Federal District Court of Southern New York (these were common-law tort cases; the Alien Tort Statute was not yet in play in relation to corporations). Union Carbide argued that the plaintiffs had no standing in U.S. courts, therefore the case should be dismissed based on the *forum non conveniens* doctrine: essentially meaning that this court is not the appropriate venue for this particular case—it should be in India's own courts. The presiding judge agreed, adding, with gratuitous rhetorical flourish: "To deprive the Indian judiciary of this opportunity to stand tall before the world and to pass judgment on behalf of its own people would be to revive a history of subservience and subjugation from which India has emerged."[20] The government of India did not see it that way and appealed, but the U.S. Court of Appeals upheld the ruling on two grounds.[21] First, that it was easier to try the case in India because the witnesses were there, many spoke no English, and the documents were mostly in Hindi, thus "India has greater ease of access to the proof than does the United States." Second, the court concluded that the relationship between UC and UCIL was arms-length, and although the parent company was responsible for the initial design, UCIL engineers had made many changes to it.

It was twenty-six years before any former members of the senior management of UCIL were convicted by an Indian court; they were sentenced to two years and fined the equivalent of US$2,100.[22] Warren Anderson, UC's CEO at the time, was declared a fugitive from justice by a Bhopal court when he failed to appear for a hearing, and it subsequently issued a warrant for his arrest. The United States declined to have Anderson extradited. In part inspired by the Bhopal case, the plaintiffs' bar in several countries began to search for different ways that corporate parents might be held legally accountable for the actions of their subsidiaries. They would soon discover one in the Alien Tort Statute.

Shell in Nigeria

By now there is a substantial literature explaining "the paradox of plenty" or "the resource curse," of how an abundance of natural resources in countries lacking good governance can end up being a curse for their people.[23] Multinational corporations in the extractive sector—mining, oil and gas—have played key roles in this detrimental dynamic, whether unwittingly or willingly. No case has attracted more attention or had a bigger impact on the business and human rights agenda than Royal Dutch Shell in what is known as Ogoniland, a tribal area of 400 square miles and 500,000 inhabitants in Rivers State, Nigeria, where Shell started pumping oil in the 1950s.

Nigeria is one of the world's largest oil producers. Oil is its single largest source of revenue, foreign exchange, and GDP. Nigeria nationalized the oil industry in the 1970s and engages in joint ventures with foreign operating companies, acting through subsidiaries. The Nigerian states in which operations are carried out receive only a small fraction of the oil revenues. It was raised to 13 percent by the country's 1999 constitution, but independent studies conclude that too little of it reaches the areas and people who are most adversely affected by the operations.[24] The misuse of public funds by state governments, as well as corruption and outright theft at all levels, take their toll. A teacher in a local Rivers State school with no desks for its students is quoted in a Human Rights Watch report: "The important things we need are textbooks, instructional materials, and a toilet."[25] Public health facilities and infrastructure fare no better. Indeed, according to the World Bank, more than half of all Nigerians live on less than $2 a day.[26]

Of all the critical issues raised by the Shell experience, I focus on two. The first relates to the fact, which is still poorly understood by many companies, that they require not only a legal but also a social license to operate. Their legal license is issued by state agencies; their social license can be granted only by communities—which, as in the Nike case, may have a transnational dimension. The second issue concerns corporate complicity in human rights abuses committed by other parties that are connected to a company. Both are key dimensions of today's globalization and governance nexus.

Shell held its Ogoniland concession—its legal license to operate—through the Shell Petroleum Development Company (SPDC), an unincorporated joint venture between Royal Dutch Shell and the Nigerian National Petroleum Corporation. From the outset there were harmful environmental effects of oil exploration and production in Ogoni territory. Land and water pollution from spills undermined livelihoods that depended on farming and fishing. In addition, "[v]illagers lived with gas flares burning 24 hours a day (some for over 30 years) and air pollution that produced acid rain and respiratory problems. Above-ground pipelines cut through many villages and former farmland."[27] As early as the 1970s, Ogoni chiefs wrote to the SPDC and the military governor of Rivers State complaining about the environmental degradation, to little effect. Shell either dismissed or discounted the extent of its operations' environmental impact.[28] Moreover, oil production, like mining, being capital intensive, provided few jobs to locals. In short, local communities were paying the cost but enjoying few if any benefits, while billions of dollars worth of oil was pumped out of the ground around them: $5.2 billion for the life of the concession, according to Shell; several multiples of that, according to the Ogoni.[29]

Gradually but steadily, civil unrest mounted. Shell began attempts to reduce tensions by investing in community development projects, such as building schools and clinics, digging wells, and constructing water storage facilities. At times these efforts actually made the problem worse because they benefited some groups but not rival groups, alienating the latter.[30] In 1992 the Movement for the Survival of the Ogoni People was established. One of its leaders was Ken Saro-Wiwa, a writer and environmental activist. The movement proclaimed an Ogoni Bill of Rights, including environmental restoration, more favorable revenue sharing, and greater political autonomy.[31] Neither the government nor the company responded. Instances of sabotage against pipelines and other company property increased. In 1993, 300,000 Ogoni, more than half of the region's population, took to the streets to protest against Shell. Shortly thereafter, in response to the beating of an SPDC worker, the company withdrew its staff from Ogoniland and suspended its operation there.[32]

In short, Shell had lost its social license to operate—the community no longer tolerated its presence. Fifteen years later, with Shell still unable to return because the security situation had deteriorated further in the interval, the Nigerian government revoked the company's legal license to operate the concession as well, although it remains a major producer elsewhere in the country. Nigeria's democratically elected President Yar' Adua concluded that "there is a total loss of confidence between Shell and the Ogoni people. So, another operator acceptable to the Ogoni will take over."[33]

Now turn to the issue of complicity. In the context under discussion, complicity refers to involvement by companies in human rights abuses committed by another party, including government agents. Its legal meaning has been spelled out most clearly in the area of aiding and abetting international crimes, where it means knowingly providing practical assistance or encouragement that has a substantial effect on the commission of a crime by another.[34] In 2009, after more than a decade of procedural wrangling in U.S. courts, Shell faced a civil trial on charges brought by plaintiffs that included Ken Saro-Wiwa's son, accusing Shell of contributing to a campaign of terror and murderous repression against the Ogoni region, culminating in what was widely agreed to have been a sham trial under Nigeria's military dictatorship and Saro-Wiwa's subsequent execution by hanging.[35]

The case against Shell might never have been possible if not for the once-obscure Alien Tort Statute, adopted by the First Congress in 1789 to provide redress for such violations of customary international law as piracy, mistreatment of ambassadors, and violation of safe conducts.[36] The statute, which lay largely dormant until it was rediscovered by human rights lawyers in the 1980s, makes it possible for foreign plaintiffs to bring civil claims in U.S. federal courts if the alleged acts rise to the level of gravity and universal condemnation of the originally recognized offenses. The pathbreaking case against a major corporation was *Doe v. Unocal* in 1997. Companies against which cases are brought need not be U.S. nationals but merely have a substantial business presence in the country.[37]

The charges against Shell take us back to where we left off above. As civil unrest in Ogoniland turned to vandalism and outright violence, government troops increasingly were called upon to protect Shell installations, including aboveground pipelines running through the territory that were often deliberately damaged or tapped—"bunkered" is the slang term—and the diverted oil sold. After Shell suspended its operation in 1993, the government began a massive crackdown on the Ogoni. Villages were burned, women raped, and some 2,000 people killed between then and 1995.[38] Shell denied any collusion with the government at the time, although it later admitted to at least one instance of providing limited assistance to the military.[39] Amid growing intra-Ogoni factionalism, four moderate chiefs were brutally hacked to death by a mob in 1994. Saro-Wiwa and fourteen others were arrested and charged with their murder. Saro-Wiwa was not present at the scene of the killings, but he was accused of having incited the mob elsewhere.[40] Nine of the accused, including Saro-Wiwa, were convicted in a special military tribunal and sentenced to hang. A worldwide campaign to prevent the executions was launched, which included appeals from other African leaders. But Nigeria's military ruler, General Sani Abacha, paid no heed. Enormous pressure was put on Shell to speak out and use its influence for clemency, but on the day the verdicts were announced, Shell issued a statement that meekly said, "A commercial enterprise like Shell cannot and must never interfere with the legal process of any sovereign state."[41]

The public outcry and condemnations following the execution of the Ogoni Nine prompted Shell to undertake considerable reflection. It revised its "General Business Principles," developed new corporate social responsibility policies and tools, and set out to become a leader on business and human rights.[42] But the situation in the oil-rich Niger Delta continued to worsen. Violence and criminality now extend well into the Gulf of Guinea, which is exceeded for acts of piracy only by the coast off Somalia. Crude oil exports from Nigeria have continued to decline.

Just as the *Wiwa v. Shell* trial was set to begin in New York in June 2009, Shell and the Ogoni plaintiffs agreed to a $15.5 million settlement. Neither side got to tell its story to a jury, no facts were established, and both sides claimed victory.[43]

Yahoo in China

The generation of business and human rights advocacy that emerged in the 1990s developed both the content and forms of its campaigns largely around the experiences of the extractive sector and working conditions in global supply chains. Bhopal continued to occupy an honored place in deference to the enormity of the tragedy, the inability of victims to hold the parent company to account, and in solidarity with the strong ongoing domestic civil society commitment in India to right the wrongs. Then suddenly, as if by a lightning bolt, a sector was struck that had been viewed as a friend to the cause, the very platforms that allowed civil society actors around the world to connect, share information, and coordinate strategies: Internet service providers.

Internet censorship is practiced in one form or another by numerous governments.[44] None has a system as sophisticated as China's. It comprises multiple layers: carefully controlled gateways—called the "Great Firewall" by the cognoscenti—separating China's Internet from the global network; powerful network control tools sold to China by such companies as Cisco; and "net nannies," or Chinese bureaucrats that scan emails, blogging sites, and instant messaging services using electronic filters to look for politically sensitive words. "But the main burden of routine censorship is left to Internet service providers [ISPs] and suppliers of content."[45] ISPs have their own watch lists, and frequently receive additional guidance from the authorities on what is and is not permissible. Moreover, they are called upon to identify users whom state agents regard with suspicion. Yahoo is one such service provider.

In April 2004, Shi Tao, a Beijing journalist, used his Yahoo China email account, which did not contain his name, to send an article, for which he used a pseudonym, to a pro-democracy publication and Web site in New York.[46] The article included a summary of a classified document containing government instructions about how the media should act to help prevent social unrest in the run-up to the fifteenth anniversary of the 1989 Tiananmen crackdown. Two days later the authorities requested information linked to Shi's email account from Yahoo. The company complied. Shi was arrested not long thereafter and in March 2005 was sentenced to ten years in prison for revealing state secrets.

The reputational hit to Yahoo in the United States and elsewhere was severe, but as late as 2006, Jerry Yang, Yahoo's CEO, said "If you want to do business [in China] you have to comply."[47] This earned Yang and Michael Callaghan, Yahoo's general counsel, a memorable reprimand at a 2007 Congressional hearing from Tom Lantos, then chairman of the House Foreign Affairs Committee and a Holocaust survivor: despite being a technology and financial giant, Lantos thundered, "Morally you are pigmies."[48]

A "Global Online Freedom Act" made it through the committee stages in the House of Representatives. Among other things, it would have required the President to designate a list of "Internet-restricting countries," and if a U.S.-based company was asked by the authorities of a designated country to hand over personal-identifying data, the U.S. Justice Department would decide if the request constituted "legitimate law enforcement purposes."[49] No comparable bill was introduced in the Senate and the effort went no further. As for Yahoo, perhaps

chastened by Yang's widely publicized and enormously embar-
rassing encounter with Lantos, it settled a legal claim filed by
Shi Tao's family and set up a "Yahoo! Human Rights Fund" to
provide assistance to persons in China who have been impris-
oned for expressing their views using the Internet. In 2008,
Yahoo went on to form the Global Network Initiative, along
with Google and Microsoft, civil society organizations, university centers, and a small number of socially responsible investment firms. Its aim is to develop common approaches regarding
how to respond to government policies and practices that violate freedom of expression and privacy.[50]

This story, like the others recounted above, is interesting in
and of itself. But I also tell it to identify a genuine dilemma posed
for multinational corporations where national law significantly
contradicts, and does not offer the same level of protection, as
international human rights standards. National authorities typically demand compliance with their law, while other stakeholders advocate adherence to international standards—as might the
company itself, for reasons of principle or simple consistency of
corporate policy. The issue of Internet privacy and freedom of
expression is a new manifestation of this dilemma. But it has
long existed over the question of freedom of association and
collective bargaining as well in relation to gender equality. Unilateral legislation alone, as was proposed in the U.S. Congress,
would not resolve the dilemma; it might make it even messier.[51]
But there are no authoritative international rules for companies,
and no international supreme court to decide what's right.

The Google story in China played out somewhat differently.
Whether driven by conscience or stagnant market share, after
a series of sophisticated online attacks that Google said originated in China, the company announced it would stop censoring
search results on its China site. Initially, Google automatically

redirected its users to its Hong Kong site, which is uncensored. But that move threatened to lose the company its legal license to operate in China. So Google reached a compromise with the Chinese government whereby the company provided a link to google.com.hk that users could click to conduct searches—an extra step that risked market share but would allow Google to avoid participating in censorship.[52] Its market share continued to plummet, and in January 2012, Google announced plans to expand its presence in China through mobile applications, product search tools, and other services that do not require censorship.[53]

I have called these cases emblematic because they, and a handful of others like them, put the issue of business and human rights firmly on the global agenda. Each raised questions for which there were no generally agreed answers at the time, either in terms of well-established social norms or international law. Thus, each posed a challenge for my mandate as well. The Nike case was the first of many to raise the question of what responsibilities a brand has toward workers in low-cost and poorly regulated jurisdictions who manufacture their products—the supply-chain issue, in short. Bhopal was an extremely complex case on the basis of which one could draw many different lessons, but the most decisive for the victims surely was their inability to "pierce the corporate veil," as it is known—that is, to reach behind the separate legal personalities of parent and subsidiary companies. Shell in the Ogoni territory is the quintessential case of unattended social license issues escalating into alleged corporate complicity in gross human rights abuses. The failure to obtain or sustain a social license to operate on numerous occasions has led companies to rely on government or private security forces to protect their assets from demonstrators or even to try to impose acquiescence on local communities, including by the illegal use of force and other forms of coercion. Finally, Yahoo illustrates the dilemma created for companies when legal demands in the host country contradict widely accepted international standards, possibly the company's own values, and the expectations of vast numbers of people whom journalist and activist, Rebecca MacKinnon, describes as "netizens"—"citizens" of online communities.[54]

I note one final point before proceeding: all of these cases involved Western multinationals. This is unexceptionable insofar as they were in the vanguard of corporate globalization—and they were most likely to be susceptible to local and transnational civic pressures, and occasionally to being hauled into a court of law. But what about the growing numbers of multinationals from emerging-economy countries? Are they not situated differently in both respects? And does this not change the picture going forward? To the extent that a firm answer is possible at this point, the picture remains mixed. Generally, non-Western multinationals lag behind their Western counterparts in adopting good practices. But they are not immune to some of the dynamics that we saw in the emblematic cases, particularly pushback by communities in which the companies operate. For example, Chinese multinationals are discovering what "social license to operate" means in places ranging from Africa to the Andes, where their operations have triggered protests and even riots. In Wasit province, Iraq, activities by the China National Petroleum Corporation led to the creation of a local human rights movement.[55] And one of the mining operations the government of Peru suspended under a state of emergency decree in December 2011 is owned by China's Zijin Mining Group.[56] Brazilian companies have encountered similar problems in Mozambique. Such firms have a way to go to catch up with their Western counterparts on better managing community relations, but reports suggest that some are trying.[57]

Having now looked at a handful of individual cases to familiarize ourselves with this terrain, I turn to examine broader patterns in corporate-related human rights challenges and the contexts in which they tend to occur.

II. PATTERNS AND CORRELATES

In the absence of any official data, the most reliable inventory of public allegations against companies around the world is the Business & Human Rights Resource Centre (BHRRC), a small London-based nonprofit.[58] Its online library includes information about company policies and practices in more than 180 countries and its Web site gets more than 1.5 million hits per month. If the Centre determines that an allegation against a company is serious enough to merit being included in its regular weekly updates, it invites the company to respond. As part of the preparatory work for developing the Protect, Respect and Remedy Framework, I examined this subset of allegations between February 2005 and December 2007. Eliminating duplicates (including ongoing news reports of legal proceedings) yielded 320 distinct cases.

Typically, complaints against companies did not come neatly packaged in human rights language, and they often included multiple claims. Although some were expressed in precise terminology, the rest had to be coded. The universe of rights I used as the benchmark for this purpose are those recognized in the International Bill of Human Rights (IBHR), which consists of the Universal Declaration of Human Rights, the International Covenant on Civil and Political Rights, and the International Covenant on Economic, Social, and Cultural Rights. To this I added the ILO's Declaration on Fundamen-

tal Principles and Rights at Work. As indicated in the Introduction, with only rare exceptions companies are not directly
subject to international law but to domestic laws wherever
they operate. Therefore, my use of the IBHR and the ILO
declaration for coding purposes is intended to indicate which
internationally recognized *rights* companies are alleged to have
violated, not which *laws*.

With these preliminaries established, we can turn to the matter at hand. I asked four questions: what, who, where, and how?
What internationally recognized human rights was the company alleged to have adversely impacted? Whose rights? Where
did the action take place—in what region and what sector? And
how was the company involved: directly, or indirectly? The following discussion summarizes the main findings.[59]

Which Rights?

Tables 1 and 2 show that companies can have adverse impacts—
or are alleged to have had such impacts—not only on a variety of labor rights, as one would expect, but also on the broad
range of human rights generally.

Table 1 lists all the labor-related rights violations that were
reflected in the 320 allegations. Those cited most frequently
were the right to work (for example, arbitrary or retaliatory
terminations of employment, mass layoffs without compensation, hiring large numbers of casual workers with limited or
no guarantees of employment); the right to just and favorable
remuneration (often pay below legal minimums and inaccurate
computation of overtime); and the right to a safe work environment (health and safety issues). Although there were numerous allegations about companies frustrating workers' rights to

Table 1: Labor Rights Impacted

Freedom of association	Right to equal pay for equal work
Right to organize and participate in collective bargaining	Right to equality at work
Right to nondiscrimination	Right to just and favorable remuneration
Abolition of slavery and forced labor	Right to a safe work environment
Abolition of child labor	Right to rest and leisure
Right to work	Right to family life

organize, freedom of association did not rank in the top three—which may tell us more about workers' low expectations than about companies' high adherence to the standard. There were also numerous claims that companies falsified or destroyed records prior to factory inspections or audits. Other allegations included tolerating routine sexual harassment as well as physical and sexual abuse of female workers; employing child labor; and seizing workers' identity papers, which can amount to forced labor. At the "egregious" abuses end of the spectrum, the cases included allegations of companies contracting security forces and collaborating with paramilitary forces that beat, tortured, and even killed labor organizers or demonstrators.[60]

Table 2 lists all the nonlabor rights reflected in the allegations. Health-related rights dominated this category and involved such issues as community exposure to pollutants and other toxins. Rights related to the security of the person were involved in nearly half of all cases (recall the Nigerian military's

Table 2: Nonlabor Rights Impacted

Right to life, liberty, and security of the person	Right of peaceful assembly	Right to privacy
Freedom from torture or cruel, inhuman, or degrading treatment	Right to marry and form a family	Right to social security
Equal recognition and protection under the law	Freedom of thought, conscience, and religion	Right to an adequate standard of living (including food, clothing, and housing)
Right to a fair trial	Right to hold opinions, freedom of information and expression	Right to physical and mental health; access to medical services
Right to self-determination	Right to political life	Right to education
Freedom of movement	Minority rights to culture, religious practice, and language	Right to participate in cultural life, the benefits of scientific progress, and protection of authorial interests

actions against the Ogoni as an extreme example). The right to an adequate standard of living was next; examples include the degradation of farmland or fishing sites as a result of corporate activity. Numerous cases concerned the displacement of communities for the benefit of extractive or infrastructure projects: the failure to obtain informed consent from community, inadequate compensation, making no provisions for relocating and rehousing displaced people, and benefiting from forcible displacement. Financial services firms were cited for funding such projects. Classic civil rights issues also came up, though in smaller numbers, including equal recognition and protection under the law as well as the right to a fair trial, stemming from alleged company interference with judicial processes.

In sum, perhaps the biggest surprise in these results lies not in any specific ranking but in the broad range of internationally recognized rights that companies have been alleged to infringe upon or abuse.

Whose Rights?

Figure 1 is a largely self-explanatory graphic showing the category of claimants or victims of alleged corporate human rights abuse. In this sample of cases, workers and communities were

Figure 1: Persons Affected

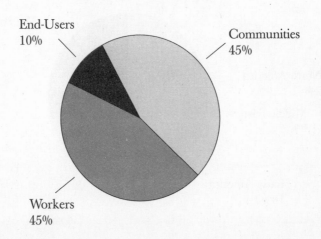

equally affected, although different sectors affect people in the
two categories differently. Not surprisingly, the footwear and
apparel industry tends to have a greater impact on workers
than on communities, while the extractive industry has a large
impact on communities as well. End-user cases in this sample
largely concerned the issue of access to essential medicines,
such as HIV/AIDS treatment drugs, due to prohibitive costs or
intellectual property rights restrictions.

Where?

I divided the where question into two: regions (Figure 2), and
sectors (Figure 3). Care is required in interpreting the regional
results. The kinds of complaints or allegations that make it onto
the Centre's Web site are more likely to concern grievances

Figure 2: Region

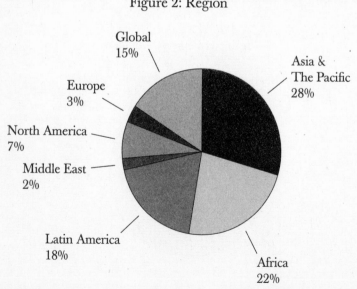

Figure 3: Sector

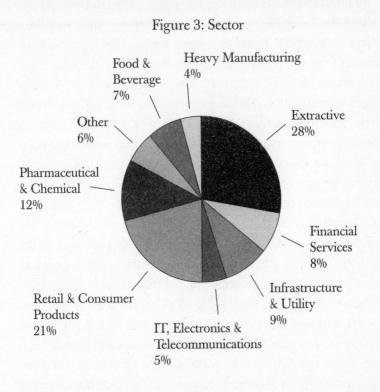

Food & Beverage 7%

Heavy Manufacturing 4%

Other 6%

Extractive 28%

Pharmaceutical & Chemical 12%

Financial Services 8%

Retail & Consumer Products 21%

Infrastructure & Utility 9%

IT, Electronics & Telecommunications 5%

that are not already being dealt with in other forums, such as a national labor relations board, nondiscrimination body, or some other regulatory institution. Also, as noted earlier, I did not include reports of ongoing court proceedings in the sample because the original allegation would likely have been included in earlier BHRRC listings. Thus, Figure 2 cannot be taken as conclusive evidence that there are fewer cases of corporate-related human rights abuse in Europe and North America than elsewhere. What it does indicate is that there are far more cases in the Asia-Pacific region, Africa, and Latin America that are not being dealt with effectively through existing forums, or that such forums don't exist there in the first place.

The term "global" in the figure refers to overall companies' policies that would have an impact wherever they operate—access to essential medicines, once again, or enterprise-wide efforts to deny workers' rights to freedom of association.

In terms of sectors, the extractive industry accounts for the largest share of allegations. It has a large local footprint in terms of the scale of its impact, often in areas inhabited by minority populations, and its main issues include inadequate procedures for (and sometimes forced) resettlement of populations, security of the person, and adverse impacts on livelihoods. Retail and consumer products were not far behind (long and complex supply chains). Infrastructure and utility companies often pose issues similar to the extractive industry, as to some extent does the foods and beverages industry (think large banana or sugar plantations, for example, or the impact on human rights of heavy water and fertilizer use). The pharmaceutical and chemical industries' third-place ranking reflects a combination of access to essential medicines and environmental hazards that can impact the right to health. Allegations against financial services firms almost invariably concern project lending by banks to companies accused of abusing rights.

How?

I also wanted to know whether a company was accused of abusing rights directly or to have been complicit in acts by others. Figure 4 provides the answer. Nearly 60 percent of the cases concern direct company acts; just over 40 percent, acts by other parties to which the company was closely connected ("complicity"). With only one exception, all reports of complicity took place in developing countries. As for the identity of the third

Figure 4: Direct or Indirect Involvement

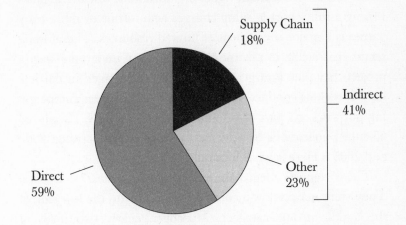

Supply Chain 18%

Indirect 41%

Other 23%

Direct 59%

party, in roughly four out of ten cases it was one of the company's supply-chain partners—for which, as we saw in the Nike case, the global buyer is expected to assume some responsibility. The majority of the other six out of ten complicity cases concerned a company's relationship to a state or state agencies, where the firm was viewed as contributing to or benefiting from direct violations by state actors.

Correlates of Egregious Abuses

It is a cardinal principle in the human rights canon that there is no hierarchy of rights, that all rights are "universal, indivisible and interdependent and interrelated."[61] This does not mean, however, that some abuses do not have worse consequences than others for rights-holders. To supplement the regional distribution reported in Figure 2, I was interested in identifying the attributes of countries in which the most egregious corporate-related abuses occurred. I drew these data from a different source. For human rights organizations, researching and issuing a full report leveling charges against one or more companies is a major investment of limited resources. Therefore, it seems reasonable to assume that when they undertake such a project they pick a target they believe has engaged in particularly egregious conduct—and which also serves their campaigning purposes. As part of my first report to the UN, I analyzed 65 such publications by advocacy groups issued between 2000 and 2005.[62] Here is what I found.

The 65 reports alleged abuses by companies in 27 countries. They were mainly low-income countries, or on the low side of the middle-income category. Moreover, nearly two-thirds of them had either recently emerged from or were still in conflict. Finally, the countries were characterized by weak governance. On-a-rule of law index developed by the World Bank, all but 2 of the 27 fell below the average score for all countries; one of the two exceptions was slightly above the global average, the other right at it.[63] On the Transparency International Corruption Perceptions Index—where 0 indicates "highly corrupt" and 10 is described as "most clean"—their average score was 2.6.[64] And on the Freedom House index of political systems—where "not free" is ranked as 1, "partially free" 2, and "free" 3—their average was 1.9.[65]

The International Council on Mining and Metals, an industry association comprising more than twenty of the world's leading mining companies, subsequently commissioned a study to see if these results held up in their sector. Their findings were broadly similar. However, in their survey 70 percent of the cases fell into the complicity category: where the actual violation of human rights was committed by another actor, more often than not a state body or armed faction, "in the vicinity of the mine, allegedly on behalf of the mine, or with alleged direct benefit to the mine."[66]

In sum, a negative symbiosis exists between the worst corporate-related human rights abuses and host countries that are characterized by combinations of relatively low national income, current or recent conflict exposure, and weak or corrupt governance.

Conflict Zones

This negative symbiosis is seen most clearly in conflict zones: countries or regions within them that the central authorities do not control and in which armed factions fight over territory and resources; or where the government itself is involved in egregious conduct against its own population that may rise to the level of international crimes. In relation to business and human rights, conflict zones attract illicit and borderline enterprises because, despite the existence of international human rights and humanitarian law standards, in practice they essentially function as "law-free" zones in which even outright looting and pillaging are possible without fear of being sanctioned. But large, legitimate, and otherwise well-governed companies also can get drawn into becoming, wittingly or unwittingly, a party to egregious human rights abuses in these contexts.

One case in point involves Chiquita Brands (bananas), indicted by the U.S. Justice Department in 2007 for making payments to a right-wing paramilitary organization in Colombia with a history of extensive massacres and population displacements, and which the United States had designated a Foreign Terrorist Organization (FTO).[67] It turned out that

Chiquita earlier had been paying Colombia's two main left-wing guerrilla groups for an even longer period; they, too, were on the State Department FTO list.[68] Fernando Aguirre, Chiquita's CEO, said in a statement: "The payments made by the company were always motivated by our good faith concern for the safety of our employees."[69] In other words, they were protection payments in an area of the country that government forces did not fully control. Notwithstanding that good-faith concern, the payments posed two problems for Chiquita: first, they were illegal under U.S. law because they were made to terrorist organizations; second, the payments to the right-wing group, Autodefensas Unidas de Colombia (AUC), allegedly financed an offensive against leftist guerilla forces, trade unionists, and social activists that was intended to force them out of Chiquita's region of operation, a campaign that may have killed hundreds. Under a plea agreement Chiquita paid a $25-million fine to settle the FTO complaint and promised to implement an effective compliance and ethics program. But it now finds itself in U.S. courts under the Alien Tort Statute on charges brought by the Colombian victims' families that Chiquita was complicit in the AUC's extrajudicial killings, torture, forced disappearances, crimes against humanity, and war crimes.[70]

There are also numerous instances of companies being accused of collaborating with the government side in a civil war. Talisman Energy's operation in Sudan is alleged to have been one.[71] NGOs, church groups, and some socially responsible investment funds pressured this Canadian company to leave Sudan, arguing that revenues from the oil flow allowed the Sudanese government to nearly double its military spending in a three-year period.[72] But what drew the most concern— including from the Canadian government—was the revelation that Sudan's armed forces used the company's airstrips to refuel helicopter gunships and bombers on more than a hundred occasions as they were on their way to bombing raids in the south of the country.[73] This led to a major campaign against the company, the battering of its stock prices, and forced its subsequent withdrawal from the country. Still, it too faced charges in U.S. courts under the Alien Tort Statute for aiding and abetting the Sudanese forces' attacks. But the 2nd Circuit Court of Appeals in an opinion I criticized publicly at the time, held that for the purposes of this statute the proper test for establishing corporate complicity was not that a company knowingly contributed to the violation of international law by another party, but that it did so "with the purpose to advance" the violation. The Court found that Talisman's actions did not meet that test. [74]

If it were possible to posit a worst-of-the-worst situation, in recent history it undoubtedly would be the Democratic Republic of the Congo (DRC). More than 4 million people are reported to have been killed in conflicts ravaging that vast country since the 1990s, and countless numbers raped, tortured, and otherwise abused. In June 2000 the UN Security Council requested that the Secretary-General establish a panel of experts on the illegal exploitation of natural resources and other forms of wealth in the DRC.[75] Its primary mission was to document how this illegal exploitation—of gold, diamonds, niobium (an alloy strengthener), coltan (used to control current flow in cell phones and laptops), cassiterite (used in circuitry), and timber, among other natural resources—fueled the conflict by financing the warring factions and keeping them supplied with arms and matériel, as well as personally enriching those who controlled these enterprises.

A regional war was triggered when, in October 1996, Rwandan troops invaded the DRC in response to attacks on Rwanda from Hutu refugee camps in eastern DRC. The Rwandan army formed a coalition with Laurent Kabila, leader of an eastern-based rebel force aiming to overthrow the central government of the notoriously kleptocratic President, Mobutu Sese Seko. Mobutu fled the country and Kabila declared himself President. After a falling out, Kabila ordered foreign troops to leave the DRC in 1998, but Rwanda and Uganda sent fresh troops instead. Angolan, Zimbabwean, and Namibian troops then intervened on behalf of the Kabila government, also supported by Sudan and Chad. Essentially, these armies "paid" themselves by taking over or otherwise controlling mining and other natural resource operations in the parts of the country they occupied. Foreign forces withdrew in 2002, but not before leaving in place networks of entities, particularly in the eastern part of the country, to maintain the mechanisms for revenue generation they had established.

The connection to business and human rights is twofold. First, the Security Council panel identified companies and their security providers who were said to be directly involved in human rights abuses—in forced labor, for example: "forcing farmers and their families to leave their agricultural land, or chasing people off land where coltan was found and forcing them to work in artisanal mines. As a result, the widespread destruction of agriculture and devastating social effects occurred, which in a number of instances were akin to slavery."[76] Second, the panel also identified what it believed to have been the wider circle of commercial enablers of this war economy: companies that bought, traded, and transported illicit raw materials; businesses that processed them; and financial institutions that provided lending and payment facilities. While their links to the DRC conflict may have been only indirect, the panel stated, they "still bore a responsibility to ensure that those links did not, albeit inadvertently, contribute to funding and perpetuating the conflict."[77]

The most contentious concept in the DRC panel's mandate was the term "illegal" in regard to the exploitation of natural resources. The panel so designated any activity that it determined to have been undertaken without the consent of the recognized government; in violation of existing national laws and regulations, whether enforced or not; sustained by the abuse of power or outright force; or in violation of international law.[78] Some parties identified by the panel complained bitterly that this definition rendered much of the commercial activity in large parts of the DRC illegal.[79] Indeed, that seems to have been precisely the message the panel wanted to convey.

On the ground, as the tragedy of the Congo makes all too clear, conflict zones currently can function as essentially law-free zones where corporate-related human rights abuses are subject only to self-restraint and the occasional lawsuit in another country based on statutes with extraterritorial reach. This constitutes the biggest gap of all between globalization and governance.

III. CONCLUSION

The 1990s introduced a new phase in the history of global markets and market actors, exemplified by the expanding reach and role of multinational corporations. There were more of them than ever before; they operated in more countries around the world, including highly challenging sociopolitical contexts; and they developed novel and far-flung cross-border manufacturing and offshore sourcing networks, often relying on contractual relationships with other business entities or joint ventures rather than on vertically integrated forms. This chapter set out to introduce some of the emblematic cases that put business and human rights on the global agenda and to provide an overall mapping of actual and alleged corporate-related human rights abuses.

When it came to business and human rights, neither governments nor companies were prepared for this wave of globalization. In the cases we surveyed, the companies initially took a strictly legalistic approach to the challenges they encountered: we don't own this problem, they said, these are independent suppliers, or this is a legally separate subsidiary; we are a business and therefore should not interfere in the domestic affairs of our host country even when the military dictatorship engages in what are widely believed to be extrajudicial killings of protesters against our operations; we must obey the law of the land even if that forces us to violate internationally recognized standards and our own business values. Movement away from these initial positions, where it occurred, was driven mainly by advocacy campaigns and occasional lawsuits, for the most part utilizing the newly rediscovered U.S. Alien Tort Statute. Zadek's rendering of Nike's evolution illustrates how some firms began to internalize new social expectations as corporate responsibilities. But there was no common understanding of precisely what these should be and what practices they should entail. Although numerous CSR initiatives would be launched over the next decade, they existed largely as disconnected fragments incorporating different commitments, with few focused specifically on human rights. My mandate was intended to address these gaps.

We learned that companies can affect virtually the entire spectrum of internationally recognized human rights and not, as had been generally assumed, merely some limited subset. In addition to the gamut of workplace issues, we saw that companies were alleged to have harmed health-related rights; rights to land, housing, and access to safe drinking water; the physical security of the person; the rights of indigenous peoples; and even such classic civil rights as free speech, privacy, peaceful assembly, and a fair trial. Of course, this made more difficult the task of devising a systematic framework for business and human rights.

Furthermore, we saw that the incidence of reported corporate-related human rights abuses is significantly higher in countries with weak governance where local laws do not exist, or where laws are not enforced even if the host country has ratified the relevant international human rights conventions. This underscores the need to define a basis for the corporate responsibility to respect human rights that does not hinge on whether or not the host state is fulfilling its duty. The dilemma companies face where host state law contradicts international standards, as in the case of Yahoo and China, requires devising more nuanced responses.

Finally, we saw that the worst cases of corporate-related human rights abuse have occurred in areas of armed conflict. Conflict zones attract marginal and illicit enterprises. But even well-recognized multinational corporations can get drawn into involvement in human rights abuses in conflict zones, typically committed by government agents or armed factions protecting company assets, or exploiting them for their own purposes. Individual companies can reduce their risk of involvement in such abuses, and national and international agencies as well as civil society organizations can help them do so. But at the end of the day this situation is the prime candidate for more robust legal measures involving home states. However, as we shall see in the next chapter, this remains highly controversial among businesses and governments.

Ultimately, the challenge of business and human rights involves nothing less than the workings of the global political economy together with the structure of the world political and legal orders. That the UN would establish a single "Special Procedure" to address these issues indicates how underdeveloped this area was, intellectually and institutionally. As I set out on my journey, I recalled the advice the taciturn highlander Scot was said to have given when asked for directions by a hiker from the city: "I wouldn't start from here if I were you."

Chapter Two

NO SILVER BULLET

A knowledgeable observer at the 2005 annual conference of Business for Social Responsibility summed up the impasse in which I seemed trapped at the start of my mandate: "On the one hand, you have NGOs with ambitious agendas for a 'treaty' on corporate responsibility and human rights. On the other hand, you have companies saying 'no, anything but that!' Cooler heads are not prevailing and in fact are hard to find at all."[1] This debate had raged on since 2003, when an expert subsidiary body of the UN Commission on Human Rights presented a treaty-like text it had drafted, called the "Norms on the Responsibilities of Transnational Corporations and Other Business Enterprises with Regard to Human Rights."[2] As noted in the Introduction, the Commission, the intergovernmental parent body, declined to act on the proposed Norms and established my mandate instead.

The same impasse dominated the first consultation I convened later in 2005, in Geneva, focused on human rights challenges in the extractive sector. The refrain from the two sets of protagonists was that I must/must not support the Norms; and that I must/must not support voluntary initiatives. Business often resists binding regulations, and this particular instrument was seen to transfer to companies responsibilities for human rights that business believed belonged to governments. Many advocacy groups discount voluntary initiatives because they believe they provide little more than whitewash for companies— or bluewash for those who want to work the UN color into the criticism—and some hold that they divert attention from the need for legal accountability. The only questions anyone wanted me to answer at the consultation were: Which way do I lean? Which side will I end up supporting? I responded that I intended to conduct an evidence-based mandate, and that I would subject the alternatives to as rigorous an assessment as time and circumstances permitted. After doing so, I found both positions wanting.

These debates still provide an invaluable point of entry to understanding the core conceptual, policy, and legal issues involved in adapting the international human rights regime to provide more effective protection against corporate-related human rights harm. Therefore, I draw on them to frame my own approach to this challenge. For context, I begin by describing briefly the current structure of international law as it concerns business and human rights. Next, I summarize the analysis of the Norms I undertook at the outset of my mandate, and explain why I rejected the idea of building on that particular instrument. Then I address why I decided against devoting the mandate to advocating my own version of an overarching business and human rights treaty. Next, I assess both the achievements but also the limits of voluntary initiatives in business and human rights. Finally, I draw key lessons from the analysis that became building blocks for the more heterodox approach I developed.

I. THE CURRENT STRUCTURE

International law does not ignore the fact that multinational corporations and other business enterprises abuse human rights. But with few exceptions, it does not impose duties directly on them to refrain from such abuses, nor does it currently possess the means that could enforce any such provisions. Instead, international law generally imposes duties on states to ensure that nonstate actors within their jurisdiction, including companies, do not abuse recognized rights by means of appropriate policies, legislation, regulations, and adjudication. This structure is reflected in United Nations declarations, human rights treaties, and in the commentaries of the treaty bodies charged with providing authoritative interpretations. The one partial exception concerns the most egregious conduct, including involvement in genocide, war crimes, and some crimes against humanity, where customary international law standards may apply directly to corporate entities under certain circumstances, though enforcement occurs through domestic courts. A brief summary follows.

The Universal Declaration

The Universal Declaration of Human Rights (UDHR) occupies a unique place in the international normative order. Its preamble proclaims that "every individual and every organ of society . . . shall strive by teaching and education to promote respect for these rights and freedoms and by progressive measures, national and international, to secure their universal and effective recognition and observance." In Columbia Law School

Professor Louis Henkin's oft-cited words: "Every individual includes juridical persons. Every individual and every organ of society excludes no one, no company, no market, no cyberspace. The Universal Declaration applies to them all."[3] Henkin surely is correct that the Declaration's aspirations and moral claims are addressed, and apply, to all humanity—and as we shall see below, many companies themselves invoke it in their own human rights policies. But that does not equate to legally binding effect.

As a Declaration, the UDHR was not intended to be legally binding. Its drafters expected that legal duties subsequently would be elaborated in treaties, as the two UN Covenants— on Civil and Political Rights (ICCPR), and on Economic, Social and Cultural Rights (ICESCR)—ultimately did. Whatever UDHR provisions may be said to have entered customary international law, they would not include the call in its preamble to "every organ of society" because preambles, even to binding international instruments, are not themselves legally binding.

The UN Treaties

The early generation of UN human rights treaties, such as the International Convention on the Elimination of All Forms of Racial Discrimination and the two Covenants, do not specifically address state duties regarding business. They impose generalized obligations on states parties to ensure the enjoyment of rights and prevent nonstate abuse. For example, the convention on racial discrimination requires each state party to prohibit such discrimination by "any persons, group or organization."

Some treaties recognize rights that are particularly relevant in business contexts, including rights related to employment, health, and indigenous communities, but the correlative duties invariably are assigned to states.

Beginning with the Convention on the Elimination of All Forms of Discrimination Against Women (CEDAW), adopted in 1979, UN human rights treaties began to address business more directly. CEDAW, for instance, requires states parties to take all appropriate measures to eliminate discrimination against women by, among other entities, any "enterprise" and, in even greater detail, including in the context of "bank loans, mortgages and other forms of financial credit." But the duty to ensure that these rights are enjoyed is assigned to the state. The treaties generally give states discretion regarding the modalities for regulating and adjudicating nonstate abuses, but emphasize legislation and judicial remedies.

Because the treaties say that states have a duty to "ensure the enjoyment" of rights, some commentators have argued that this implies a direct legal obligation for all social actors, including corporations, to respect those rights in the first place. How can this claim be tested? One means is by examining the treaty bodies' commentaries and concluding observations—which I did for each treaty body, sampling them over a ten-year period.[4] The claim is not borne out. A General Comment on the right to work by the treaty body monitoring the ICESCR is typical: it recognizes that various private actors, including multinational enterprises, "have a particular role to play in job creation, hiring policies and non-discriminatory access to work."[5] But it then goes on to say that business enterprises are "not bound" by the Covenant. Similarly, the committee on civil and political rights has said that the treaty obligations "do not . . . have direct horizontal effect as a matter of international law"—that is, they take effect between nonstate actors only under domestic law.[6]

International Labor Conventions

On purely logical grounds one might expect that direct corporate responsibilities would feature more strongly under the International Labour Organization's conventions. The ILO is a tripartite organization, comprising representatives of governments, business associations, and workers organizations. The conventions address all types of employers, including corporations; business enterprises generally acknowledge greater responsibility for their employees than for other stakeholders; and the ILO's supervisory mechanism and complaints procedure specify roles for employer organizations and trade unions. But logic alone does not make law, and corporations' legal responsibilities under the ILO conventions remain indirect, while states remain the direct duty bearer.

Egregious Conduct

The United Nations General Assembly has recognized the category of "gross" violations of international human rights law and "serious" violations of international humanitarian law, also known as the law of armed conflict.[7] The acts in question are commonly described as "egregious." While no all-inclusive definition exists, it is generally agreed that they include genocide, war crimes, and such crimes against humanity as torture, extrajudicial killings, forced disappearances, enslavement, slaverylike practices, and apartheid. Few legitimate businesses may ever commit such acts, but there is greater risk of their facing allegations of complicity—aiding and abetting—in their commission by, for example, security forces protecting company assets and facilities, as in the case of Shell and the Nigerian military or Chiquita Brands and the paramilitary in Colombia. The enforcement of the duty of companies not to commit such acts is left to national courts, but in some instances they have drawn on international standards in doing so.

The main legal mechanism under which this incorporation has occurred is the already-discussed U.S. Alien Tort Statute (ATS), under which foreign plaintiffs have brought civil claims (monetary compensation for harms) against companies with a business presence in the United States for human rights violations abroad. Under the statute, U.S. courts have looked to international standards—both treaty-based and customary law standards as developed by the international criminal tribunals for the former Yugoslavia and Rwanda, for example—to inform their own deliberation whether "the law of nations" was breached. The presumption has been that, provided they meet certain criteria, such standards developed for natural persons also apply to legal persons. But in September 2010, the U.S. 2nd Circuit Court of Appeals, the first ever in modern times to uphold a ruling permitting a case to be brought against an individual under the ATS, decided that the statute did not apply to corporations as legal persons.[8] Subsequent rulings by other circuit courts in different cases contradicted this view. The question is currently under review by the Supreme Court, and I take it up in chapter 5.

A second route through which international standards could enter domestic legal systems and be applied to corporate entities involves the International Criminal Court's Rome Statute. The ICC itself does not have jurisdiction over business entities—the issue was discussed in the drafting stage, but agreement could not be reached because a number of countries do not recognize criminal liability of corporations. Nevertheless, where a country has ratified the statute and incorporated its standards for individual criminal liability into its domestic criminal law, and where the national legal system does provide for criminal punishment of companies, it is possible that the standards for natural persons may get extended to corporate entities as legal persons.[9] No actual case has yet been brought against a company under this scenario, but there have been reports of preliminary investigations by authorities in Australia and Canada.

Extraterritoriality

Through combinations of unilateral and multilateral measures, the extension of national jurisdiction abroad has evolved in a number of international policy domains—antiterrorism, money laundering, anticorruption, aspects of environmental protection, and child sex tourism, for example. But with the partial exception of the types of egregious conduct discussed above, it remains limited in other areas of human rights.[10]

The various UN human rights treaties differ in their possible extraterritorial implications. The Genocide Convention, for example, includes no jurisdictional limit, therefore in principle none apply. In contrast, state duties to respect and ensure the enjoyment of rights under the Covenant on Civil and Political Rights are explicitly limited to individuals "within its territory and subject to its jurisdiction." Finally, the ICESCR includes a provision that each state party "take steps, individually and through international assistance and co-operation, especially economic and technical, to the maximum of its available resources, with a view to achieving progressively the full real-ization of the rights recognized in the present Covenant by all appropriate means"—which governments generally view as a call to provide financial and other forms of assistance to devel-oping countries.

The UN treaty bodies traditionally paid relatively little atten-tion to business-related issues. Their general guidance suggested that the treaties do not require states to exercise extraterritorial jurisdiction over business abuse, but that they are not generally prohibited from doing so either, provided there is a recognized jurisdictional basis: for example, where the actor or victim is a national, where the acts have substantial adverse effects on the state, or where specific international crimes are involved. More recently, the committee monitoring the economic, social, and cultural rights covenant began to recommend that states parties "should" take steps to "prevent their own citizens and companies" from violating rights in other countries, particu-larly in relation to the rights to food, water, and health.[11] For the most part, states do not consider the treaty bodies to constitute a source of law. But the committees' increased attention to the question of extraterritorial obligations signals a growing con-cern with the inadequacy of the status quo.

Soft Law

States have addressed the human rights responsibilities of busi-ness enterprises most directly in soft-law instruments. Soft law is "soft" in the sense that it does not by itself create legally bind-ing obligations. It derives its normative force through recogni-tion of social expectations by states and other key actors. States may turn to soft law for several reasons: to chart possible future directions for, and fill gaps in, the international legal order when they are not yet able or willing to take firmer measures; where they conclude that legally binding mechanisms are not the best tool to address a particular issue; or to avoid having more binding measures gain political momentum.

Apart from the foundational Universal Declaration, the most prominent soft-law instruments in the business and human rights space originate with the International Labour Organization (ILO) and the Organization for Economic Cooperation and Development (OECD). The ILO Tripartite Declaration of Principles Concerning Multinational Enterprises and Social Policy, first adopted in 1977, was endorsed by states as well as global employers' and workers' organizations, through the ILO's tripartite decision-making system. It proclaims that all parties, including multinational enterprises, "should respect the Universal Declaration of Human Rights and the corresponding international Covenants." The ILO Declaration on Fundamental Principles and Rights at Work was adopted by the International Labour Conference (the ILO's tripartite assembly) in 1998. It commits its member states to respect and promote principles and rights in four categories, whether or not they have ratified the relevant ILO conventions: freedom of association and the effective recognition of the right to collective bargaining, the elimination of forced or compulsory labor, the abolition of child labor, and the elimination of discrimination in respect to employment and occupation.

The OECD Guidelines for Multinational Enterprises were first adopted in 1976 and revised in 2000 (their 2011 update is discussed in chapters 3 and 4). The 2000 text recommended as a general principle that firms "respect the human rights of those affected by their activities consistent with the host government's obligations and commitments," which ruled out international standards the host state did not recognize. The Guidelines also require the adhering states to establish a government office called the National Contact Point to which anyone can bring a "specific instance" (i.e., complaint) of noncompliance by a multinational corporation domiciled or operating in an adhering country, although negative findings have no automatic official consequences.

To sum up, the structure of current international law is such that human rights duties for the most part are imposed on states, not on companies directly. Of course, the human rights treaties apply only to states that have ratified them. The most consequential hard-law development in recent years has been the gradual extension of potential liability to companies for egregious acts that may amount to international crimes, under domestic law but reflecting international standards. But this trend is largely an unanticipated by-product of states' strengthening the legal regime for natural persons, not legal persons, and its actual operation reflects wide variations in national practice. There have also been a handful of cases in the United Kingdom, The Netherlands, and Canada in which charges have been brought against a parent company under national law for its contribution to or negligence in permitting harmful acts by overseas affiliates, sometimes described as "direct foreign liability" cases. But overall, in terms of the law, a large governance gap exists in business and human rights. The central question is how most effectively to narrow or bridge it.

II. THE NORMS

The Norms were the first international effort to develop legally binding international human rights standards for companies. The Commission on Human Rights had not requested the

Sub-Commission (a group of experts nominated by governments but acting in their personal capacity) to produce a draft, and only the Commission had the authority to adopt the product, which it declined to do.

The case for the Norms went like this. The Universal Declaration is addressed to all organs of society. Multinational corporations, being among those organs, have greater power than many states to affect the realization of rights, and "with power should come responsibility."[12] Therefore, these corporations must bear responsibility for the human rights affected by business activities. And because some states are unwilling or unable to make them do so under domestic law, international law must impose uniform standards not only on states, as in the existing human rights regime, but on corporations directly. To determine violations, the Norms recommended that companies be monitored by the UN human rights machinery even before further legalization and, where abuses were found, that reparations be made.

It would be surprising if governments and businesses did not react negatively to the Norms, based at least in part on their perceived interests. Those interests were not my primary concern, however. If the proposal was sound, I was prepared to back it. My assessment of the Norms focused on five questions: Which human rights did the Norms include? What human rights duties did they attribute to business enterprises? On what basis were they attributed? With what consequences? And with what legal justification? I found the effort flawed on every count.

The Norms enumerated rights that their authors believed to be particularly relevant for business, including nondiscrimination, the security of the person, labor standards, and indigenous peoples' rights. But they also would have imposed on companies responsibilities for rights that states had not yet recognized at the global level, including a "living wage," consumer protection, and the precautionary principle for environmental impacts. Moreover, the text stated that not all internationally recognized rights pertained to business, but it provided no principled basis for determining what was in and what was out. In response to criticism that the list was overly inclusive, some Norms' advocates suggested a shorter list of "core" rights said to enjoy the most widespread support and which business could easily grasp.[13] But that idea triggered the riposte that the concept of core rights is "a very significant departure from the insistence within the international human rights regime on the equal importance of all human rights."[14] In any event, we saw in chapter 1 that business can affect virtually the entire spectrum of internationally recognized rights, therefore any delimited list of rights in what purports to be a comprehensive and foundational legal framework will provide inadequate guidance in practice.

A far more serious problem concerned the Norms' proposed formula for attributing duties to corporations. After acknowledging that states are the primary duty-bearers under international human rights law, the General Obligations article added: "Within their respective spheres of activity and influence, transnational corporations and other business enterprises have the obligation to promote, secure the fulfillment of, respect, ensure respect of and protect" nationally and internationally recognized human rights.[15] But these are exactly the same duties states have. The distinction between primary and secondary duty-holders was not defined. And as a basis for attributing legal duties to companies, "spheres of influence" proved problematic.

The UN Global Compact had introduced the concept of "corporate spheres of influence" as a spatial metaphor to help companies think about their effects on human rights beyond the workplace and to identify opportunities for them to support human rights, which is the Compact's objective. The Office of the High Commissioner for Human Rights subsequently published a paper graphically depicting the "sphere" as a set of concentric circles: company operations at the core, moving outward to suppliers, the community, and society as a whole—premised on the logic that as a company's influence declines from one circle to the next, so too, by implication, would its responsibility.[16]

In a legal context, there are three problems with the sphere-of-influence concept. First, the emphasis on proximity can be seriously misleading. Of course companies should be concerned with their impact on workers and surrounding communities. But their activities can equally affect the rights of people far away from the source—as, for example, violations of the right to privacy by Internet service providers can endanger dispersed end-users. Interestingly, the Norms did not specifically enumerate this right; the Yahoo case, described in chapter 1, had not yet occurred.

Second, attributing responsibility for human rights to companies based on their influence requires the assumption, in moral philosophy terms, that "can implies ought." But companies should not be held responsible for the human rights impacts of every entity in society over which they may have influence because this would include sources of harm to which they are entirely unrelated. At the same time, such an attribution could absolve companies from responsibility for adverse impacts when they could show they lacked influence even if they were connected to the harm. It is one thing to ask companies to support human rights voluntarily where they have influence, as the Global Compact does; but attributing legal obligations to them on that basis for meeting the full range of human rights duties is quite another.

Third, "influence" is a relational term and thus is subject to strategic gaming. By this I mean that a government can deliberately fail to perform its duties—as we saw in the discussions of Cajamarca and Nigeria—in the hope that the company will yield to social pressures to promote or fulfill certain rights. For its part, a company can minimize its apparent influence by creating any number of hollow subsidiary entities, and thereby seek to diminish or duck its responsibilities.

In short, the boundaries within which corporations' duties would take effect under the Norms were indeterminate, and the distinction between primary and secondary duties undefined. With scope and threshold conditions both underspecified, it seemed highly likely that corporate duties in practice would have come to hinge on the respective *capacities* of states and corporations in particular situations—so that where a state was unable or unwilling to do its job, the pressure would be on companies to step in. But with what consequences?

Philip Alston, a leading academic authority on human rights law and former chair of the UN Committee on Economic, Social and Cultural Rights, identifies one resulting dilemma:

> If the only difference is that governments have a comprehensive set of obligations, while those of corporations are limited to their "spheres of influence" . . . how are the latter [obligations] to be delineated? Does Shell's sphere of influence in the Niger Delta not cover everything ranging from the right to health, through the right to free speech, to the rights to physical integrity and due process?[17]

Alston raises the concern that this formula could undermine corporate autonomy, risk-taking, and entrepreneurship, and asks, "What are the consequences of saddling [corporations] with all of the constraints, restrictions, and even positive obligations which apply to governments?"[18] Corporations may be "organs of society," in short, but they are specialized organs, established to perform specialized economic functions, and the obligations imposed on them must recognize that fact.

The impact the Norms would have had on the roles and obligations of governments is equally troubling. The international human rights regime recognizes the legitimate need of governments, within the constraint of "progressive realization," to exercise discretion for making trade-offs and balancing decisions, and especially for determining how best to "secure the fulfillment" of, precisely those economic, social, and cultural rights on which corporations have the greatest impact. Imposing the entire range of human rights duties on multinational corporations directly under international law, including fulfilling rights, by definition reduces individual governments' discretion in making those balancing decisions. The Norms attempted to square the circle by requiring companies also to follow national laws and policy priorities, but this merely added a layer of conflicting prescriptions for firms to follow. And it was contradicted outright by yet another requirement that firms adopt "the most protective standards" wherever those may be found. Furthermore, where governance is weak to begin with, shifting obligations onto corporations to protect and even fulfill the broad spectrum of human rights may undermine domestic political incentives to make governments more responsive and responsible to their own citizenry, which surely is the most effective way to realize human rights.

Finally, the legal claims and justifications made for the Norms were puzzling to many observers, including mainstream international lawyers, further fueling controversy. Their chief author described the Norms as "a restatement of international legal principles applicable to companies."[19] Yet they would have imposed the full range of human rights duties on companies, including fulfilling rights, and done so directly under international law. Moreover, they would have required a significant restructuring of domestic corporate law regimes, in effect replacing the "shareholder" model of fiduciary duties that is dominant in many countries in favor of a broad "stakeholder" model. Whatever the intrinsic merits of those moves, they would have amounted to fundamental revolutions in existing law, not a mere restatement. As law professor John Knox later wrote, "the proponents of the Norms sometimes seemed oblivious to the size of the revolution in international law that they were seeking to realize."[20]

Similarly, the Norms were described as the first such initiative at the international level that was "non-voluntary" in nature, and thus in some sense automatically binding on companies. This pleased human rights NGOs but surprised governments and business because no intergovernmental body had approved them, nor had any government ratified them. It turned out subsequently that the authors merely meant that if the Norms ever took effect through treaty law or customary international law, then companies would be bound by them even if they didn't sign up to them, as they would to a voluntary initiative. The UN Human Rights Commission resolved any possible confusion by stating in a formal resolution that the Norms had no legal standing.

Thus, even leaving aside the contentious proposal for some unknown and unspecified entity to ensure reparation to victims worldwide, and apart from the near-universal political opposition beyond NGO circles, I found the Norms to be deeply flawed. In December 2005, I signaled these reservations in a London speech and in a private meeting with human rights NGOs. Not long thereafter, having been pressured previously that I must "build on" the Norms, I received this email message

from one of those organizations: "We . . . would be concerned
if you felt it necessary in your report to take a position on the
UN Norms . . . . We feel that doing so may unnecessarily compromise the outcome of your work."[21] By now it had become
clear that only a clean break would free my mandate from
the shadow cast over it by the Norms. And so, in the words
of Edward Mortimer, Kofi Annan's speechwriter at the time, I
committed "Normicide." In my first report to the Human Rights
Commission, I concluded, in deliberately undiplomatic language, that the Norms suffered from "exaggerated legal claims
and conceptual ambiguities," and that they were "engulfed by
[their] own doctrinal excesses." Therefore, I added, they constituted "a distraction from rather than a basis for moving [my]
mandate forward."[22] Yet the Norms' flaws as well as the visceral
responses the initiative triggered on all sides provided both substantive and political insight that was very useful in developing
my own approach.

Not surprisingly, the human rights NGOs that had strongly
supported the Norms were unhappy. " 'Principled Pragmatism'
or Mere Antagonism?" read the headline in one newsletter.[23]
The International Commission of Jurists (a Geneva-based
NGO promoting the rule of law) subsequently convened several
meetings with leading human rights organizations, including
Human Rights Watch and Amnesty, to discuss possible ways
of derailing my mandate when it came up for renewal in 2007
and for NGOs themselves, with the help of supportive academic
human rights lawyers, to draft a new instrument that would
try to fix the Norms' flaws and then promote it to "friendly"
governments. But these efforts came to naught and public references to the Norms declined thereafter.

The business community and most governments were
relieved that the Norms would not feature in my work. Both

began to take seriously my claim that I would take a rigorous evidence-based approach and search for practical solutions, not be driven by doctrinal preferences. This opened the door to constructive engagement with the business community—individual companies as well as business associations. At the same time, a number of governments began to respond favorably to my requests for voluntarily funding the mandate at a level that would enable me to recruit a team of professionals, conduct the necessary research, and consult widely with affected individuals and communities, other stakeholder groups and experts.

With the Norms issue settled, the attention of my interlocutors turned to the more general question of whether I would advocate "mandatory" or "voluntary" measures. This put the cart before the horse, I explained; let's first focus on the substance of what should be done and then address form. Nevertheless, as part of the initial mapping phase of my mandate, I turned next to an assessment of the relative feasibility and utility of my proposing a comprehensive treaty negotiation or promoting voluntary initiatives.

III. THE TREATY ROUTE

A perfectly understandable reaction to the emblematic cases described in chapter 1 is to say there ought to be a law, one international law, that binds all business enterprises everywhere under a common set of standards protecting all human rights. International standards become legally binding for adhering states when the requisite number of countries have ratified a treaty or when they become part of customary international law—established patterns of state practice based on a sense of legal obligation, not merely self-interest or etiquette. Because custom cannot be created at will, seeking to establish binding standards for business and human rights means launching an international treaty negotiation—whether the treaty seeks to impose obligations on states or on companies directly. Advancing this paradigm is a core aim of the UN human rights system: identifying the need for new standards, drafting instruments, creating procedures intended to secure their adoption, and then providing commentary on and recommendations for state compliance. It is also a core objective of many international human rights organizations, representing both their moral and institutional commitments.

But advocacy groups made no specific proposals for an international legal instrument after the Norms' demise. Amnesty's new position, for example, was conveyed to me in a letter from Irene Khan, then AI's Secretary-General. It called generically for "the creation of international legal standards and of corporate legal accountability for human rights."[24] Should this include some internationally recognized rights, or all? If the latter, was it plausible that uniform global legal liability standards could be created for corporate violations of every single internationally recognized human right, where the conduct in question can range from failure to pay overtime to complicity in extrajudicial killings? Or should some be prioritized? Would corporate accountability be imposed under national law or directly under international law? If the latter, would this require the creation of an international tribunal for corporations, or would it be enforced by states, not all of which have ratified all human rights treaties addressing state abuses of those same rights? Advocacy groups did not address these and related foundational questions, neither then nor throughout the rest of my mandate. I felt obliged to do so.

After assessing the prospects, I judged that the foundations for *any* treaty negotiations simply did not exist at that time, least of all for some comprehensive legal framework. Moreover, not only would such an effort achieve little for current victims of corporate-related human rights harm, but forcing the issue of international legalization prematurely would set the agenda back rather than advance it. Finally, even if the highly improbable were to occur and a treaty was adopted, it would not deliver all that its advocates hoped for and expected, suggesting the need for complementary approaches from the start. I explain my reasoning in the paragraphs that follow.

Foundations

Human rights treaties can take a long time to negotiate and enter into force: generally, the broader their scope and the more controversial the subject, the longer the duration. This is true even of soft-law instruments focused on relatively circumscribed subjects such as the Declaration on the Rights of Indigenous Peoples which, as already noted, took twenty-six years to negotiate and yet includes only one of the scores of issues that a comprehensive business and human rights treaty would need to encompass. Thus, even if treaty negotiations were to have begun the next day, more immediate solutions would be needed to deal with existing challenges. Louise Arbour, the then UN High Commissioner for Human Rights, put it succinctly in 2008: "It would be frankly very ambitious to promote only binding norms considering how long this would take and how much damage [to victims] could be done in the meantime."[25] But why not start such a treaty-making process while simultaneously taking shorter-term practical steps? Four impediments stood out when I considered this question.

First, the issue of business and human rights is still a relatively new concern for governments, and there was little agreement among them beyond "we need to consider doing something about the problem." As a case in point, governments initially limited my mandate to two years, as opposed to the normal three. And initially they gave me the task merely of "identifying" and "clarifying" things: applicable international standards, best practices, and the meaning of key concepts such as corporate complicity in human rights abuses committed by others and corporate spheres of influence. Not much of a shared knowledge base existed, let alone consensus on desirable international responses. In the past, political coalitions might have formed around the north-south or east-west axis, although this had never yielded significant concrete results in relation to multinational corporations.[26] But even that possibility no longer existed, thanks to the rapidly rising number of multinationals based in emerging market countries, such as Brazil, China, India, Indonesia, Malaysia, Russia, and South Africa, which are at least as protective of "their" multinationals as Western home states are of theirs. Greater shared understanding and consensus needed to be built from the bottom up.

Second, prevailing institutional arrangements and practices within governments concerning business and human rights were also a factor militating against the initiation of a business and human rights treaty process. My research, including a questionnaire sent to all UN member states, indicated that the responsibility for this issue typically is lodged in small, mid-level units, usually in foreign offices, occasionally in economics ministries. In contrast, the numerous government entities whose job it is to promote and protect business interests invariably are larger and have considerably greater institutional clout. Typically, the two exist in isolation from one another. Business and human rights issues have risen to the top of a government's agenda only momentarily in the wake of some major event or crisis. For example, South Africa was shocked to learn that it had signed bilateral investment treaties that enabled mining interests from Italy and Luxembourg to sue the government for monetary damages under binding international arbitration because of certain provisions in the Black Economic Empowerment Act, perhaps the single most significant piece of human rights legislation adopted by the postapartheid government. An official inquiry into how the government got itself into that situation concluded that "the Executive had not been fully apprised" of the possibility—the connection between investment treaties and human rights either was not considered or was ignored.[27] In light of such realities it seemed highly likely that a business-and-human-rights-treaty negotiating process would lock in commercial interests at the expense of human rights. Ways needed to be found to address what I called "horizontal policy incoherence" within governments around business and human rights.

Third, where states are reluctant to do much in the first place, they tend to invoke ongoing treaty negotiations as a pretext for not taking other significant steps, including changing national laws under pressure from domestic groups—arguing that they would not want to preempt the ultimate treaty outcome. Moreover, while negotiations are ongoing, proposals for other steps tend to be viewed through the lens of what they ultimately might mean for treaty-negotiating tactics and commitments, thus reducing the scope for experimentation and innovation—which is precisely what this policy domain demands. The counterargument is sometimes made that bargaining "in the shadow of the law" can yield productive outcomes, but that only works where there is a realistic prospect of meaningful legal measures being adopted.

Fourth, even some of the most progressive countries on the subject of human rights, such as Sweden, expressed concern about imposing the broad range of international human rights obligations on companies directly under international law, fearing that this would diminish states' essential roles and duties. This suggested the need to establish a clear differentiation between the respective obligations of states and businesses, one that recognized the different social roles they play, not intermingling the two as the Norms had done. That would take considerable effort in itself.

In short, these would have been inauspicious starting points for any treaty negotiation, consuming substantial time and energy to little positive effect. But because this may not always be so, it is also important to become aware of and develop adequate responses to even more fundamental issues related to the implementation of any business and human rights treaty. I take up three below: the effectiveness of human rights treaties generally, how a business and human rights treaty would be enforced, and the need for governments to avoid, or figure out how to reconcile, conflicting obligations under different bodies of international law.

Effectiveness

How effective are human rights treaties at changing actual behavior? How are they effective? And can they be made more so? These are big questions, difficult to answer definitively and briefly at the same time. Here I simply summarize key findings from systematic empirical studies conducted over the past decade to assess whether and how the ratification of international human rights treaties changes the conduct of states that ratify them. These studies have focused on political, civil, and personal integrity rights (the prohibitions against genocide and torture, for example), as well as women's rights and the rights of the child. Differences in methodology can affect the results, but the studies agree on one fact: human rights treaties are least effective in the case of those countries where they are needed most.[28] Moreover, strong positive correlations between treaty ratification and improved state behavior are the exception, not the rule.

Statistically, the positive effects of treaty ratification tend to be associated with one or more of the following country attributes: it is at least partly democratic; has strong civil society institutions; is relatively secular; has an existing commitment to the rule of law and reasonably well-functioning domestic legal institutions; and the protection of a particular right (prohibiting child labor, for example) is promoted by some external incentive mechanism, such as development assistance or a preferential trade agreement to which the country is a party. Effects within the same category of rights can vary. For example, ratification of the relevant treaties appears to have a greater effect on women's political rights than on their social rights, and on reducing child labor more than on improving basic health care for children. Moreover, the most recent assessment by a group of leading scholars on this subject concludes that limited capacity on the part of states to live up to their commitments "is much more widespread in the contemporary international system than is usually acknowledged."[29]

When all is said and done, the indirect role of treaty ratification—what it may make possible by way of mobilizing internal and external pressure against human rights violators—may be as important as the formal processes of translating commitments into compliance. In the case of multinationals this does raise the question of whether functional equivalents to such leverage points might exist when treaty negotiations seem problematic in the first place. I sought to identify what such equivalents might be, as elaborated in later chapters.

Enforcement

We have already seen that UN human rights treaties lack an international enforcement mechanism as such. What additional enforcement challenges might exist in the case of business, especially transnationally operating enterprises? Few observers believe that establishing a world court for multinationals is a realistic prospect in the foreseeable future. For the time being, therefore, that leaves national enforcement by host and/or home states, UN "monitoring," and whatever social compliance mechanisms exist.

Host states are states in which companies operate. As discussed earlier, if they have ratified existing human rights treaties, they already have obligations flowing from them to protect individuals against human rights abuses committed within their jurisdiction, not only by state agents but also by third parties, including business enterprises. A robust and widely adopted multilateral business and human rights treaty might give those states greater incentives to enforce their obligations by reducing collective action problems. But in the immediate context I found that many governments understood poorly both the substance and the extent of their existing international human rights duties vis-à-vis business, so as a first step I sought to spell them out in some detail. Of course, host states that have not ratified existing human rights treaties do not have correlative duties under those treaties—and it is not self-evident why they would sign on to a new treaty requiring them to enforce such duties. Essentially, this means that adding yet another enforcement obligation on host states could be either redundant or irrelevant.

Home states are those in which companies are "domiciled"—meaning incorporated or headquartered. To date, in the business and human rights domain, home states generally still tend to worry more about the competitive position of "their" companies, and business remains strongly opposed to extraterritorial jurisdiction. Moreover, even developing countries that express concern about the power of multinationals typically also resist interference by other countries in their domestic affairs. As discussed in later chapters, I sought to identify ways in which and circumstances under which home states could take certain actions to regulate overseas human rights harm by corporations domiciled in their jurisdiction without arousing serious host state ire. But as a general solution to the overall human rights challenges posed by multinational corporations, extraterritorial jurisdiction remains unacceptable to governments. Therefore, pushing it aggressively could backfire by reducing the already limited willingness to take steps within the currently permissible scope of such actions.

A UN business and human rights treaty presumably would establish a treaty body to monitor and guide implementation, as is the case with all such treaties. Depending on the treaty's provisions, either the states parties would be required to report periodically to that committee on their progress in dealing with corporate-related human rights abuses within their jurisdictions, or they would have to require businesses to do so directly. In either case, the committee would issue comments and recommendations, as they do in relation to other human rights treaties. If the reporting was the duty of the states, many would lack the capacity to do so adequately, as is already the case today with reporting on their current state-related obligations.

And if the reporting was to be done by companies directly, then presumably states would have to enforce the obligation upon them—which would take us back to some of the enforcement challenges discussed in previous paragraphs. In addition, the overall arithmetic for the treaty body would be daunting. These committees cannot keep up with monitoring the limited universe of states parties today, and yet each committee deals only with a specific set of rights or one affected group. How a treaty body would cope with the incalculably larger universe of businesses, while addressing all rights of all persons affected by them, is unclear. What is clear is that additional means of authoritative "monitoring" would be required.

Finally, there is a risk that a treaty would establish too low a ceiling. Consider this scenario. In the unlikely event that some overarching business and human rights treaty emerged from the inauspicious circumstances under which I began my mandate, it would have been based on a very low common denominator with potentially adverse consequences for social compliance mechanisms. In the wake of a treaty with low standards, external pressure on companies that are not in the corporate social-responsibility vanguard to aspire to the highest voluntary levels—pressure from NGO campaigns, socially responsible investment funds, consumer groups, and so on—might well become less effective because those companies could reasonably respond that they are dutifully following newly enacted international law. The loss of social leverage would be even more consequential if a treaty with low standards was not ratified by enough states to enter into force as law, or if it was ratified by the bare minimum required but by few or no major home states of multinationals.

Raising these concerns does not imply that we should give up on the current international human rights machinery. On the contrary, it is meant to identify additional ways in which preventing harm and providing remedy are necessary. The same is true of one final feature of the international treaty system I want to address and which has received far too little attention in relation to human rights: a pronounced trend toward fragmentation in the international legal order itself.

Legal Fragmentation

States are simultaneously subject to numerous bodies of international law, such as investment law, trade law, and environmental law, along with human rights law. How are conflicting international legal obligations to be resolved? Human rights discourse is infused with the assumption of a rights-based hierarchy—the idea that human rights trump not only in a moral sense but, if enough international legal instruments were added, that they would do so in terms of the law as well. This belief is one driver behind the quest for additional legalization. But the current practice of international law reflects this hierarchy only in part, discussed below. More generally, the authoritative International Law Commission (ILC) and a bourgeoning academic literature find that the predominant trend in international legalization in recent decades is toward the "fragmentation of international law" into separate and autonomous spheres of law. In an influential report to the UN General Assembly, the ILC concluded that "no homogenous hierarchical metasystem is realistically available" within the international legal order to resolve the problem of incompatible provisions, including when different tribunals that have overlapping jurisdictions address exactly the same set of facts and yet reach different conclusions.[30] This outcome has been described as "regime collision."

Illustrating the phenomenon, in the 1990s Argentina privatized the delivery of water to households and entered into a contract with a consortium of international water companies to provide the service. Subsequently, the government denied a request by the companies to increase the tariffs they could charge, made necessary, the companies said, by additional costs as well as a severe devaluation of the peso. The companies sued Argentina under binding international arbitration, as permitted by bilateral investment treaties that Argentina had signed. In the hearing, Argentina among other defenses invoked its obligation to fulfill the human right to water as justification for denying the rate increase. The international tribunal hearing the case agreed with the companies and concluded:

> Argentina and the amicus curiae submissions received by the Tribunal suggest that Argentina's human rights obligations to assure its population the right to water somehow trumps its obligations under the BITs [bilateral investment treaties] and that the existence of the human right to water also implicitly gives Argentina the authority to take actions in disregard of its BIT obligations. The Tribunal does not find a basis for such a conclusion either in the BITs or international law. Argentina is subject to both international obligations, i.e. human rights and [investment] treaty obligation, and must respect both of them equally.[31]

In other words, the country itself has to figure out how to reconcile its various international legal obligations—several of which may have implications for human rights.

One exception to the fragmentation challenge, conceptually if not always in practice, is the category of norms called "*jus cogens,*" or "peremptory." This is the name given to norms of general international law that permit no exemption under any circumstances, and which are said to trump any contrary norm, including treaty provisions.[32] No definitive list exists, but it is generally believed to include the prohibition of such egregious conduct as genocide, war crimes, and some crimes against humanity. Nevertheless, at an everyday level "*jus cogens* does not dispose of most 'ordinary' value conflicts" among different bodies of law—for example, between the promotion of free trade and the protection of the environment—because most such conflicts do not rise to that level of severity.[33] Similarly, the category of *jus cogens* norms does not encompass the broad spectrum of "ordinary" human rights harms with which companies may be involved, and therefore it doesn't take us far enough.

In short, at the global level no hierarchy of legal norms can be taken for granted beyond *jus cogens* norms. Therefore, a business and human rights treaty would not resolve the type of "regime collision" illustrated by the Argentine water case. "Legal fragmentation cannot itself be combated," write two leading legal theorists. "At best, a weak normative compatibility of the fragments might be achieved. However, this is dependent upon the ability . . . to establish a specific network logic, which can effect a loose coupling of colliding units."[34] In other words, the heavy lifting in attempting to reconcile different state obligations under international law has to take place in the realm of practice, where objectives are defined and can be aligned so as to achieve greater "normative compatibility." The Guiding Principles begin to address this challenge.

To sum up: International law has an important role to play in constructing a better-functioning global regime to govern business and human rights. But I did not believe that promoting some overarching global legal framework for corporate accountability was a productive objective for my mandate; the foundations were lacking, the issues too complex, and states too conflicted; it offered no short-term benefits while posing long-term risks; and whatever the ultimate outcome might be, it would take a long time to get there. Thus, "interim" measures would be required in any event. This brings me to the polar opposite of the juridical paradigm: voluntarism.

IV. VOLUNTARY INITIATIVES

By the 1990s, corporate social responsibility (CSR) initiatives had emerged in many sectors of business. Illustrating the trend, each of the cases discussed in chapter 1—Nike, Bhopal, Shell, and Yahoo—generated campaigns and/or lawsuits against the companies involved, and they, in turn, adopted business principles or codes of conduct pledging to follow responsible practices. Moreover, as noted in the Introduction, a general policy shift in the 1990s toward greater reliance on market mechanisms provided government support for voluntary CSR initiatives rather than mandatory regulations in such areas as business and human rights.

Origins

CSR morphed out of corporate philanthropy. Philanthropy itself became more strategic over time as companies began to make social investments where they operate. Depending on industry sector, this might include building housing for workers, community health clinics, schools, and roads, or hooking up nearby towns and villages to the company's electrical grid or fresh water supplies. Over time, this practice extended to increasing local procurement and training local suppliers. From there, two distinct strands emerge, focused on business opportunity and risk respectively. With regard to the first, social entrepreneurs began to experiment with microenterprises such as consumer lending and mobile telephones or other forms of what came to be known as "bottom of the pyramid marketing" or "socially inclusive business models."[35] Most recently, Harvard business guru Michael Porter has advocated a grand strategy of "creating shared value"—companies creating economic value for themselves "in a way that also creates value for society by addressing its needs and challenges."[36] My mandate was meant to encompass the second and less glamorous CSR strand: the risk that companies cause or contribute to adverse social impacts.

In response to such risks, companies began to adopt voluntary standards and verification schemes. These go beyond meeting local legal requirements—and in fact they can conflict with them. The antiapartheid campaign against South Africa gave rise to a precursor. The Reverend Leon Sullivan, an African-American pastor in Philadelphia's Zion Baptist Church and longtime civil rights advocate, was appointed to the General Motors Board in 1971. GM was the largest employer of blacks in South Africa at the time. As an alternative to the push for divestment from the country, Sullivan developed a code of conduct known as the Sullivan Principles, adopted by more than one hundred U.S. companies operating in South Africa. It demanded nonsegregation in those companies' workplace facilities, equal treatment and equal pay for equivalent work regardless of race, training nonwhites for better jobs, and increasing their numbers in management positions.

Unilateral company codes for offshore vendors were introduced in the early 1990s; Gap and Nike adopted theirs in 1992. Internal audit teams were established to verify that contractors were complying, and gradually a social audit industry emerged. Unilateral efforts were soon followed by collective initiatives involving other firms in the same sector; the chemical industry moved early, largely in response to Bhopal. Multistakeholder initiatives were pioneered in the late 1990s. Prominent examples include the Fair Labor Association (FLA) to monitor and improve factory conditions in suppliers for certain premium brands in the athletic footwear and apparel industry, including Nike, Puma, Phillips Van Heusen, and Patagonia; and an accreditation system developed by Social Accountability International (SAI) that allows for compliance certification of entire facilities in any industry. Fair trade schemes promised that products were manufactured or grown in accordance with certain social and environmental standards. Companies also began to develop more systematic means for engaging external stakeholders at global and local levels, enabling them to better understand operating contexts, build trust, and avoid surprises.

Public-private initiatives came along in the early 2000s. In areas related to business and human rights, the best known are the Kimberley Process, intended to stem the flow of conflict diamonds through a certification and tamperproof packaging system; the Extractive Industry Transparency Initiative, whereby oil, gas, and mining companies agree to publish what they pay to participating host governments and those governments commit to certain transparency standards for the corresponding revenue, in the hope that this will reduce corruption; and the Voluntary Principles on Security and Human Rights, prescribing vetting, training, and reporting practices for the private and public security forces extractive companies use to protect their assets. The UN Global Compact became a leading CSR advocacy and learning forum, as well as a provider of tools for companies to manage social and environmental challenges.

Today it is rare for multinational corporations and many other businesses not to have or participate in one or more CSR initiatives. As noted at the outset of this chapter, the business community, led by the major international business associations, urged that I devote my mandate to advocating and supporting the further development of voluntary initiatives in the business and human rights area, and to identifying and disseminating best practices. In contrast, many human rights organizations were and remain skeptical of such initiatives precisely because they are voluntary, not legally binding, believing that they permit companies merely to burnish their image without changing their behavior.

A Profile

As I did with the treaty route, I set out as best I could to assess voluntarism as a general strategy for advancing the business and human rights agenda. The empirical literature was (and largely remains) spotty; even today no comprehensive studies exist. Therefore, I undertook three projects in 2006 and 2007. One was a questionnaire survey of the Fortune Global 500 firms (FG500); the second was a Web-based survey of actual CSR policies of a broader cross section of more than 300 firms from all regions; and the third was a Web-based survey of the policies of 25 major Chinese companies, including in Mandarin where no information in English was available.[37] I wanted to know what if any human rights provisions companies had adopted, and what if any patterns existed across regions and industries. The surveys were hardly exhaustive and these were not "average" firms, but the results did provide useful grounding.

Very few companies at the time had what could be described

as fully fledged human rights policies. But nearly all of the 102 firms that responded to the FG500 survey stated that they had incorporated some elements of human rights into their policies and practices. Workplace issues dominated the list. All respondents referenced nondiscrimination as a core corporate responsibility, at minimum meaning recruitment and promotion based on merit. Workplace health and safety standards were cited almost as frequently. Almost three-fourths said they recognized freedom of association and the right to bargain collectively; the prohibition against child and forced labor; and the right to privacy. Not surprisingly, workplace issues dominated in manufacturing and issues related to communities in the extractive sector. In virtually all respects the broader cross-section of 300 companies roughly tracked the FG500 pattern but at considerably lower levels of adoption—so company size clearly seemed to matter.

Where did the standards come from that companies referenced in their codes? ILO declarations and conventions topped the list, followed by the Universal Declaration. The Global Compact was also cited, but beyond recapitulating ILO labor standards, its human rights principles are very general, simply asking companies to "support and respect the protection of human rights" and to not be complicit in human rights abuses committed by others. The OECD Guidelines were referenced as well, but at that point the Guidelines merely linked corporate human rights responsibilities to the host country's human rights commitments, not to any international standards. In any event, companies did not "adopt" international standards in any literal sense; they reported "support" for the principles of the various instruments they invoked and of being "influenced by" them. This could make for elastic interpretations: I learned in one admittedly extreme case that what a company's code described as "engaging in dialogue with employees about issues of mutual interest" was intended to be its version of freedom of association and collective bargaining. Premier initiatives such as the FLA and SAI meet or exceed ILO standards, but the number of companies participating in them is small.

Despite the proclaimed universality of human rights, the political culture of a company's home country seemed to affect which rights it recognized. European multinationals were more likely than their American counterparts to reference the rights to health and to an adequate standard of living. They were also more likely to state that their human rights policies extended beyond the workplace to include their impact on the communities where they operate. U.S. and Japanese firms tended to recognize a narrower spectrum of rights and rights holders. The most widely cited right by Chinese companies at the time—and that was by only 5 in the sample of 25—was the right to development, which few Western governments or companies recognize.[38] Moreover, even among companies domiciled in the same country and operating in the same sector, the particular home market segment also seemed to shape their human rights policies. For example, the FG500 survey indicated that some form of supply-chain monitoring was common. Anecdotally, it was known that premium brands like Nike, trading on cachet, tended to have more ambitious supply-chain standards and protocols than value brands such as Walmart, where price points dominate. Because it is not uncommon for the same supplier to manufacture for different brands, different workers in the same factory, say in China, Bangladesh, or Honduras, therefore might be covered by different standards.

How did these companies assess and report on their human

rights impact? One-third of the FG500 stated that they routinely included human rights criteria in their social and environmental impact assessments—although I knew of only one company at the time that had ever conducted a full-scale human rights impact assessment of a major project (BP, of a planned liquefied natural gas facility in the Indonesian province of Papua). Most FG500 respondents said they had internal reporting systems in place to track performance. Three-fourths indicated that they also reported externally; of those, fewer than half utilized a third-party medium like the Global Reporting Initiative, which provides detailed templates, or the far less demanding Global Compact Communication on Progress. The rest issued varying forms of narrative reports, often adorned with photos of smiling children, on their own company-based Web sites and periodic publications. Here, too, national differences appeared: European companies were more likely to engage in external reporting than U.S. firms; Japanese companies lagged well behind both; and there were only two references to reporting in the sample of Chinese companies.

I also inquired about stakeholder engagement. Most FG500 respondents indicated that they worked with external stakeholders in developing and implementing their human rights policies and practices. U.S. firms were somewhat less likely to do so than their European or Australian counterparts, perhaps reflecting the stronger "shareholder" model in U.S. corporate law and culture. Japanese firms lagged behind both. NGOs were the most frequently mentioned external partner, except by Chinese and Japanese firms. Industry associations also featured prominently. International institutions such as the UN were next except for U.S. firms, which ranked them last, behind labor unions and governments, reflecting the standoffish posture of America's political culture toward such institutions more generally.

Assessment

So what did these surveys indicate about the state of play at the time? For starters, they suggested a number of encouraging trends. Most notably, such a mapping scarcely would have been possible a decade earlier because there would have been too few data points. Not only had uptake increased rapidly; the scope of initiatives was also expanding. For example, when the leading brands in the apparel industry first began supply-chain monitoring, they focused on the factories where items are cut and sewn; then they discovered the need to push further down to fabric and textile mills, and to makers of buttons and such; most recently they have begun to address working conditions on cotton farms. Voluntary initiatives also expanded into the financial sector, initially through project lending banks that demand certain assurances with regard to projects' social and environmental impacts.

Yet another encouraging finding in the FG500 survey was that fewer than half of the firms that reported having adopted elements of a human rights policy said they had themselves experienced what the questionnaire described as "a significant human rights issue." This suggests that norm diffusion and learning from others' mistakes was taking place. No doubt this was facilitated by rapidly expanding CSR staffs within companies, an increase in nonprofit and for-profit service providers to advise and assist firms, the demands of socially responsible investors and large public sector pension funds, and the dissemination activities of entities like the Global Compact and its national networks, especially in key emerging markets.

Clearly, voluntary initiatives were a significant force to build on. But the surveys also indicated that in the area of business and human rights the overall universe of company-based initiatives fell short as a stand-alone approach. Although growing rapidly, the numbers remained small. With few exceptions, managing the risk of adverse human rights impacts was not strategic for firms; most were still in a reactive mode, responding to external developments they experienced or witnessed. Moreover, companies typically determined for themselves not only which human rights standards they would address but also how to define them, and these could reflect the preferences of home markets and market segments as much as the needs of affected people in the host country. External accountability mechanisms for ensuring adherence to voluntary standards were weak or did not exist at all. From extensive discussions with company personnel, I also found that CSR activities as a whole tended not to be well integrated with firms' core business functions. Finally, business-based initiatives rarely provided affected individuals and communities with any means of recourse.

In supply-chain contexts, the fact that different workers in the same factory could be covered by different codes is inherently odd—though each code may well exceed locally prevailing standards. It also created enormous duplication of factory audits, generating "audit fatigue" on the part of suppliers, which is one reason they engage in cheating by keeping different sets of books and coaching workers and managers how to respond to audit interviews. As I was conducting this research, groups of companies—including large retailers like Walmart, Tesco, Carrefour, and Migros—were beginning to collaborate on code consolidation as a response. But at the same time, leading initiatives like the FLA were discovering that supply-chain monitoring by itself did not appreciably improve performance on the factory floor—that greater investments in training managers in basic human resources skills, let alone human rights, would also be required. Indeed, they found that the capacity shortfall that affected shop floor performance included the need to have more and better-resourced public labor inspectors.

Moreover, the further the leading brands moved to expand their CSR scope and deepen its reach—beyond suppliers to thousands of cotton farms and millions of farmers, for example—the more daunting their task became. At minimum, this required extensive cooperation with other brands, which is never easy because the companies are competitors, and also with public authorities. At that time the extractive sector as a whole lagged well behind on the learning curve.

To sum up: Voluntary initiatives emerged relatively quickly and evolved to include aspects of human rights. Like international law, they provide an essential building block in any overall strategy for adapting the human rights regime to provide more effective protection to individuals and communities against corporate-related human rights harm. But my research also indicated that they had significant and systematic limits, and therefore were not likely by themselves to bridge business and human rights governance gaps. And yet here, too, as with the treaty route, the analysis of shortcomings provided insights on how to proceed: simply put, finding ways to drive more authoritative guidance into market practices.

In drawing my foundational considerations to a close, I advised the Human Rights Council in 2007 that "no single silver bullet can resolve the business and human rights challenge. A broad array of measures is required, by all relevant actors."[39] But, I added, those measures must cohere and generate cumulative progress over time. The Council rolled over my mandate for another year and asked me to come back with specific recommendations.

V. CONCLUSION

The debate that pitted "mandatory" approaches against "voluntary" ones had induced policy stalemate at the international level. Yet neither was capable by itself of narrowing global governance gaps in business and human rights anytime soon. Now I had an official invitation to identify a path forward. The overriding lesson I drew from the assessment of the two approaches was that a new regulatory dynamic was required under which public and private governance systems—corporate as well as civil—each come to add distinct value, compensate for one another's weaknesses, and play mutually reinforcing roles—out of which a more comprehensive and effective global regime might evolve, including specific legal measures. International relations scholars call this "polycentric governance." But practical guidance, not merely a new concept, was needed to persuade governments, the business community, and other stakeholders to move in this direction.

One reason that existing initiatives, public and private, do not add up to a more coherent system capable of truly moving markets is the lack of an authoritative focal point around which the expectations and behavior of the relevant actors can converge. Thus, my immediate objective was to develop and obtain agreement on a normative framework and corresponding policy guidance for the business and human rights domain, establishing both its parameters and its perimeters.

For starters, such a framework needed to spell out the respective responsibilities of states and business in relation to human rights, and equally important, what actions those responsibilities entailed. Of course, states knew that their legal duties and policy requirements under the international human rights regime extended beyond abuses by state agents. But actual state practice indicated that even the most committed had not addressed the full range of actions these implied in relation to business. For its part, business acknowledged some responsibility for human rights, if nothing else by virtue of adopting CSR initiatives. But here, too, actual practice indicated considerable divergence and shortcomings in the understanding of what those responsibilities were and implied. To avoid ambiguity and strategic gaming on the ground, it also was critical that the two sets of obligations be clearly differentiated from one another, and that they reflected the different social roles of the actors who are expected to meet those responsibilities.

In addition, the scope of the framework had to coincide with the scope of the business and human rights domain in two respects. First, because business can affect virtually all internationally recognized rights, the framework needed to encompass all such rights, not only some arbitrary subset. Second, the framework needed to reach beyond the relatively small and often weak units in governments and business enterprises that currently have responsibility for managing business and human rights: in the case of states, to include agencies that promote trade and investment, or that deal with securities regulation, to mention but a few; and in the case of businesses, to the different business functions that impact directly on workers and communities, companies' own internal oversight and compliance systems, as well as closer engagement between businesses and their internal and external stakeholders.

For similar reasons, business and human rights was far too

big for the UN's human rights machinery alone. Many other international organizations had developed corporate responsibility standards over time, addressed to their particular missions and mandates. Ideally, the human rights dimensions of these efforts would become aligned with the UN framework, creating convergence and cumulative effects. This required establishing relationships with those organizations and constructing the framework as a platform of core norms and policy guidance that others could build on in their particular institutional contexts.

In addition, as an initial priority, I deliberately stressed preventative measures and alternative dispute resolution techniques, as a complement to, not a substitute for, judicial measures. They can be established more readily than legal regimes can be built and judicial systems reformed, and if successful they should have the effect of reducing the incidence of harm directly. Moreover, states, firms, and civil society organizations can play important roles in establishing and supporting nonjudicial grievance mechanisms even as the longer-term project of judicial reform and capacity building continues. I considered closer engagement between companies and the individuals and communities they impact to be a central element in this strategy.

There was one other requirement: to move this agenda forward, governments would have to endorse such a framework, and governments were more likely to endorse it if it enjoyed broad stakeholder buy-in.

These were the key aims behind the Protect, Respect and Remedy Framework and the Guiding Principles for its implementation, to which I turn next.

Chapter Three

PROTECT, RESPECT AND REMEDY

The international community is still in the early stages of adapting the human rights regime to provide more effective protection to individuals and communities against corporate-related human rights harm. Chapter 1 illustrated how governance gaps provide permissive environments for wrongful acts by companies, even where none may be intended, without adequate sanction or remedy. In chapter 2, I explained why neither the treaty route nor the voluntary corporate social responsibility approach by itself is likely to bridge these gaps sufficiently anytime soon. A successful way forward, I concluded, needs to recognize, better interconnect, and leverage the multiple spheres of governance that shape the conduct of multinational corporations.

The Protect, Respect and Remedy Framework (Framework) and Guiding Principles (GPs) for its implementation aim to establish a common global normative platform and authoritative policy guidance as a basis for making cumulative step-by-step, progress without foreclosing any other promising longer-term developments. The Framework addresses *what* should be done; the Guiding Principles *how* to do it. The present chapter outlines their key features, the thinking behind them, and their reception by the major stakeholder groups: states, businesses, and civil society. Although the GPs incorporate and build on the Framework, for the sake of clarity this chapter separates the Framework's foundational considerations from the additional operational guidance provided by the GPs. Chapter 4 provides an analytical reprise of the strategic paths by which they were produced, endorsed by the UN Human Rights Council, incorporated by other standard-setting bodies, and taken up directly by other key actors.

To remind: The Framework and the GPs rest on three pillars. The first is the state duty to protect against human rights abuses by third parties, including business enterprises, through appropriate policies, regulation, and adjudication. The second is the corporate responsibility to respect human rights, which means that business enterprises should act with due diligence to avoid infringing on the rights of others and to address adverse impacts with which they are involved. The third is the need for greater access by victims to effective remedy, both judicial and nonjudicial. Each pillar is an essential component in an interrelated and dynamic system of preventative and remedial measures: the state duty to protect because it lies at the very core of the international human rights regime; the corporate responsibility to respect because it is the basic expectation society has of business in relation to human rights; and access to remedy because even the most concerted efforts cannot prevent all abuse.

For reasons discussed in the previous chapter, my stipulation of what should be done was intended to be broadly consistent with existing international law rather than to advocate for new legal standards that would either trigger an inconclusive debate or be ignored altogether—and in my judgment, those would have been the inevitable outcomes. The normative novelty was the way in which the Framework's components were defined and linked together within a single and coherent human-rights–compatible template. The GPs move more directly in a prescriptive direction by elaborating how existing commitments must, should, or can be met.

I. THE FRAMEWORK

The Framework identifies the legal duties and related policy rationales of states with regard to business and human rights; the independent social responsibilities of companies, particularly multinational corporations, in relation to human rights–where "independent" means that they exist irrespective of whether states are living up to their commitments; and the remedial mechanisms associated with both. The Framework establishes foundational principles and also lays down markers for an array of complex and relatively new issues for the human rights field that would require further development and consideration–several of which were later taken up in the GPs.

The State Duty to Protect

In international human rights discourse, states' legal duties typically are differentiated according to the typology of "respect, protect, and fulfill," with some usage adding "promote" between the latter two. The category of "protect" refers to protection by the state against human rights abuse by third parties–that is, by private actors. Much of the early thinking concerning third parties had focused on the likes of armed rebel groups. But by definition, third parties include business enterprises. Thus, the state duty to protect against business-related human rights abuse became the point of departure for the Framework. The first step was to make its meaning clear, and then to identify ways for states to discharge this duty more effectively.

The state duty to protect against third-party abuse, including business, is grounded in international human rights law, both treaty-based and customary law. The specific language employed in the main UN human rights treaties varies, but all include two sets of obligations. First, the treaties commit states parties themselves to refrain from violating the enumerated rights of persons within their jurisdiction ("respect"). Second, the treaties require states to "ensure" (or some functionally equivalent verb) the enjoyment or realization of those rights by rights-holders.[1] Ensuring that rights-holders enjoy those rights, in turn, requires protection by states against other social actors, including businesses, whose actions impede or negate the rights.

It is generally agreed that the state duty to protect is a standard of conduct, not result. What this means in relation to business is that states are not per se responsible when a business enterprise commits a human rights abuse. But states may breach their international human rights law obligations if they fail to take appropriate steps to prevent such abuse and to investigate, punish, and redress it when it occurs; or when the acts of an enterprise may be directly attributable to the state, for example because it merely serves as the state's agent. In this sense, states themselves may bear some responsibility for the acts of state-owned enterprises. Within these parameters, international law gives states broad discretion as to how to discharge their duty to protect. The main human rights treaties generally contemplate legislative, administrative, and judicial measures.

Current guidance from UN human rights treaty bodies generally suggests that states are not required to regulate the extraterritorial activities of businesses incorporated in their jurisdiction, but nor are they generally prohibited from doing so provided there is a recognized jurisdictional basis—for example, where abuses are committed by or against their nationals. We saw in chapter 2 that some treaty bodies are increasingly recommending that states should take steps to prevent abuse abroad by multinational corporations domiciled in their jurisdiction. In addition, there are strong policy rationales for home states to encourage such companies to respect rights abroad. This is particularly the case where the state itself is involved in the business venture—whether as owner, investor, insurer, procurer, or simply promoter. Doing so gets home states out of being in the untenable position of indirectly contributing to overseas corporate abuse through its support for a firm that is involved in such abuse. Moreover, it can provide much-needed support to host states that lack the capacity to implement fully an effective regulatory environment on their own.

In my 2008 report presenting the Framework, I stipulated this formulation of the state duty to protect as a foundational element of the international human rights regime as it applies to business enterprises. The report went on to say:

> The general nature of the duty to protect is well understood by human rights experts within governments and beyond. What seems less well internalized is the diverse array of policy domains through which states may fulfill this duty with regard to business activities, including how to foster a corporate culture respectful of human rights at home and abroad. This should be viewed as an urgent policy priority for governments.[2]

I identified four such policy clusters focused on broadly preventative measures; adjudication and punitive measures are addressed in the "remedy" pillar, along with non-state-based forms of remediation.

The first policy cluster concerns international investment agreements—the point of entry for a multinational corporation into a host country market. They include state-to-state bilat-eral investment treaties (BITs) that spell out the protections accorded by the capital-importing country to investors from the capital-exporting country, as well as investor-state contracts for specific investment projects, such as the delivery of water services or oil and mining concessions. These agreements pro-tect foreign investors against arbitrary treatment by host gov-ernments. But they also potentially pose two problems for host governments' regulatory policy space. One is that the agree-ments can lock in existing domestic regulatory requirements for the duration of a project, thus allowing the foreign investor to seek exemption from or compensation for the host government adopting, say, a new labor law, even if it raises costs equally on all enterprises in the country, domestic as well as foreign. If the government does not comply, the investor may be able to sue under binding international arbitration, in which an ad hoc panel of arbitrators considers only the treaty or contract text ("the law applicable"), not any broader public interest consid-erations that may be at stake. Research conducted by my team and others showed that provisions protecting foreign inves-tors' interests and the rulings of arbitration panels had become increasingly expansive over time, particularly where host gov-ernments lacked bargaining power.[3] In some instances even the definition of "investor" and "investment" expanded to extend protections to would-be investors (preestablishment rights), intermediate holding companies, and minority shareholders—and by extension potentially to various other forms of economic transactions: "sales presence; market share through trade; loan agreements and construction contracts; promissory notes and other banking instruments; and even establishing law firms."[4] Even where no claim is brought against the state, the possibility of a suit itself may have chilling effects on the willingness of the host government to adopt adequate regulations in the best interests of its own population. The second problem results from the extensive fragmentation within governments, and the greater bureaucratic clout of investment promotion policy and agencies compared to entities concerned with the protection of human rights. This is what the government of South Africa discovered in the Black Economic Empowerment case I referred to in chapter 2. More balanced investment agreements and better alignment among host government agencies and policies are required to redress both problems.

The second policy cluster requiring greater attention concerns corporate law and securities regulation—incorporation and listing requirements, directors' duties, reporting requirements, and related policies. This body of law and regulation directly shapes what companies do and how they do it. Yet its implications for human rights are poorly understood. Traditionally, the two have been viewed as distinct legal and policy spheres, populated by different communities of practice. As a result, there is a lack of clarity in virtually all jurisdictions regarding not only what companies or their directors and officers are required to do regarding human rights, but in many cases even what they are permitted to do without running afoul of their fiduciary responsibilities to shareholders. In addition, there is little if any coordination between agencies that regulate corporate conduct and agencies responsible for implementing human rights obligations. Prior to 2008 a handful of governments and stock exchanges encouraged, and in far fewer cases required, some form of CSR reporting. Others promulgated voluntary CSR guidelines. But relatively few such policies referred specifically to human rights. For the most part, therefore, governments were not providing companies with meaningful guidance on how to do deal with their rapidly escalating human-rights-related risks.

The third policy cluster I identified as requiring further development concerns business operations in areas affected by conflict—over the control of territory, resources, or a government itself. Some of the most egregious human rights abuses, including those related to business enterprises, occur in such areas. As we saw in chapter 1, people in the Democratic Republic of Congo have been cursed by a wealth of natural resources coupled with poor and in some areas nonexistent public governance. The international human rights regime cannot possibly be expected to function as intended in such situations. Here the home states of multinationals need to play a greater role. But home states typically lack the policies, and their embassies the capacity, to advise companies on how to ensure that they avoid involvement in human rights abuse in those situations—and to warn companies when they get too close to such involvement.

Fourth, domestic policy fragmentation spills over into the international arena when states participate in multilateral institutions. International human rights norms are debated in the UN Human Rights Council, trade policy in the World Trade Organization, and development financing, including private sector investment, in the World Bank Group. The same country may—and often does—pursue policies in those arenas that are inconsistent with one another. I had a personal encounter with this phenomenon in 2011, when some of the same governments that supported the GPs at the Human Rights Council in Geneva pushed back on the International Finance Corporation moving too far in the same direction in Washington, D.C. The simple explanation is that Human Rights Council policy is set largely by foreign ministries and policies for the World Bank/ IFC by treasury departments. The two may reflect quite different institutional interests and priorities.

I made no specific recommendations on any of these issues in 2008. Many were entirely new territory for the Human Rights Council, and progress would require more extensive discussions and greater national policy alignment. But I put them on the agenda for further consideration on the grounds that effective responses to business and human rights challenges required that they be addressed.

This brief formulation of the core international human rights law principles and policy rationales regarding the state duty to protect was not met entirely without controversy. Representatives of several states, including the United Kingdom, questioned whether states in fact had a general duty to protect against corporate abuse of human rights.[5] They maintained that the duty is strictly treaty-based, and that the various treaties differed in this regard. The United States, in turn, challenged my use of the term "jurisdiction" to define the duty's geographic scope, insisting on "territory."[6] I suspect they had precedents for Guantánamo prisoners in mind—which is not U.S. territory but arguably is under U.S. jurisdiction. In both instances I modified the language slightly (tightening it in response to the first, and using the clumsier formula "territory and/or jurisdiction" in response to the latter), which sufficed to prevent formal objections while maintaining the essence of what I sought to achieve. For their part, some advocacy groups contended that I understated the extent to which extraterritorial obligations on the home states of multinationals already exist. But that was a tough sell when home states that are generally supportive of human rights were prepared to challenge even the extent of the duty's domestic scope. At the same time, states, the busi-ness community, and the advocacy community supported the emphasis on state duties as the bedrock of protection against corporate human rights abuse.

The Corporate Responsibility to Respect

How do corporations fit into the picture? Companies have legal duties in relation to human rights. They know they must comply with all applicable laws to obtain and sustain their legal license to operate. For multinationals this includes the laws of both host and home states. We have seen that it may also include certain international law standards proscribing egregious conduct, enforced in some national courts. But the international law standards encompass only a narrow range of conduct; not all states have ratified all international human rights treaties; and states vary in their ability and willingness to enforce the obligations they have undertaken. This is where the independent corporate responsibility to respect human rights comes into play. Of the Framework's three pillars, this required the most significant conceptual departure from standard human rights discourse, but it became a centerpiece of the Framework and GPs.

Prior efforts to establish standards governing corporate con-duct in relation to human rights, such as the Norms, sought to identify a limited list of rights for which business enterprises might bear responsibility. Typically, they coupled this with an imprecise and expansive array of corporate duties (in the case of the Norms, "to promote, secure the fulfillment of, respect, ensure respect of and protect"). In doing so they often blurred the distinctions between legal norms, social norms, and moral claims, seeking to make each equally binding under international law. The Protect, Respect and Remedy Framework differs on all dimensions. I begin with the second.

Within the Framework, the specification of the corporate responsibility to respect human rights begins with the observation that this responsibility already exists as a well-established social norm. My use of the term "responsibility" was intended to signal that it differs from legal duties. Social norms exist over and above compliance with laws and regulations. And of course some social norms become law over time; in many countries there were social norms against racial bias in employment, for example, or against smoking in restaurants, long before laws prohibited the practice. Social norms exist independently of states' abilities or willingness to fulfill their own duties. In the case of business, noncompliance with social norms can affect a company's social license to operate: recall from chapter 1 that Shell irretrievably lost its social license to operate in Nigeria's Ogoni territory more than a decade before the government revoked its legal license. Thus, business enterprises are subject to two distinct external governance systems: the system of public law and authority, and a nonstate-based social or civil system grounded in the relations between corporations and their external stakeholders. The system of corporate governance reflects the requirements not only of the former but also the latter—in varying degrees, to be sure, depending upon circumstances. What was lacking, and what the Framework sought to provide, was a more precise and commonly accepted definition of the corporate responsibility to respect human rights, what specific measures it entails, and how it can be linked more effectively with the public-law construction of internationally recognized rights.

But exactly what is a social norm, how do we know that one exists, and how does it function? A social norm expresses a collective sense of "oughtness" with regard to the expected conduct of social actors, distinguishing between permissible and impermissible acts in given circumstances; and it is accompanied by some probability that deviations from the norm will be socially sanctioned, even if only by widespread opprobrium.[7] Now, different people and different countries may hold different expectations of corporate conduct in relation to human rights. But one social norm has acquired near-universal recognition within the global social sphere in which multinationals operate: the corporate responsibility to respect human rights.

By "near-universal recognition" I mean two things. First, the corporate responsibility to respect human rights is widely acknowledged by business itself. At the outset of my mandate, I asked the three largest international business associations to consult their constituents on the question of what standards should apply to business operations in countries where human rights laws are poorly enforced or don't exist at all. They submitted an official policy brief stating that companies "are expected to obey the law, even if it is not enforced, and to respect the principles of relevant international instruments where national law is absent."[8] Moreover, virtually every company and industry CSR initiative acknowledges the corporate responsibility to respect human rights. To take just one example, on human rights day in 2008, the sixtieth anniversary of the adoption of the Universal Declaration, ExxonMobil published a quarter-page infomercial on the op-ed page of the *New York Times* highlighting the Framework and stating that respecting human rights "is a responsibility that the more than 80,000 ExxonMobil employees around the world work to uphold every day."[9] The corporate responsibility to respect human rights is one of the commitments companies undertake in joining the UN Global Compact, expressed in a letter from the CEO to the UN Secretary-General. It is enshrined in soft-law instruments, including ILO declarations and the OECD Guidelines for Multinational Enterprises. And it is increasingly reflected in national CSR guidelines, including in a growing number of emerging-market-economy and developing countries.

Second, of all the human-rights-related expectations that diverse publics may hold of business enterprises, in the global sphere deviation from the corporate responsibility to respect human rights is the most likely to be socially sanctioned, which is how social norms are "enforced." The allegations against companies mapped in chapter 1 were about their not respecting human rights. Advocacy campaigns against companies allege failure to respect human rights. Complaints against multinationals for not respecting human rights are brought to the National Contact Points under the OECD Guidelines. The $525-billion Norwegian Government Pension Fund has divested from companies, including Walmart, for not respecting human rights; for similar reasons the Dutch civil service pension fund has divested from PetroChina. Socially responsible investment funds screen companies for evidence that they respect human rights.

Moreover, the rapid increase in CSR initiatives, whatever their limits, reflects recognition by companies of their need to develop the capacity to respond to these social compliance mechanisms. Indeed, my survey of the Fortune Global 500, summarized in chapter 2, indicated that roughly half of the respondents that had incorporated human rights elements into their CSR policies did so even without having faced a serious human rights event themselves, presumably learning from others' mistakes. In some companies CSR staff report to the chief compliance officer. And a small number of companies have established board-level CSR committees. Among them are major international mining companies, none of which is a household name, so mere consumer-oriented brand burnishing cannot be the full explanation. Such steps pull internal oversight responsibility up into the higher levels of corporate governance.

It is true that these social compliance mechanisms apply unevenly across and within countries and industry sectors—but that does not differentiate them radically from legal compliance mechanisms in many jurisdictions. Yet it is also the case that their role is greatest precisely in relation to multinational corporations operating in countries with weak regulatory environments. Originally, this was due to the fact that transnational social compliance mechanisms—pressure by civil society organizations, organized labor, socially responsible investors, and others—were rooted in the home countries of Western multinationals where brand, reputation, and access to capital might be affected. But in recent years, Chinese companies operating in, say, Peru, South Africa, or Zambia have begun to encounter resistance from local communities and other stakeholders that are empowered and mobilized by the very social norms that had built up around their European and North American counterparts, often assisted by transnational networks of committed advocates and other agents of social compliance.[10] Thus, certain core social norms regarding corporate conduct are taking root within the transnational economic sphere that multinationals themselves have created.

In short, the corporate responsibility to respect human rights is a widely recognized and relatively well-institutionalized social norm, particularly in relation to multinational corporations. But its implications for what companies need to do to meet this responsibility had never been spelled out authoritatively. That became my next task. Building on this foundation, I adapted the standard human rights definition of "respect," elaborated on the substantive content and scope of the corporate responsibility to respect, and stipulated the means for companies to discharge this responsibility.

As we saw in relation to states, in human rights discourse "respecting" rights means to not violate them, to not facilitate or otherwise be involved in their violation. And it entails a correlative responsibility to address harms that do arise. The Framework paraphrases this definition in simple and intuitive terms: as business goes about its business, it should not infringe on the human rights of others. In some situations companies may be asked, or they may volunteer, to do more than "respect" human rights. But not infringing on the rights of others is the baseline norm with the widest global recognition. Moreover, there is no equivalent to buying carbon offsets in human rights: philanthropic good deeds do not compensate for infringing on human rights.

The next question is: to which human rights does the responsibility to respect rights apply? The quest to determine a delimited list of rights that are relevant for business enterprises had been a major preoccupation for some time, including by the drafters of the Norms. But such efforts inevitably run into the fact that companies can affect just about the entire spectrum of internationally recognized rights—the thirty-plus that are so recognized—as we saw in chapter 1. Therefore, any such list will provide inadequate guidance, and as a matter of principle the corporate responsibility to respect human rights must include all internationally recognized rights. In practice, some rights will be at greater risk than others in particular industries or operating contexts, and thus should be the focus of heightened attention. Internet service providers are likely to pose a greater risk to privacy rights and freedom of expression than other lines of business; extractive companies a greater risk in relation to resettlement issues; and athletic footwear manufacturers to rights at work. Likewise, a company operating in the eastern region of the Democratic Republic of Congo is far more likely to be involved in a range of adverse impacts on human rights than one operating in Denmark. But because no such impacts can be ruled out ex ante by any business anywhere, all rights should be considered.

Moreover, an authoritative "list" of internationally recognized rights already exists and does not need to be reinvented. Its core is contained in the International Bill of Human Rights (the Universal Declaration and the two Covenants), coupled with the ILO Declaration on Fundamental Principles and Rights at Work, all of which are widely endorsed by the international community. Depending on circumstances, business enterprises may need to consider additional standards: for example, those found in international humanitarian law when they operate in conflict zones; or the rights of indigenous peoples where they are affected; or of migrant workers, women, or children where they require particular attention—all of which are elaborated in international instruments. In short, an authoritative list of human rights that business enterprises should respect already exists.

There had been a long-standing doctrinal debate whether these international instruments, or which provisions in them, applied directly to business enterprises as legal obligations. My specification of "the list" circumvented this debate. The point is moot when the question is where companies should look for an authoritative enumeration, not of human rights *laws* that might apply to them, but of human *rights* they should respect. For the purposes of social compliance, "the list" provides authoritative benchmarks. Several useful efforts have "translated" the list of internationally recognized rights into business terminology and functions, including one by a group of leading multinationals in the Business Leaders Initiative on Human Rights.[11]

Having established which human rights corporations must respect, it was necessary to further clarify the scope of their responsibility. What acts or attributes of companies does it encompass, and how far does it extend? Here the debate preceding my mandate focused on whether or not the concept "corporate sphere of influence" was an appropriate delimitation of scope; indeed, the resolution establishing my mandate specifically requested that I clarify the meaning of the term. In essence, the concept of corporate sphere of influence was intended as a business analogue to the concept of national jurisdiction: whereas national jurisdiction is defined territorially, the corporate sphere of influence was conceived functionally—the spatial extension over which companies project influence. For reasons elaborated in chapter 2, I found this formulation highly problematic. Among other things, it would have held companies responsible for things unconnected to their business but which in some sense might fall within their capacity to influence, while at the same time possibly absolving them from responsibility for adverse impacts where they could show they lacked influence. Moreover, it would have encouraged endless strategic gaming by states and companies alike about who was responsible for what in particular situations.

Instead, I drew the scope of the corporate responsibility to respect human rights from the definition of respect itself: noninfringement on the rights of others. Thus, the Framework defines scope in terms of the actual and potential adverse human rights impacts arising from a business enterprise's own activities and from the relationships with third parties associated with those activities. In the case of multinational corporations the "enterprise" is understood to include the entire corporate group, however it is structured. And business relationships are understood to include business partners, other entities in the enterprise's value chain, and any other nonstate or state entity directly linked to its business. To adapt the warning sign in the pottery shop, YOU BREAK IT, OR CONTRIBUTE TO BREAKING IT, YOU OWN IT. We saw how Nike's initial response to the campaign concerning its Indonesian supplier factories—that it didn't own the problem because it didn't own the factories—was socially unsustainable.

Corporate complicity in human rights abuses can grow out of business relationships. This was another concept my original mandate asked me to clarify, and on which I produced a report in 2008.[12] Complicity has legal and nonlegal pedigrees, and the implications of both are important for companies. It refers to indirect involvement by companies in human rights abuse—where the actual harm is committed by another party, whether state agents or nonstate actors, but the company contributes to it. The legal meaning of "complicity" has been spelled out most clearly in the area of aiding and abetting acts that may rise to the level of internationally recognized crimes: knowingly providing practical assistance or encouragement that has a substantial effect on the commission of a crime—as, for example, when Chiquita Brands was accused of recruiting right-wing paramilitary forces in Colombia to protect its facilities, who then allegedly killed left-wing guerillas and labor organizers. But even where no law is broken, corporate complicity—contributing to human rights harm, as Apple did with its purchasing practices from Foxconn—is an important benchmark for other social actors. It can impose reputational costs and even lead to divestment, illustrated by the examples of pension funds that I noted earlier.

Now we come to what I considered to be the most important question. How can companies ensure that they meet their responsibility to respect human rights? Claims that they respect rights are all well and good. My questions to them: Do you have systems in place that enable you to support the claim with any degree of confidence? Can you demonstrate to yourselves that you do, let alone to anyone else? In fact, most companies did not and still do not have such systems. And even those that do often exhibit the shortcomings described in the previous chapter. To discharge the responsibility to respect human rights requires that companies develop the institutional capacity to *know* and *show* that they do not infringe on others' rights. For guidance I looked at systems that companies already use to satisfy themselves in other domains that they are accounting for risks. Companies have long conducted transactional due diligence, to ensure that a contemplated merger or acquisition, say, has no hidden risks. Starting in the 1990s, they began to add internal controls for the ongoing management of risks to both the company and to stakeholders who could be harmed by the company's conduct—for example, to prevent employment discrimination, to comply with environmental commitments, or to prevent criminal misconduct by employees. Drawing on these established practices, I introduced the concept of human rights due diligence as a means for companies to identify, prevent, mitigate, and address adverse impacts on human rights.

But human rights due diligence must reflect what is unique to human rights. Because the aim is for companies to address their responsibility to respect rights, it must go beyond identifying and managing material risks to the company itself, to include the risks the company's activities and associated relationships may pose to the rights of affected individuals and communities. Moreover, because human rights involve rights-holders, human rights due diligence is not simply a matter of calculating probabilities; it must meaningfully engage rights-holders or others who legitimately represent them. And because situations on the ground may change—often by the sheer fact of a company's presence— human rights due diligence is not a one-off task, but must be conducted periodically over the life cycle of the particular project.

I acknowledged that the juxtaposition within the Framework of companies complying with national legal requirements and the corporate responsibility to respect human rights may pose difficult dilemmas for multinational corporations in some situations, because the two may conflict. There may be significant host country restrictions on freedom of association, gender equality, and privacy rights, for example. Where that occurs, the Framework recommends that companies honor the principles of internationally recognized human rights to the greatest extent possible, and be able to demonstrate their efforts to do so. At the same time, they should treat the risk of becoming complicit in egregious human rights abuses committed by another, including those host governments' agents, as a legal compliance issue and consider severing the relationship where the risk is high.

Let me sum up how I conceptualized the corporate responsibility to respect human rights. It exists independently of and yet complements the state duty to protect. It is defined in terms of the classic human rights meaning of respect: noninfringement on the rights of others, and addressing harms that do occur. Its substantive content consists of internationally recognized human rights. And its scope follows from its definition: actual or potential adverse human rights impacts by an enterprise's own activities or through the business relationships connected to those activities. This formulation provides greater clarity and predictability for all concerned, including business, than using either the general idea of human rights as moral claims, companies' own "homemade" human rights standards, or an elusive and elastic notion of corporate "influence" as the basis for attributing human rights responsibilities to business enterprises. This formulation won broad approval, though some business associations and government representatives expressed the concern that human rights due diligence should not increase corporate liability or impose undue burdens on small and medium-sized enterprises.

The fact that the corporate responsibility to respect human rights did not propose new legal requirements for business was criticized by some advocacy groups. And yet it does have "bite"—indeed, it has several bites. First, it was precisely this feature that made it possible for states and businesses to accept linking the content of the responsibility to respect specifically to international human rights instruments—even though not all states have ratified all relevant treaties or voted in favor of all relevant declarations, and even though those instruments generally do not apply legally to companies directly. Second, this specification made it clear that unless a company can know and show that it respects human rights its claim that it does remains just that—a claim, not a fact. Third, the concept of human rights due diligence brought the issue of identifying and addressing companies' adverse human rights impacts into a familiar risk-based framing for them. And it provided the basis for a process standard that can be adopted by companies themselves, advocated by stakeholders, and required by governments—which, as discussed below, began to happen almost immediately. Fourth, due diligence by companies can be expected to reduce the incidence of corporate-related human rights harm, thereby benefiting impacted individuals and communities while also lowering the burden on other, more difficult to construct, regime components. Finally, endorsement of this specification by the UN and other international standard-setting bodies gave it official recognition in the system of public governance, thus beginning to pull it beyond the realm of "social expectations" from which it had emerged.

Access to Remedy

Even under the most favorable circumstances, corporate-related human rights harm will occur. As part of their duty to protect under international human rights law, states are required to take steps to investigate, punish, and redress corporate-related abuse of the rights of individuals within their territory and/ or jurisdiction—in short, to provide access to remedy. Without such steps, the duty to protect could be rendered weak or even meaningless. These steps may be taken through judicial, administrative, legislative, or other means. Equally, under the corporate responsibility to respect human rights, business enterprises should establish or participate in effective grievance mechanisms for individuals and communities that may be adversely impacted, without prejudice to legal recourse. The Framework differentiates among three types of grievance mechanisms through which remedy may be sought: judicial, state-based nonjudicial, and nonstate-based.

States often point to the existence of their criminal and civil law systems to demonstrate that they are meeting their international obligations in this regard. But these systems often are weakest where they are most needed. The Framework affirms that states must ensure access to effective judicial remedy for human rights abuses committed within their territory and/or jurisdiction, and that they should consider ways to reduce legal and practical barriers that could lead to its denial. Although the ability of claimants to bring cases against multinational corporations in the courts of the home country has expanded, the practice remains contested in the business and human rights domain. Business remains strongly opposed; home states fear disadvantaging "their" corporations; and host states often resist it on the principle of noninterference in their domestic affairs. Extraterritorial jurisdiction cases also routinely encounter obstacles of legal principles, such as how liability is to be attributed among members of a corporate group, which can be difficult to resolve even in purely domestic situations; as well as procedure, such as who has standing to sue. And it involves serious financial costs for all concerned, above all for claimants and the agencies investigating and prosecuting alleged acts that took place overseas. Chapter 4 discusses how I sought to deal with some of these impediments.

In the area of business and human rights the potential of state-based nonjudicial mechanisms, alongside judicial, is often overlooked. They can play a complaint-handling role as well as other key functions, including promoting human rights, offering guidance and providing support to companies as well as stakeholders. National human rights institutions are one promising vehicle. These are administrative entities, established constitutionally or by statute, to monitor and make recommendations regarding the human rights situation in their respective countries. Some seventy are fully accredited for compliance with UN standards for their independence from, but access to, governmental institutions, and they exist on all continents. But many lack the mandate to address business-related human rights grievances, or are permitted to do so only when business performs public functions or impacts certain rights. I recommended that those mandates be expanded. The National Contact Points (NCPs) under the OECD Guidelines for Multinational Enterprises also have the potential of providing effective remedy. But prior to 2011 the Guidelines had no human rights chapter; they required that an "investment nexus" exist, which some NCPs interpreted as ruling out contractual relationships such as between a brand and its supply-chain partners, as well as lending institutions; and findings against companies lack official consequences. As I will discuss later, I collaborated extensively with the OECD on updating its Guidelines.

The most underdeveloped component of remedial systems in the business and human rights domain is grievance mechanisms at a company's operational level. These can be provided directly by a company, through collaborative arrangements with other stakeholders, or by facilitating recourse to a mutually accepted external expert or body. As already noted, my own research indicated that serious human-rights-related confrontations between companies and individuals or communities frequently began as lesser grievances that companies ignored or dismissed, and which then escalated. This has been particularly true in the extractive industry, as we saw in the case of Shell in Nigeria and in the Cajamarca example. The same pattern is evident in many workplace disputes and in other industry sectors. To make it possible for such grievances to be addressed early and remediated directly, the Framework recommends that companies establish or participate in operational-level grievance mechanisms, with the proviso that they must be dialogue-based or use third-party mediation to avoid having companies be the sole judge of their own actions.

Reactions

The Protect, Respect and Remedy Framework was deliberately heterodox because the standard repertoire of responses had not succeeded in establishing a common basis for thinking about business and human rights challenges, let alone a common platform for acting on them. Providing those was the main legacy I hoped to leave behind even if the mandate had ended then and there. As it turned out, in June 2008 the Human Rights Council unanimously "welcomed" the Framework and extended my mandate by another three years, tasking me with developing more concrete guidance for its implementation. How and why was the Framework received as well as it was in 2008? Chapter 4 maps out the strategic paths I followed throughout the mandate; for now, I let representatives of various stakeholders explain their reactions.

United Nations High Commissioner for Human Rights Navi Pillay described the Framework as "an important milestone."[13] A Norwegian government white paper called it "groundbreaking" and drew on it extensively in assessing its own national policy.[14] In a joint statement the main international business associations said it provides "a clear, practical and objective way of approaching a very complex set of issues."[15] The Business Leaders Initiative on Human Rights stated that the Framework "moves the business and human rights debate forward significantly both by setting out the key responsibilities of companies in relation to all rights they may impact and by stressing that governments must do more to foster corporate cultures which respect rights and close the governance gaps."[16] Forty socially responsible investment funds sent a joint letter to the Human Rights Council stating that the Framework aided their work by promoting greater disclosure of adverse corporate human rights impacts as well as appropriate steps to mitigate them. A joint statement by leading human rights NGOs found the Framework to be "valuable and meriting further attention."[17] A separate statement by Amnesty International said the Framework "has the potential to make an important contribution to the protection of human rights."[18] NGOs and international workers organizations began to use the Framework in their advocacy, governments in policy reviews, and companies in internal gap analyses. Not long thereafter, the United Kingdom's National Contact Point under the OECD Guidelines issued a finding against Afrimex, a UK-based minerals-trading company, for failing to exercise adequate human rights due diligence in its supply chain in the Democratic Republic of Congo, and drew the company's attention to the Framework for the core elements of a socially responsible corporate policy.[19]

The Guiding Principles built on this foundation.

II. GUIDING PRINCIPLES

These positive reactions to the Framework indicated that the major players in business and human rights found it to be new and useful. Though differences among them remained, the divisiveness and discourse disconnects of the previous decade had yielded to a common conversation. My stressing that the Framework did not create new legal obligations undoubtedly contributed to its acceptance by governments and the business community even as it limited the enthusiasm of some advocacy groups. The next phase would be trickier, however, because it was intended to be more prescriptive. In developing it, I implicitly drew on an analytical distinction from the academic study of norms: between "the logic of consequences" and "the logic of appropriateness." The former refers to conduct based on expected gains and losses. In contrast, under the logic of appropriateness "notions of duty, responsibility, identity and obligations [also] may drive behavior."[20] Reflecting on this distinction suggested the following questions for the next phase: given the widely supported commitments embedded in the Framework, what are the "appropriate" steps required to move toward their realization? What additional concrete acts do these commitments imply? The GPs then elaborated on those implications.

However, I should add that this would not simply be an exercise in pure logic—which some of my friends in the academic world did not fully appreciate when noting my failure to provide a robust moral theory or a full scheme for the attribution of legal liability to underpin the Framework. The reason is straightforward: in order to maximize the prospect that states, businesses, and other relevant actors adopt and act on the GPs, I would have to go right back to the Human Rights Council for its up-or-down vote on whether to endorse them. Council members and others seeking to influence their decisions could be expected to adhere not only to "the logic of appropriateness" but also to apply "the logic of consequences" in judging my proposals—calculations of how it would affect them specifically. Accordingly, the GPs needed to be carefully calibrated: pushing the envelope, but not out of reach.

The GPs and related Commentaries are lengthy and complex, and they came with a companion report plus four even longer addenda providing additional information and guidance on specific elements. The following summary can do no more than highlight the key provisions under each of the three pillars. I cite portions of the GPs' text to convey a sense of the actual language the Human Rights Council and other stakeholders had in front of them in reaching their decisions.

The State Duty to Protect

The Guiding Principles reaffirm the foundational elements of the state duty to protect, as described earlier in this chapter.

Then they lay out a series of regulatory and policy measures for states to consider in meeting this duty; stress the need to achieve better internal alignment among relevant national (and international) policy domains and institutions; and introduce the idea that in some circumstances states should require companies to exercise human rights due diligence. This set of GPs can be divided into two broad categories: those that are generally applicable in any situation, and additional provisions for particular types of situations.

The GPs remind states of the need to enforce existing laws that already regulate business respect for human rights (for example, labor, nondiscrimination, and criminal law), and to review whether these laws provide the necessary coverage in light of evolving circumstances (GP 3a). But we know that business conduct is directly shaped by areas of law and policy that are largely silent on the subject of human rights. Therefore, the GPs also stipulate that states should:

- Ensure that other laws and policies governing the creation and ongoing operation of business enterprises, such as corporate law, do not constrain but enable business respect for human rights [GP 3b].

Doing this, in turn, requires better alignment among the relevant state entities. Thus:

- States should ensure that governmental departments, agencies and other State-based institutions that shape business practices are aware of and observe the state's human rights obligations when fulfilling their respective mandates, including by providing them with relevant information, training and support [GP 8].

Better alignment also requires that "states should maintain adequate domestic policy space to meet their human rights obligations when pursuing business-related objectives with other states or business enterprises, for instance through investment treaties or contracts" (GP 9). This provision addresses the need for host governments to avoid signing overly restrictive investment agreements that constrain their ability to adopt bona fide public interest legislation and regulation, including for human rights protection, under the threat of being sued by foreign investors because the measures alter the economic equilibrium assumed under an investment agreement.

In provisions that are applicable to all business enterprises but which are particularly relevant for multinational corporations, the GPs stipulate:

- States should set out clearly the expectation that all business enterprises domiciled in their territory and/or jurisdiction respect human rights throughout their operations [GP 2]; [and they should] provide effective guidance to business enterprises on how to respect human rights throughout their operations [GP 3c].

The Commentary summarizes a distinction I drew in my 2010 report and elsewhere, between domestic policy measures that have extraterritorial effects, and actually adjudicating conduct in one's own courts that took place within another jurisdiction, pointing out that the former do not raise the same jurisdictional challenges as the latter. For example, a securities regulator is well within its authority in imposing disclosure rules on companies listed in its jurisdiction, whether domestic or foreign, requiring them to report on certain types or magnitudes of risk in their entire global operations, on the grounds that domestic investors need to be informed about and protected against such risks, no matter where they may be incurred. This section of the Commentary was intended to encourage states to explore the use of such measures in relation to significant human-rights-related risks posed by companies throughout their operations.

In addition to these general provisions, the GPs also address two types of situational variants: one where the state is itself involved in a business venture, and the other where business operations take place in conflict-affected areas.

The Commentary observes that states individually are the primary duty-bearers under international human rights law, and collectively they are the trustees of the international human rights regime. Moreover, where the acts of a business enterprise can be attributed to the state, a human rights abuse by the enterprise may also entail a violation of the state's own international law obligations. Therefore:

- States should take additional steps to protect against human rights abuses by business enterprises that are owned or controlled by the state, or that receive substantial support and services from state agencies such as export credit agencies and official investment insurance or guarantee agencies, including, where appropriate, by requiring human rights due diligence [GP 4].

The Commentary makes it clear that the phrase "where appropriate" applies to situations "where the nature of business operations or operating contexts pose significant risk to human rights." The GPs also add that states do not relinquish their international human rights obligations when they outsource the delivery of services that may impact upon the enjoyment of human rights (GP 5)—for example, when they privatize prisons or water delivery services—but that states are required to provide continued oversight; and that states "should promote respect for human rights by business enterprises with which they conduct commercial relations" (GP 6), as in government procurement.

From the outset of the mandate I made the case that business operations in conflict zones require special attention from states and businesses alike. A lengthy Guiding Principle addresses preventative steps states should take (again, judicial recourse is addressed under "remedy"). Although the provision applies to all states, it has particular relevance for home states of multinational corporations, both at the level of the capital and through in-country embassy or consular services:

- Because the risk of gross human rights abuses is heightened in conflict-affected areas, states should help ensure that business enterprises operating in those contexts are not involved with such abuses, including by:
  (a) Engaging at the earliest stage possible with business enterprises to help them identify, prevent and mitigate the human rights-related risks of their activities and business relationships;
  (b) Providing adequate assistance to business enterprises to assess and address the heightened risks of abuses, paying special attention to both gender-based and sexual violence;
  (c) Denying access to public support and services for a business enterprise that is involved with gross human rights abuses and refuses to cooperate in addressing the situation;

(d) Ensuring that their current policies, legislation, regulations and enforcement measures are effective in addressing the risk of business involvement in gross human rights abuses [GP 7].

As a supplement to the GPs, I appended a separate, more detailed report on business and human rights in conflict-affected regions.

The Corporate Responsibility to Respect

In the fall of 2010, not long before posting a discussion draft of the Guiding Principles, I previewed their core message for the corporate responsibility to respect in my annual remarks to the UN General Assembly: "The era of declaratory CSR is over," I stated. "The corporate responsibility to respect human rights cannot be met by words alone: it requires specific measures by means of which companies can 'know and show' that they respect rights."[21] In all, 14 of the 31 GPs are addressed to business. They reaffirm the Framework's foundational concepts and elements, and lay out specific steps entailed by them. These comprise three main parts: a policy commitment by business enterprises to meet the responsibility to respect human rights; a human rights due-diligence process to identify, prevent, mitigate, and account for the way they address their impacts on human rights; and processes to enable the remediation of any adverse human rights impact they cause or to which they contribute (GP 15). The GPs stress the need to engage affected individuals and communities in a meaningful way at several stages throughout the process, thereby strengthening the links between businesses and their workers as well as businesses and the communities in which they operate.

An explicit policy commitment is necessary in order to embed the responsibility to respect human rights within a company. The GPs provide that it should *set out* the company's expectations of personnel, business partners, and other parties directly linked to its operations, products, or services; be *approved* by senior management; *informed* by internal and external sources of expertise; *communicated* to all relevant parties; and *reflected* in the company's operational policies and procedures (GP 16).

The means for companies to "know and show" that they respect rights is by exercising human rights due diligence: "The process should include assessing actual and potential human rights impacts, integrating and acting upon the findings, tracking responses, and communicating how impacts are addressed" (GP 17). Potential adverse impacts should be addressed through prevention or mitigation. Actual impacts, those that have already occurred, should be a subject for remediation. "Human rights due diligence can be included within broader enterprise risk-management systems, provided that it goes beyond simply identifying and managing material risks to the company itself, to include risks to rights-holders" (GP 17, Commentary).

Additionally, human rights due diligence:

(a) Should cover adverse human rights impacts that the business enterprise may cause or contribute to through its own activities, or which may be directly linked to its operations, products or services by its business relationships;

(b) Will vary in complexity with the size of the business enterprise, the risk of severe human rights impacts, and the nature and context of its operations;

(c) Should be ongoing, recognizing that the human rights risks may change over time as the business enterprise's operations and operating context evolve [GP 17].

Thus, the due-diligence requirement applies not only to a company's own activities, but also to the business relationships linked to them—for example, its supply chain, security forces protecting company assets, and joint venture partners. The Commentary elaborates that where a company causes or contributes to an adverse impact, it should take the necessary steps to cease or prevent the impact. Where a company neither causes nor contributes to an adverse impact, but its operations, products, or services are directly linked to the impact through another entity in its value chain—for example, a supplier using bonded labor, unknown to the company and in violation of contractual terms—the company should use whatever leverage it has over that entity to prevent or mitigate the impact, and if it is unsuccessful, it should consider terminating the relationship (GP 19, Commentary).[22]

The Commentary also indicates that for small companies due diligence typically will remain informal. At the other end of the size spectrum, where an enterprise has large numbers of entities in its value chain that would make it unreasonably difficult to conduct ongoing due diligence across them all, the process should identify areas where the risk of adverse human rights impacts is most significant, whether due to the operating context or to the nature of the product or service, and prioritize those.

Each of the components of human rights due diligence—from assessing impacts to communicating results—is spelled out in a separate GP and Commentary, which can only be telegraphed here. Assessment means "to understand the specific impacts on specific people, given a specific context of operations" (GP 18, Commentary.) Depending on the size of the business enterprise and the nature and context of its operations, assessments should involve meaningful engagement with potentially affected individuals and groups (GP 18); where that is not possible, legally or logistically, other relevant stakeholders or independent experts should be consulted. Integrating and acting upon the findings of human rights impact assessments requires that the company assign specific responsibilities across business functions and within corporate reporting lines, and that these are enabled by adequate internal budget allocations, incentive systems, and oversight processes (GP 19).

Conducting appropriate human rights due diligence should help companies address the risk of legal claims against them by showing that they took every reasonable step to avoid involvement with an alleged human rights abuse. However, they should not assume that, by itself, this will automatically absolve them from liability for causing or contributing to human rights abuses (GP 17, Commentary).

Even with the best policies and practices in place, a company may cause or contribute to an adverse human rights impact that it has not foreseen or been able to prevent. Therefore:

- Where business enterprises identify that they have caused or contributed to adverse impacts, they should provide for or cooperate in their remediation through legitimate processes [GP 22].

Moreover:

- Where it is necessary to prioritize actions to address actual and potential adverse human rights impacts, business enterprises should first seek to prevent and mitigate those that are most severe or where delayed response would make them irremediable [GP 24].

Severity is defined in terms of the scale, scope, and irremediable character of impacts (GP 14, Commentary); and it is intended not as an absolute concept, but relative to any other human rights impacts the company has identified (GP 24, Commentary).

Verifying that adverse impacts are being addressed should involve affected stakeholders (GP 20). Finally, companies should disclose sufficient information to make it possible to evaluate the adequacy of their response to adverse impacts, particularly when concerns are raised by or on behalf of affected stakeholders (GP 21). Finally: "Formal reporting by enterprises is expected where risks of severe human rights impacts exist, whether this is due to the nature of the business operations or operating contexts" (GP 21, Commentary).

Access to Remedy

In the ideal world, state-based judicial and nonjudicial mechanisms would form the foundations of a wider system of remedy for corporate-related human rights abuse. Within such a system, company-level grievance mechanisms would provide early-stage recourse and possible resolution in at least some instances. Collaborative initiatives, whether industry-based or multistakeholder in character, would contribute in a similar manner. But "reality falls far short of constituting such a system," I concluded in my 2010 report to the Council.

The state duty to protect requires states to provide for access to remedy, and the GPs reaffirm this obligation. The GPs also urge states to "not erect barriers to prevent legitimate cases from being brought before the courts in situations where judicial recourse is an essential part of accessing remedy" (GP 26, Commentary). The text elaborates on several key legal and practical barriers I raised in the Framework, drawing on extensive research and also collaborative work with human rights organizations.[23] The challenge was to identify barriers that were specific to, or particularly problematic in, the business and human rights domain. Clearly, it was not possible to promote uniform answers to certain questions—such as class action provisions—given the sheer diversity of national legal systems, and the implications of any such recommendations in a whole host of other areas of the law apart from human rights. But the experience of advocates and my own research did identify several barriers that needed to be addressed.

For example, I highlighted situations "where claimants face a denial of justice in a host state and cannot access home state courts regardless of the merits of the claim" (GP 26, Commentary) because of objections to extraterritorial adjudication. Nevertheless, having explored this challenge extensively and with a broad spectrum of governments, other stakeholders, and legal experts, I concluded that it was not possible to reach a consensus on it among governments at this time, and that my putting forward an overly prescriptive recommendation in the GPs could well jeopardize the entire initiative because the Human Rights Council process dictated that states either support or reject the GPs as a whole. Therefore, in a separate note I was invited to submit to the Council offering suggestions for the follow-up process to my mandate, I proposed that governments consider the possibility of "an intergovernmental process of drafting a new international legal instrument" to establish clearly "the applicability to business enterprises of international standards prohibiting gross human rights abuses, potentially amounting to the level of international crimes," and—importantly—clarity over who may take jurisdiction under what conditions.[24] I return to this initiative in chapter 5.

On the nonjudicial front I was able to draw on several years of research and pilot projects conducted by the mandate to specify a set of effectiveness criteria for grievance mechanisms. Whether state-based or nonstate-based, such mechanisms should be:

(a) Legitimate: enabling trust from the stakeholder groups for whose use they are intended, and being accountable for the fair conduct of grievance processes;

(b) Accessible: being known to all stakeholder groups for whose use they are intended, and providing adequate assistance for those who may face particular barriers to access;

(c) Predictable: providing a clear and known procedure with an indicative timeframe for each stage, and clarity on the types of process and outcome available and means of monitoring implementation;

(d) Equitable: seeking to ensure that aggrieved parties have reasonable access to sources of information, advice and expertise necessary to engage in a grievance process on fair, informed and respectful terms;

(e) Transparent: keeping parties to a grievance informed about its progress, and providing sufficient information about the mechanism's performance to build confidence in its effectiveness and meet any public interest at stake;

(f) Rights-compatible: ensuring that outcomes and remedies accord with internationally recognized human rights;

(g) A source of continuous learning: drawing on relevant measures to identify lessons for improving the mechanism and preventing future grievances and harms;

Operational-level mechanisms should also be:

(h) Based on engagement and dialogue: consulting the stakeholder groups for whose use they are intended on their design and performance, and focusing on dialogue as the means to address and resolve grievances [GP 31].

Reactions

Having conducted forty-seven formal consultations around the world, made numerous visits to key capitals, and maintained close informal contacts with governments, their Human Rights Council representatives, and other stakeholders throughout the six years of the mandate, I was quite confident that the Council would support the GPs. The outstanding questions were whether it would be a divided vote—and if so, the number and relative importance of negative votes—and what verb the Council would use to express its support. Verbs in UN resolutions matter for legitimacy purposes. The Framework had been "welcomed," which is high praise. A relatively good response is "take note with interest." Merely to "take note" means that the effort may have been for naught. Anything less amounts to an outright rejection, as happened to the Norms initiative discussed in the previous chapter. In order to establish the most robust foundation possible, I proposed "endorse" to my mandate's sponsors, even though it had never been used in relation to a text that governments did not negotiate themselves. Norway led the way in promoting the idea and the sponsors were persuasive: the Council decision was unanimous and the verb used was "endorse."

By the time of the Council vote in June 2011, statements of support had been issued by business associations, individual companies, corporate law firms, socially responsible investment funds, pension funds, and workers organizations—from the United States and Canada, numerous European and Latin American countries, Hong Kong, India, Malaysia, Russia, and South Africa among others.[25] For example, GE wrote that the Guiding Principles "will further help business entities and governments operationalize their respective approaches to human rights in a business context, as well as respond to the need for remedies where deprivations nevertheless occur." Clifford Chance, the world's largest corporate law firm, said the GPs "provide immediately useful guidance to the business community and the legal profession on the steps which business (and their professional advisors) should take in pursuit of their responsibility to respect human rights." The CEO of Sakhalin Energy in Russia wrote: "It is my sincere hope that the Human Rights Council will endorse the Guiding Principles . . . helping to establish them as the authoritative reference point for states, companies and civil society." The International Trade Union Confederation added: "The 'Protect, Respect and Remedy Framework' adopted in 2008 changed the entire discussion on human rights and business in a positive way. We see the Guiding Principles as the next important step at the international level."

Some of the international human rights NGOs were less enthusiastic. In a joint statement at the time of my final presentation to the Council, several leading advocacy groups acknowledged that the GPs "do address a range of topics in a

useful manner; however some important issues that merit attention are not adequately reflected or addressed," chief among
them being an international legal instrument covering business
and human rights. A number of NGOs also felt leery about
operational-level grievance mechanisms, arguing that these
would reflect the power imbalance between companies and
rights-holders and fearing that they might become substitutes
for judicial processes—though both of these issues are specifically addressed in the GPs' provisions for how such processes
should be structured. A group of anticorporate-antiglobalization
NGOs actually urged the Council to reject the GPs on grounds
of their "insufficiencies."

The uptake of the GPs by other international standard-setting
bodies was swift; chapter 4 describes in greater detail how this
came about. ISO, the International Organization for Standardization, had adopted a social responsibility standard in late
2010, approved by 93 percent of its national member bodies,
including China. It explicitly drew upon, and is fully aligned
with, the Framework's second pillar, the corporate responsibility to respect human rights—using the same concepts, definitions, and required steps for discharging the responsibility. The
significance of ISO standards is that they have particular appeal
in Asia because of their historical emphasis on quality management systems that grew out of Japan's experience of becoming an industrial powerhouse; and they engage an established
global consulting industry that provides compliance advice to
companies.

As already noted, the OECD updated its Guidelines for Multinational Enterprises in May 2011. Chairing the ministerial
meeting at which the decision was taken, U.S. Secretary of State
Hillary Clinton said: "The current update is particularly notable for its incorporation of a new human rights chapter, drawing

on the Guiding Principles for business and human rights developed by the UN Special Representative for Human Rights and Business, John Ruggie, and the incorporation of guidance on exercising due diligence in the context of supply chain relationships."[26] The OECD's unique contribution lies in the fact that the forty-two adhering governments are required to maintain a designated office to which complaints of noncompliance may be brought against multinationals domiciled in those countries, wherever they may operate. The Guidelines' new human rights chapter, due diligence requirement, and explicit extension to include supply chains, drawn from the GPs, expands the scope of this mechanism.

The International Finance Corporation adopted a new "sustainability policy" in mid-2011 that for the first time recognizes the business responsibility to respect human rights. Again, the core concepts are identical to the GPs: the responsibility exists independently of states' duties; "respect" means to avoid infringing on the rights of others; and the "list" of human rights is provided by the International Bill of Human Rights and the ILO's eight core conventions.[27] The performance standards the IFC requires its clients to meet include having adequate due-diligence systems for the assessment and management of social and environmental risks, and they are tracked by more than seventy private sector financial institutions and by several regional development funding agencies and national export credit agencies. Thus, the significance of this development lies in the fact that it can affect companies' access to capital.

In October 2011, the European Commission issued "A Renewed EU Strategy 2011–2014 for Corporate Social Responsibility."[28] It abandons the EU's prior bifurcation of mandatory and voluntary approaches to corporate responsibility, which

I had criticized in a speech at the European Parliament.[29] And it proposes "risk-based due diligence" for business enterprises, "including through their supply chains," referencing the updated OECD Guidelines, the UN Guiding Principles, and ISO 26000 among sources for "authoritative guidance." The strategy document is intended to serve as the basis for EC work in this area during the next phase, including any possible new regulatory proposals.

The concept of human rights due diligence has had particular resonance. Mark Taylor, of the Norwegian research institute Fafo, has written that "multilateral organizations, business associations, governments, and NGOs latched on to the concept of due diligence as the solution to one of the more vexing issues of corporate responsibility, that of companies sourcing metals and minerals from war zones where serious human rights abuses and armed conflicts were rampant."[30] He traces a path from the concept's introduction and specification by my mandate to OECD work on responsible supply chains of minerals, which was subsequently endorsed by the eleven member states of the International Conference on the Great Lakes Region in Central Africa; then found its way into UN Security Council Resolutions on minerals exploitation in the Democratic Republic of the Congo; and ultimately into Section 1502 of the Dodd-Frank Wall Street Reform Act, which includes a due-diligence requirement for U.S.-listed companies sourcing minerals from conflict-affected areas in the Congo. Global Witness, a British NGO focused on the role of natural resources in fueling conflict and corruption, played a key role in connecting these dots. Taylor concludes: "Thus, even before the Guiding Principles were addressed by the UN Human Rights Council in June 2011, core elements of the business responsibility to respect human rights were being integrated into national and international legislation."[31]

III. CONCLUSION

At the end of the day, what are these Guiding Principles? What do they do? And how are they expected to achieve their aim? Clearly, the Guiding Principles are not an international treaty, although they include both hard- and soft-law elements. Nor are they intended to be a tool kit, its components simply to be taken off the shelf and plugged in, although they are meant to guide policy and practice. The Guiding Principles constitute a normative platform and high-level policy prescriptions for strengthening the protection of human rights against corporate-related harm. They provide a foundation for expanding the international human rights regime to encompass not only countries and individuals, but also companies. In doing so, they embrace the moral value and intrinsic power of the idea of human rights, but also recognize that in the context of the global economy human rights can be realized in relation to business only by leveraging the multiple governance systems that shape the conduct of multinational corporations: public, civil, and corporate. Maximizing their combined leverage, however, requires a common platform from which reinforcing effects and cumulative change can be generated. The GPs provide that common platform.

And yet it is essential that this common platform rest on clearly differentiated pillars—or bases of obligation. The corporate responsibility to respect human rights exists independently of the willingness or capacity of the state to exercise its duty to protect human rights. Likewise, the state duty to protect exists independently of whatever influence corporations may choose or be able to exercise over the state. For similar reasons it is also important to differentiate between preventative measures and remedy, and on the remedy side between judicial and nonjudicial forms. Providing judicial remedy is a state duty. Access to judicial remedy is an entitlement of human-rights-holders. Beyond that, states, businesses, and civil society all have roles to play in relation to preventative measures and nonjudicial remedy, including operational-level grievance mechanisms in which companies may participate to provide early-stage recourse. They all may have different rationales for doing so, and those rationales need to be mobilized if the overall effort is to succeed. In sum, the Guiding Principles are based on distinct yet complementary pillars, forming an integrated, logically coherent, and comprehensive platform for action.

The Guiding Principles take us beyond the stalemate induced by the mandatory-vs.-voluntary divide. They reaffirm that the state duty to protect human rights includes the creation of legally binding rules and the provision of effective judicial remedy. They frame the corporate responsibility to respect human rights in terms of risk-based due diligence, which is familiar territory for business, but also embed both its content and scope in classic human rights definitions established in the realm of international public governance. The endorsement by states of the corporate responsibility to respect human rights and how to discharge it gives official recognition to a norm that was previously grounded only in the realm of social expectations. And its adoption by companies turns them into regulators through their own internal management systems and via contracts with suppliers and service providers. International legal instruments must and will play a role in the continued evolution of the business and human rights regime but, as I noted in a 2007 article, "as carefully crafted precision tools complementing and augmenting existing institutional capacities."[32]

The rapid and widespread uptake by other international

standard-setting bodies of the core provisions of the corporate-responsibility-to-respect pillar—what it means and how it should be discharged—has produced an unprecedented international convergence in this domain. We are no longer in a situation where multiple competing standards are vying for attention in the area of business and human rights. This contributes to creating a more level playing field for companies. It clarifies what is expected of them in relation to human rights and provides predictability on where and how to focus their energies in response. It also provides a greater role for, and more focused guidance to, affected individuals, communities, and other stakeholders in determining whether companies, especially those in difficult sectors and operating contexts, have adequate systems in place to manage human-rights-related risks. And it provides agreed benchmarks by which business and civil society can assess the performance of states. The fact that elements of the corporate responsibility to respect human rights have already been incorporated into policy requirements and legislation adds weight to the standard. Moreover, with the GP's uptake there is now a built-in dynamic for cumulative change. Each entity that has adopted variants of the GPs has its own implementation mechanisms and knock-on effects, and all will be pushed by their own internal deliberations and by external pressures for further specification of these requirements and improved corporate performance.

I closed my final presentation to the Human Rights Council with these words: "I am under no illusion that the conclusion of my mandate will bring all business and human rights challenges to an end. But Council endorsement of the Guiding Principles will mark the end of the beginning."[33] What I meant was this. The GPs, as their name suggests, provide principled guidance to states and business enterprises. More detailed work will be required in order for governments, businesses, and other stakeholders to turn the GPs into rules and tools for specific industry sectors and operating contexts, different scales of operations, various forms of financial intermediaries, and so on. But for the first time those efforts will have a common platform on which to build, and a set of authoritative benchmarks against which they can be assessed.

Before addressing further steps on this journey in the concluding chapter, I offer some reflections on the way we got "from there to here"—the strategic paths that led to the adoption and uptake of the Framework and Guiding Principles, which may help inform comparable efforts to address other global governance gaps.

Chapter Four

STRATEGIC PATHS

My mandate began modestly with the initial task of "identifying and clarifying" things, amid contentious debates and deep divisions reflecting the different interests and preferences of the major players: states, businesses, and civil society. It ended six years later with unanimous Human Rights Council endorsement and widespread uptake of what essentially is a soft-law instrument that enjoys strong support from them all. There was no script, no user's manual, to follow because there had never been a UN mandate like it. So how did we get from there to here? And what if any lessons can be drawn from my particular journey for other efforts to narrow governance gaps created by globalization?

Every case has unique features, and this one is no exception. It may not be possible—or necessary—for future initiatives of this kind to travel along the specific paths I did. Nevertheless, retracing them may provide signposts for others and help separate out the idiosyncratic factors from more general features of how international norms are established and get disseminated and acted upon. This chapter outlines six strategic paths I identified and followed. I conclude by locating the Guiding Principles in a more general discussion of how new norms emerge and displace competing norms; how they cascade through rapid uptake; and, if successful, how they then are internalized by relevant actors and begin to assume a "taken-for-granted quality"—the ultimate measure of successful normative change.[1]

The six strategic paths comprised the following:

1. creating a minimum common knowledge base that permits a shared conversation to take place;
2. ensuring the legitimacy of the mandate process, quite apart from questions of substance;
3. bringing new players to the table whose insights and influence could advance the agenda;
4. road testing core proposals to demonstrate that they actually can work on the ground;
5. having an end-game strategy and effective political leadership to execute it; and where the opportunities exist or can be created,
6. working toward convergence among standard-setting bodies in order to achieve scale and benefit from the broadest possible portfolio of implementing mechanisms.

I. CREATING A COMMON KNOWLEDGE BASE

When I began in 2005, there was relatively little that counted as shared understanding regarding business and human rights among the major stakeholder groups involved in UN norm setting. There being no authoritative repository of information concerning corporate-related human rights abuse, anecdotal evidence ruled, coupled with evidentiary fragments from Alien Tort Statute cases, less than a handful of which had ever gone beyond procedural questions to address the actual merits of a case. Debates tended to be doctrinal, and doctrinal preferences tended to reflect institutional interests: business stressed its positive contributions to the realization of human rights coupled with the rapid growth of voluntary initiatives, while activist groups focused on the worst abuses and, with some of their academic supporters, demanded that some overarching global system of corporate liability be established. Since my initial mandate required me to "identify and clarify" the existing state of play, as a first step I conducted a set of baseline studies which I hoped might provide, if nothing else, some perspective for assessing proliferating claims and counterclaims. Over time, the research took a more strategic direction intended to help inform if not resolve difficult dilemmas encountered along the way.

Baseline Studies

Mapping a descriptive baseline for the mandate consisted of three main research streams. One was to identify prevailing patterns of corporate-related human rights abuse. Chapter 1 draws on this research: surveying allegations against companies over a two-year period; summarizing what abuses were alleged to have been committed, where, by whom, and how; and demonstrating that business can have adverse impacts on virtually any internationally recognized right so that attempts to come up with "the" definitive list is a fool's errand. The second body of work clarified existing legal standards and their application to states and business enterprises, and is reflected in chapter 2: documenting that UN human rights treaties generally do not impose direct legal obligations on companies; that there is an expanding web of potential corporate liability for egregious abuse that can amount to international crimes, imposed through national courts but drawing on customary international law standards, and potentially on the standards defined in the Rome Statute of the International Criminal Court as incorporated into national laws; that states have international law obligations to protect against corporate-related human rights abuse within their territory or jurisdiction; and that states as a general rule are neither required to nor prohibited from exercising extraterritorial jurisdiction in fulfilling those duties, while UN treaty bodies in a growing number of instances have encouraged and even urged home states of multinationals to take steps to prevent such firms from committing human rights abuses in their overseas operations and hold them to account if they do. The third body of research, also summarized in chapter 2, mapped the attributes and rapid expansion of voluntary corporate social responsibility initiatives, pointing out their strengths as well as their shortcomings.

In addition, I benefited enormously from similar kinds of mapping research that numerous academic and other volunteers undertook on behalf of the mandate, including research on the workings of all regional human rights systems in the world, the impact of the international trade regime on human rights, and obstacles to effective judicial remedy specifically related to business and human rights, on which I also drew in my reports to the Human Rights Council and posted on my Web site.[2]

More strategically, the existing state of play clearly showed that thinking and action concerning business and human rights needed to be pushed beyond the relatively narrow conceptual and weak institutional boxes in which it was framed and contained by governments, companies, and civil society organizations. In the first instance I sought to promote this development by means of empirical and conceptual work and by discussing its results with stakeholder groups. The combination of relevance of subjects and my capacity constraints to address them all in a serious manner led to research in four areas: corporate and securities law, international investment agreements, the costs to companies of conflicts with local communities, and extraterritorial jurisdiction.

Corporate and Securities Law

Corporate and securities laws address what companies, their directors and officers must do to comply with standards of corporate governance, risk management, and market safeguards. I stressed from the outset of my mandate the need to have a systematic conversation at the global level regarding the relationship of these bodies of law and policy to business and human rights. This took on a sense of urgency in May 2008 when, only weeks before the Human Rights Council was to take its decision on the Protect, Respect and Remedy Framework, one of Wall Street's leading law firms issued a blistering critique. "The framework could impose on businesses an array of expansive obligations," wrote a senior partner of Wachtell, Lipton, Rosen & Katz, in a five-page advisory memo to its clients. "The Report bears significant, potentially harmful implications for global business and for meaningful accountability in various social actors' duties to fulfill the promises of international human rights instruments [and] will invite immense pressure on corporations and their directors."[3] Needless to say, I feared the negative effects this missive might generate within the business community. But because I had no standing in the world of corporate law at the time, I did not think that a response by me would be sufficiently effective. Fortunately, through the good office of Oxfam I was introduced to another leading Wall Street law firm, Weil, Gotshal & Manges, where a team led by senior partners studied the Framework, listened to my explanations of it, and then issued its own six-page memo just in time for the Council meeting. "We believe the basic concepts embodied in the Report are sound and should be supported by the business community," they wrote. "Rather than being alarmed, U.S. corporations should welcome the Special Representative's proposals. . . ."[4] And so the conversation began.

Inspired by this experience, in 2009 I launched a research project that involved more than twenty corporate law firms from around the world assisting on a pro bono basis to identify whether and how corporate and securities law encourages or impedes companies' respect for human rights in thirty-nine jurisdictions the firms were able to cover. Full reports on each jurisdiction and a summary report are posted online; the latter is also appended to the Guiding Principles.[5] The surveys constitute the most extensive comparative study of this subject currently available. They indicated that for the most part corporate law and securities law intersect with human rights only indirectly. In most of the jurisdictions surveyed, regulatory bodies do not provide effective guidance on how best to ensure or oversee corporate respect for human rights or to report on the company's human rights processes or performance. None of the surveys identified laws expressly requiring companies, at incorporation, to recognize a duty to society. Directors are rarely expressly required to consider nonshareholders' interests. In most jurisdictions, companies must disclose all information that is "material" or "significant" to their operations and financial condition, and where a company's human rights impacts reach that threshold, most surveys suggested that it would be required to disclose them. But again there is little official guidance on when a human rights impact might reach that threshold.

Modest exceptions may be found in a number of jurisdictions. In the case of director's duties, UK law provides that in promoting the success of the company, directors must have specific regard to "the impact of the company's operations on the community and the environment," among other factors. A provision in Brazilian law similarly requires directors "to achieve the company's corporate purposes and to support its best interests, satisfying the requirements of the public at large and the social role of the company." This type of provision has been described as reflecting an "enlightened shareholder" model: whereas the directors' duty remains to the company, in exercising it they need to "have regard" to broader social and environmental factors—although nowhere is it crystal clear what this means. Some stock exchanges have listing rules that touch on these issues (CSR in Paris and the Bursa Malaysia, environmental protection and community development in Shenzhen and Shanghai); others operate voluntary socially responsible investment indexes (Johannesburg, Bovespa in Brazil, the Dow Jones Sustainability Index in New York, FTSE4Good in London, and similar indices in the Nordic countries). Several countries require some form of corporate social responsibility reporting for some types of companies (China, Indonesia, Sweden); where they exist, these provisions tend to focus on the reporting of policies rather than on impacts and how they are dealt with, and the reports are not subject to the standardization, verification, and distribution requirements of financial reports.

The direct consequences for the mandate of this research and related consultations were to draw the subject of corporate and securities laws more centrally into the business and human rights debate; to help inform the development of key elements of the Guiding Principles; and to engage an enormously important community of practice, which I discuss separately below.

International Investment Agreements

History has witnessed successive waves of states expropriating foreign investments—and, in prior eras, the "gunboat diplomacy" that could be triggered in response. The modern investment regime is based on international investment treaties and contracts, often coupled with binding investor-state arbitration—some 3,000 bilateral and regional investment treaties are currently in effect. Such agreements are necessary to protect foreign investors against arbitrary treatment by host governments. However, in successive rounds of negotiations, capital importers that lack significant market power have felt increasingly pressured to compete with one another for foreign investments by accepting ever-more-expansive provisions, even regarding such basic issues as to what constitutes an investment, an investor, and expropriation. As a result, under threat of binding international arbitration, foreign investors may be able to insulate their business venture from new laws and regulations, or seek compensation from the host government for the cost of compliance, even if the policy enacted legitimate public interest objectives such as new labor standards or environmental and health regulations, and even if it applied in a nondiscriminatory manner to domestic and foreign investors alike. I set out to analyze this phenomenon and its possible implications for the ability of host states to fulfill their duty to protect human rights, with the aim of contributing to a broader dialogue concerning the need for more balanced—and more human-rights-compatible—investment agreements.

For large-scale projects, the formal relationship between the host government and a multinational corporation typically begins with a host government agreement: a contract between the two parties for specific projects, whether a mining operation, a telecommunications system, a sugar plantation, or toll-road construction. The investor is likely already to be protected under an international investment treaty that the home and host states will have concluded; indeed, foreign investors are free to incorporate individual projects in any "home" state that offers the most favorable treaty protections for "its" investors vis-à-vis the target host state. In addition, project contracts often include provisions that "stabilize" the host country's existing regulatory context as further protection for the foreign investor. Thanks to the cooperation of the International Finance Corporation, I gained access to and examined some ninety such contracts. Among the key findings were: (1) no contract between a multinational corporation and an OECD country offered the investor exemptions from new laws and, with minor exceptions, they tailored stabilization clauses to preserve public interest considerations; (2) a majority of the contracts with non-OECD countries did have provisions to insulate investors from compliance with new environmental and social laws or facilitated compensation for compliance; (3) the most sweeping stabilization provisions were found in contracts signed with Sub-Saharan African countries, where seven of the eleven contracts to which I had access specified exemptions from or compensation for the effect of all new laws for the duration of the project—a half-century in one case—irrespective of their relevance to protecting human rights or any other public interest.[6]

This research generated considerable interest, particularly

among African government contract negotiators, with whom we convened several meetings to discuss the results—which had the additional benefit of contributing to the strong support the mandate enjoyed from the African group in the Human Rights Council. The findings were also of interest to leading law firms that negotiate contracts on behalf of companies and governments, which discovered that provisions they believed had been abandoned some time ago because their impact on states was unacceptably onerous in fact were still being used. The combination of these two factors encouraged me to develop a set of "Principles for Responsible Contracts" with the help of government negotiators, leading law firms, and NGOs that have expertise in this area. It, too, was issued as an addendum to the Guiding Principles.[7]

Costs of Conflict

Corporate-related human rights abuse harms people. That should be sufficient reason for avoiding adverse impacts and mitigating or remediating them where they occur. But escalating conflicts with local communities are not cost-free for companies either. I was curious about the magnitude of such costs and how companies account for them. The World Resources Institute published a handful of case studies on extractive and infrastructure projects in 2007, which indicated that financial risks to companies associated with pushback from communities and other stakeholders can include delays in design, siting, granting of permits, construction, operation, and expected revenues; problematic relations with local labor markets; higher costs for financing, insurance, and security; reduced output; collateral impacts such as diverted staff time and reputational hits; and possible project cancellation, forcing a company to write off its entire investment and forgo the value of the lost reserves, revenues, and profits, which could run into several billion dollars for large-scale operations.[8] A 2008 Goldman Sachs study of 190 projects operated by the international oil majors provided greater details on this sector.[9] It found that the time it takes for new projects to come onstream—to pump the first drop of oil—had nearly doubled over the previous decade, causing significant cost inflation. Delays were attributed to the projects' "technical and political complexity," with the category "political" including resistance from communities and other external stakeholders.

An independent and confidential follow-up analysis commissioned by one such company of a subset of the projects covered by the Goldman Sachs study, to which I had access, indicated that nontechnical risks accounted for nearly half of all risk factors faced by the oil majors, with "stakeholder-related risk" constituting the single largest category of nontechnical risk. It further estimated that this particular company may have accrued $6.5 billion in such costs over a two-year period, amounting to a double-digit percentage of its annual profits. Those are big numbers. Did no one in the company notice? Looking into it further, I learned that such costs tended to be atomized within companies, rolled into local operating costs across different business units and functions, and not aggregated into a single category that would trigger the attention of senior management and boards. I undertook additional research in the mining industry.[10] This showed, for example, that a mining operation with start-up capital expenditures in the $3–$5-billion range suffers losses of roughly $2 million per day of delayed production, in net present value terms. Think back to the frequent closures of Yanacocha, and now Minas Conga, discussed in the Introduction, which operate on that scale. Perhaps the single most overlooked cost is the staff time that has to be devoted to managing conflicts with communities. The working assumption in the mining sector is about 5 percent of an asset manager's time. Yet the research identified instances where it was as high as 50 and occasionally even 80 percent. If those conflicts are left unattended, they may escalate, which can lead to property damage and injury, or worse, to community members and company employees.

This is a lose-lose situation: a company harms human rights and incurs serious costs in turn. Adding to the perversity, the costs of *avoiding* conflicts with communities—by building closer links through active stakeholder engagement, adequate due diligence, and effective grievance procedures—*do* show up as direct costs on the company's balance sheet. This asymmetry disadvantages companies' own CSR and community engagement efforts, which are seen as pure cost centers, vis-à-vis the operating units that bring in revenue.

I reported these findings to the Human Rights Council and have mentioned them in virtually every speech to business groups. Now that the fact of these costs is better known, they are also becoming better aggregated and are drawing the attention they deserve from management, boards, shareholders, and regulators.

Extraterritorial Jurisdiction

We come, finally, to the difficult issue of extraterritorial jurisdiction (ETJ). It was the subject of one of the mandate's first multistakeholder expert consultations, and one of the last. For reasons already discussed, ETJ in relation to human rights remains highly contentious. "Legitimate issues are at stake and they are unlikely to be resolved fully anytime soon," I noted in my 2010 report to the Human Rights Council. "However, the scale of the current impasse must and can be reduced."[11] I took two steps in the attempt to move beyond the impasse.

First, I pointed out in that Council report that a critical distinction between two very different phenomena is usually obscured in the heated arguments about ETJ in business and human rights. One is jurisdiction exercised directly in relation to actors or activities that take place overseas, such as criminal regimes governing child sex tourism that rely on the nationality of the perpetrator no matter where the offence occurs. This literally involves one national court, say in Germany, adjudicating conduct by one of its nationals that took place in another sovereign state, say Thailand. The other form of ETJ involves domestic measures that may have extraterritorial implications: for example, requiring companies that are listed on domestic stock exchanges, no matter what their nationality, to report on their worldwide risks, no matter where they may be incurred. To be sure, the latter has extraterritorial implications, but it relies entirely on territory as the jurisdictional basis, and its justification is protecting domestic investors. Indeed, I argued that the issue of territoriality and extraterritoriality should not be viewed in binary terms at all; it comprises a range of measures, not all of which are equally subject to objections on jurisdictional grounds. I proposed ways of differentiating a spectrum of measures in business and human rights.

Second, states clearly have agreed to certain instances of exercising extraterritorial jurisdiction in policy domains other than business and human rights. In order to understand better what factors contribute to variations in the perceived reasonableness of ETJ, I commissioned a study of ETJ in anticorruption, securities law, antitrust, environmental regulation, as well as criminal and civil jurisdiction generally.[12] The main conclusions were that multilateral measures are likely to be seen as more acceptable than unilateral measures; principles-based approaches are less problematic than prescriptive rules-based approaches; the extent of international consensus on the wrongfulness of an act or activity plays a significant role; and the acts or activities in question tend to be relatively specific and definable—not an entire policy domain, such as the whole bundle of business and human rights issues. I drew on this conceptual and empirical work in formulating the Guiding Principles. The European Commission subsequently conducted a study exploring ETJ issues in relation to the human rights and environmental impacts of EU-based companies and is considering further CSR policy developments, discussed below.

There surely are other areas of strategic research my team and I could have pursued, and several other subjects were explored less intensely. But the mandate's capacity was limited, even when augmented by pro bono assistance from law firms and universities, think tanks and committed individuals, throughout the world. Moreover, even six years are surprisingly short, and additional paths toward achieving a successful outcome required attention.

II. ENSURING PROCESS LEGITIMACY

Building a common knowledge base is important in establishing a viable foundation for policy development. However, whether proposals based on it gain any traction with decision-makers is also a function of the perceived legitimacy of the process. In United Nations contexts—particularly for the independent and institutionally weak human rights "special procedures" such as my mandate—inclusiveness, in turn, can be a significant determinant of perceived legitimacy. Have victims been engaged? Have all stakeholder groups been given the opportunity to be heard? Have the varying situations of different countries and regions been considered—including their levels of economic development, the character of their legal systems, and the different ways business activity is organized and governed? Professor Karin Buhmann of Copenhagen University refers to this as "process legitimacy," and she attributes at least part of the mandate's success to having achieved it.[13]

One aspect of process legitimacy is the sheer geographical and substantive inclusiveness of the process I undertook. It included forty-seven formal consultations around the world. Some were large multistakeholder meetings—in Bangkok, Bogotá, Buenos Aires, Johannesburg, Moscow, and New Delhi—involving participants from those countries and the surrounding region. Two global consultations were held at the UN European Headquarters in Geneva. Sweden convened an EU-wide consultation in Stockholm when it held the EU presidency. Expert meetings on the many technical subjects addressed by the mandate were convened in the capitals of countries willing to fund them, at the offices of supportive law firms, or at universities including my Harvard home base. Great care was taken in each case to strive for geographical balance of participants. My team and I made site visits to the operations of firms and consulted with local stakeholders in more than twenty countries. I held numerous bilateral meetings with officials in capitals. An annotated outline of the Guiding Principles was posted online for public comment and discussed at separate consultations with Human Rights Council delegations, business enterprises and associations from all continents, and with civil society groups. Later a full draft of the GPs was posted online for public comment, attracting 3,576 unique visitors from 120 countries. The draft was also discussed at an informal Council session and at a multi-stakeholder retreat. The mandate's work benefited significantly from this diversity of views and experiences. And Council resolutions praised "the comprehensive, transparent and inclusive consultations conducted with relevant and interested actors in all regions."[14] Indeed, the only criticism any government ever made on "inclusiveness" grounds was when a delegate from France remarked at one Council session that I had referenced relatively few French sources in that year's report.

Buhmann notes that while this level of consultation is quite extensive by UN human-rights-mandate standards, the practice itself is not unusual. What is unusual, she continues, was "consulting with prospective duty-holders that do not have direct access to the conventional process of international law-making is."[15] The "duty-holders" Buhmann is referring to are business enterprises. She points out that their involvement in my mandate was in sharp contrast to the earlier Norms process. That text was drafted by a small expert working group in Geneva conference rooms in collaboration with human rights NGOs and academic human rights lawyers, with only limited participation by business associations (or governments, for that matter), and that only came late in the day, by which time business was in pure damage-limitation mode.

Inviting extensive business participation was not without its critics in civil society. But I considered it essential for three reasons. The first was substantive. Before prescribing systems that companies should put in place to identify, prevent, mitigate, and remedy human rights harm in which they may be involved, I felt the need to understand better how companies manage their risks of adverse impacts in other areas, such as health and safety, anticorruption, and environmental issues, or the risk of criminal activity by personnel. Having business participate in consultations and invite members of my team and me to visit their operations were means to that end. I gained access to information I would never have had otherwise: for example, the sources for my research on the costs of conflict with communities came from businesses themselves. (We typically combined site visits to companies with independently organized meetings with communities and civil society representatives.)

The second reason was strategic. Students of international law and regulatory policy have long maintained that the perceived legitimacy of a rule-making process by those to whom the rules apply exerts a "compliance pull," increasing the chances that they will adhere to the rules.[16] This is particularly true where the rule-making system lacks powerful enforcement mechanisms, as is the case in the business and human rights domain. I do not mean to imply that business representatives always agreed with my views and positions. That was hardly the case; indeed, some tried to be outright spoilers. The German business association, BDA (Bundesvereinigung der Deutschen Arbeitgeberverbände), more conservative-leaning than others, was a case in point, though most of the time were pulled along by others in the end. But throughout, business knew that its views and positions were heard and had been taken into account. Moreover, because the company representatives involved typically had CSR responsibilities, having them participate in mandate consultations gave them and their mission greater visibility within their companies, advancing both of our aims.

The third reason was political. Excluding business from an international rule-making process that directly and significantly affects its interests will simply mean that it will lobby national governments in the attempt to undermine the process—which is what happened to the Norms. In contrast, when the United States threatened to make trouble at the Human Rights Council over the scope of the Framework's stipulation of the state duty to protect human rights in 2008, which would have opened the door to objections by other countries with far less congenial attitudes toward human rights, the U.S. Council for International Business helped persuade the government to back down.

My engagement with NGOs was equally sustained but took two slightly different forms depending on the type of organization: one with pure advocacy groups, the other with NGOs that also have on-the-ground operational activities that involve business. The former—for example, Amnesty International, Human Rights Watch, and the International Commission of Jurists—participated actively in mandate consultations and helped identify participants from the global south who could genuinely represent affected individuals and communities. But we agreed to disagree on several substantive and methodological matters.

In terms of substance, although we were both driven by the desire to promote and protect human rights, in one fundamental respect our objectives were different. The animating vision for the legally minded advocacy groups is the further development of international human rights law. My animating vision was to generate a regulatory dynamic that would reduce the incidence of corporate-related human rights harm to the maximum extent possible in the minimum amount of time. While their aims may overlap, the two visions are not identical in terms of where to start and how to proceed. Moreover, for reasons elaborated in chapter 2, I found it hard to imagine even conceptually how to make the entire bundle of business and human rights the subject of some overarching international legal framework—their preferred position—given the breadth, magnitude, and diversity of issues involved, let alone how to achieve it politically.

In terms of methodology these groups consistently sought to push my mandate into a more traditional human rights mold, based on the way things have been done in relation to state-based abuses. In contrast, I was trying to move beyond the confined opportunity space afforded by that methodology for the business and human rights context. For example, when the Human Rights Council was considering extending my mandate in 2008 to "operationalize" the Framework, the heads of the leading advocacy organizations wrote to the foreign ministers of the resolution's five cosponsors stating that I had done too little to represent victims of corporate-related human rights abuse, and urging them to include investigations of specific allegations against companies in my new mandate. I understand and appreciate that bearing witness and giving voice to victims is an essential component of human rights tactics to raise public awareness and in naming-and-shaming campaigns. But I did not believe that a highly sensitive and complex effort to develop and secure the adoption of universally applicable principles would mix well with getting drawn into adjudicating specific adversarial situations. I feared that whatever positions I took on individual disputes would become the lens through which my broader proposals would be viewed by concerned companies and their governments alike. Besides, I met with affected individuals and communities throughout the world to learn from their experiences, and some of my encounters were facilitated by those same NGOs. But once I felt that I had a grasp of the problems, I wanted to focus all energies on developing effective ways of addressing them, not identifying even more variations on their manifestations. The foreign ministers agreed and the mandate remained unchanged.

NGOs that have on-the-ground operations in business and human rights are every bit as committed as the pure advocacy groups to holding companies to account. But they pursue a greater variety of routes toward that end and thus viewed my mandate more flexibly. For example, Global Witness, best known for its pathbreaking work on the international regulation of conflict diamonds, went so far as to assign (and pay the salary of) one of its researchers to work with the mandate on human rights and conflict zones for several months—and then, as noted in chapter 3, campaigned to promote the application of human rights due-diligence requirements to companies sourcing minerals in the Democratic Republic of Congo. Oxfam cosponsored a workshop with the mandate on developing operational-level grievance mechanisms, and the Clean Clothes Campaign on assessing the effectiveness of multistakeholder initiatives in improving workplace conditions in global supply chains.

I maintained excellent relations with workers organizations through their Geneva-based global federations and the Trade Union Advisory Committee to the OECD. Their main concern with human rights initiatives is that they may rewrite hard-won labor standards that have been extensively negotiated within the ILO's tripartite system, involving states, business, and workers. This had been a main source of friction between workers' organizations and the Norms process. I had no such aspirations and relied extensively on the ILO and the union federations to inform the mandate on issues related to international labor standards.

Transparency is another key factor in process legitimacy. The London-based Business & Human Rights Resource Centre kindly agreed to host a Web portal for my mandate.[17] Virtually everything produced by and for the mandate is posted there, as is all criticism of my work that anyone chose to post. When significant issues were at stake, I responded to critics, thereby triggering an ongoing public dialogue. Apparently, this had not been done before by UN human rights special procedures. Also breaking with precedent, and possibly protocol, I sent numerous research reports and occasionally my speeches and other updates directly to individual Human Rights Council delegates (for which I first had to construct my own email contact list). This made it possible to establish informal relationships with delegates rather than relying solely on once-a-year appearances at the Council or the occasional unofficial consultations with Council members, and to convey views and information to them that could not be included in annual reports that had a 10,700-word limit.

Finally, to provide strategic guidance as well as greater visibility and additional legitimacy, I established an advisory group for the mandate comprised of recognized leaders from various sectors and regions, cochaired by Kofi Annan and Mary Robinson, the former President of Ireland and UN High Commissioner for Human Rights.[18]

III. ENGAGING NEW COMMUNITIES OF PRACTICE

Having originally been created to deal with human rights violations by state agents, it is standard procedure for UN human rights mandate-holders to engage with certain groups of actors: victims and their representatives, state entities and international bodies involved in human rights protection, civil society organizations and human rights lawyers, national human rights institutions, and occasionally legislative forums considering new standards. However, in the business and human rights context there are additional communities of practice whose actions can have powerful effects on business conduct in relation to human rights—but who may have little or no awareness of this fact, and whose institutional mission is driven by very different interests and concerns. Therefore, it became one of my key objectives to identify ways to engage such communities of practice, learn from them, raise human rights awareness among them, and possibly find ways of leveraging their influence.

In a previous section, I briefly described my project involving investment contract negotiators representing states and companies. This project ultimately resulted in a ten-step guide for responsible contracting, incorporating human rights concerns in investment projects from the initial contracting phase. It also prompted me to take a closer look at the international arbitration procedures under which foreign investors can sue states for breaches of these agreements. These procedures can be problematic for states because they draw their rules and practitioners largely from the world of private commercial arbitration, and yet in many cases they determine matters of profound public interest. Even fully understanding how the process works and subjecting it to public scrutiny can be difficult because of a lack of transparency: if an arbitration is conducted under the rules of the UN Commission on International Trade Law (UNCITRAL), nothing may be known publicly about it—not even the existence of the case itself. As a result, neither experts nor the public at large are in any position to assess deals the government has signed with foreign investors. ICSID, the World Bank's International Centre for Settlement of Investment Disputes, does keep a roster of cases and makes known their outcome, but deliberations themselves remain confidential unless both parties agree to public disclosure. At the invitation of UNCITRAL officials, I made presentations on my mandate at several Commission meetings, where I took the opportunity to advocate for a change of rules to provide greater transparency which, I contended, is essential when human rights issues are involved. UNCITRAL eventually set up a working group to review those rules in the context of investor-state arbitration.

My most consequential engagement with nontraditional stakeholders was with the corporate-law community, through the corporate-and-securities-law project and other pro bono work firms conducted for the mandate over the course of several years. This included law firms and other experts not only from North America and numerous European countries, but also Australia, Argentina, Botswana, Brazil, Chile, Colombia, Hong Kong, India, Kenya, Malaysia, Mexico, Morocco, South Africa, and Thailand. I convened several meetings with participating law firms, in-house counsel as well as academic and advocacy group attorneys. These relationships with the corporate-law community generated at least four benefits for the mandate. The first was simply the extensive mapping of how, if at all, corporate and security law intersected with human rights in the thirty-nine jurisdictions the collaborating firms were able to examine. Second, this group of experts became an initial sounding board for the development of the due-diligence requirements under the corporate responsibility to respect human rights. They had extensive experience with the ways companies conduct due diligence in other domains, what makes for a successful process, and what if any requirements regulators already impose in different jurisdictions. Third, their engagement began to generate publicity for the mandate within the legal profession: an article in the *American Lawyer*, a cover story in a Canadian magazine for corporate lawyers, a symposium of articles by corporate law experts in the *Journal of Business Ethics*, press coverage in India, a blog in Singapore, among others. My favorite was a presentation by a corporate law firm at an international mining conference. One of the PowerPoint bullets read: "Race by leading mining companies (Anglo American and BHP Billiton, for example) to determine whether their policies are 'Ruggie-Proof.'"[19] (No doubt the law firm was prepared to help companies become so.) This level of engagement and publicity led to a fourth benefit: it bumped the mandate's visibility up within corporate hierarchies, beyond the confines of corporate social responsibility departments, into general counsels' offices and "C-suites"—chief compliance officers and occasionally the CEO and boards of directors. Getting companies to integrate change management requires commitment from the top, and engagement with the corporate law community helped provide access. As a final bonus from lawyers, in February 2012 the House of Delegates of the American Bar Association, the association's official policy-making body, endorsed the Guiding Principles and urged governments, the private sector, and the legal community itself to integrate them into their respective operations and practices.[20]

IV. ROAD TESTING

A routine objection by those who would be affected by new rules and don't like them is to claim that the rules won't work in practice. The most effective rejoinder is to be able to demonstrate that they already have worked. Accordingly, I looked for opportunities to test the practical feasibility of the two most novel and potentially far-reaching elements of the Guiding Principles: that companies should conduct human rights due diligence, and that they should establish or participate in operational-level grievance mechanisms. Several projects involving companies assessed the core elements of both as outlined in the 2008

Framework document. Additionally, I convened a small but representative group of states to explore practical steps that states should take to address the risk of corporate involvement with human rights abuses in conflict zones.

Due Diligence

Ten Dutch companies under the umbrella of the Netherlands' Global Compact Network agreed to conduct a feasibility study of the various elements involved in the corporate responsibility to respect human rights, with a particular focus on the due diligence requirement. The companies included such well-known names as AkzoNobel, ABN AMRO, Philips, Shell, and Unilever. The group recruited a former member of my team to manage the eighteen-month project, which consisted of three parts. The first was a confidential "gap analysis" that mapped each company's systems and practices against the various elements of the corporate responsibility to respect human rights as outlined in the Framework. It examined which corporate functions—human resources management, procurement, production, security, marketing, R&D, and so on—could affect which internationally recognized right, and how well each company was currently equipped to meet its responsibility to respect those rights. The second part consisted of a series of workshops and seminars with members of my team and a broad range of stakeholders in which the companies exchanged views and experiences on such subjects as corporate governance and human rights, human rights risk and impact assessments, and the Framework's grievance mechanisms provisions. Finally, the project published a guidance tool for business based on lessons learned. It found that the companies had bits and pieces of relevant policies and practices in place, but often they were not focused on human rights specifically nor were they always systematically connected; and it also identified gaps. It concluded that "human rights due diligence is a practical and attainable approach to guide companies in respecting human rights in their business."[21]

A follow-up study by the London-based Institute for Human Rights and Business examined the efforts of twenty-four leading multinational corporations, representing a broader geographical spread, to put human rights due-diligence processes into practice. It concluded that none of the companies studied had fully integrated concern for human rights into all aspects of its management. Although this was a challenging task for companies, the experience to date indicated that "for businesses committed to doing so, human rights due diligence is possible."[22]

Grievance Mechanisms

Even under ideal circumstances things will go wrong, and when they do, remedy is required. Much of the focus in business and human rights understandably had been on judicial systems. I also wanted to explore early-stage recourse in the form of grievance mechanisms that companies could establish themselves or participate in, but I could find few instances of such mechanisms. Therefore, I initiated a year-long study and a series of workshops.[23] Operational-level grievance mechanisms potentially can perform two key functions in relation to the corporate responsibility to respect human rights. The first is as an early warning system, making it possible for grievances against the company to be addressed and remediated before they escalate, thereby preventing harm from compounding. The second is as a feedback loop, providing the company with information about its current or potential adverse human rights impacts. By analyzing trends and patterns in complaints, companies can identify systemic problems and adapt their practices accordingly. At the same time, however, such grievance mechanisms face particular challenges given that companies are closely involved in their design and administration, which can raise questions of bias or the critique that they are illegitimate sources of remedy. Robust criteria for effectiveness and legitimacy are important in addressing this risk. Our research had suggested a set of such criteria that I wanted to test.

In March 2009, the International Organization of Employers, the International Chamber of Commerce, and the Business and Industry Advisory Committee to the OECD agreed to collaborate with the mandate on organizing pilot projects for this purpose. Four companies in four sectors volunteered to take part: Carbones del Cerrejón, in Colombia, a large coal-mining joint venture of Anglo American, BHP Billiton, and Xstrata Coal; the Esquel Group in Hong Kong, piloting a mechanism at its apparel facility in Viet Nam; Sakhalin Energy Investment Corporation in the Russian Federation, an oil and gas joint venture of Gazprom, Royal Dutch Shell, Mitsui & Co., and Mitsubishi Corporation; and Tesco Stores, a major UK supermarket chain working with a group of its fruit suppliers in South Africa. In addition, an adjunct project was conducted in collaboration with the technology company Hewlett-Packard to review its recent efforts to help two of its suppliers in China enhance their grievance procedures for workers. The pilot projects involved collaboration with the companies and with their local stakeholders to design or amend grievance procedures in line with the mandate's draft effectiveness criteria. The purpose of the pilots was twofold: to test the benefits that mechanisms aligned with the GPs can have as a means of remedy for impacted stakeholders and as a means of risk management and accountability for companies; and to learn how the principles can be further refined to reflect operational realities and enable their practical application by companies. The pilot projects ran for approximately eighteen months. Team members conducted periodic site visits. The results are reflected in Guiding Principle 31 and its Commentary—stipulating eight criteria for the effectiveness of grievance mechanisms. A detailed report, which includes a frank discussion of challenges, is appended to the Guiding Principles.[24]

Given the slow pace of legal reform, and in view of the fact that legal recourse may not always be necessary or even the preferred course of action by victims, I also sought to identify and promote effective alternative dispute resolution mechanisms more generally. To that end, I established an online resource: Business and Society Exploring Solutions.[25] BASESwiki is a collaborative work space for sharing information and learning about how dispute resolution between business and society works around the world. It offers information, in multiple languages, about available mechanisms at global, regional, national, and local levels, and it continues to evolve to meet the needs of its diverse audience. Its value as a resource derives from the wealth of experiences and information its users bring to the community. Launched in 2008, it currently describes 370 dispute resolution mechanisms, provides business and human rights profiles of more than 140 countries, and has had approximately 1,500 users. BASESwiki also hosts three documentary films, produced by my team, of successful community-company dialogue and mediation efforts in Nigeria, Peru, and the Philippines. Work begun under the mandate on the feasibility of establishing a global network of national and local mediators in business and human rights disputes continues under the auspices of the Harvard Kennedy School Corporate Social Responsibility Initiative, in collaboration with the World Legal Forum.

A common thread running through the three initiatives—human rights due diligence, operational-level grievance mechanisms, and alternative dispute resolution more generally—is that they expand the portfolio of available means for reducing the incidence of human rights harm in the first place, and provide timely and local remedy for some harms where they do occur.

Conflict Zones

My interest in and concern with business operations in conflict zones stemmed from the fact that the worst forms of human rights abuses involving companies tend to take place in such contexts. Not only does this demand special attention, but no government can claim credibly that the current international human rights regime is able to function as intended in such contexts.

To explore the possibility of developing more robust measures, I invited a small group of states to participate in three off-the-record workshops at a UN-dedicated conference facility on the outskirts of New York City. I deliberately did not want participants merely to voice their country's foreign policy views on specific events, so the workshops did not address actual conflicts. Instead, each was structured as a brainstorming session built around a different scenario that I shared with participants beforehand—a simulated road test, as it were. Moreover, I invited participants not only from foreign ministries but also from agencies with economic responsibilities, including development assistance and export credit agencies.

At each session participants were asked to work through a scenario with a view to identifying the range of policy options that home, host, and neighboring states have, or could develop, to prevent and deter corporate-related human rights abuses in conflict contexts. The nature of the business activity differed from one scenario to the next, and each scenario assumed escalating and variegated forms of violence. States were invited to participate based on their known interest in dealing with the issue; their previous or current exposure to it; their willingness to engage in such a process; as well as representation and balance between home, host, and neighboring states. Belgium, Brazil, Canada, China, Colombia, Ghana, Guatemala, Nigeria, Norway, Sierra Leone, Switzerland, the United Kingdom, and the United States agreed to participate. Guiding Principle 7 and the report on conflict-affected areas that I submitted to the Human Rights Council along with the GPs were directly informed by this project. In some cases it also provided an excellent back channel to national capitals on related issues. And it provided informal guidance on the question of a possible legal instrument in this domain.

V. GAINING ENDORSEMENTS

Strong Human Rights Council backing for the Guiding Principles was necessary for them to take root. Without it they would merely constitute yet another initiative vying for attention in a crowded field where none had reached scale. The momentum behind the mandate suggested that a positive Council response was highly likely. But the prospects for outright endorsement would be enhanced by two additional steps: expressions of support for such an endorsement by credible external stakeholders, and effective internal politics to achieve consensus.

When the draft Norms were first presented to the Commission on Human Rights, the Council's predecessor, the major international human rights advocacy organizations were strongly in favor. Although we worked together extensively throughout my mandate, these groups were unlikely to be equally enthusiastic about the GPs. I have already discussed why, beginning with the fact that my first official act was to commit "Normicide." Thus, the most I could expect from them was acknowledgment that the GPs had utility, coupled with statements that they don't go far enough—which is precisely the position they took. More important, many NGOs, including the main human rights organizations, were already using the Framework and the draft GPs in their own advocacy and operational work, and that fact spoke louder than words.

That some advocacy groups lacked enthusiasm or voiced criticism may have been an advantage with the business community. Indeed, as the Council session approached, I encouraged business associations, individual companies, and law firms, particularly those we had worked with in our various research and pilot projects, to send letters of support to their governments, directly to the Council, or to me, and to post them online. A significant number from diverse regions did so, which helped to solidify backing among many Council delegations.

The intergovernmental process of drafting and negotiating the resolution endorsing the GPs and establishing a follow-up mechanism that is consistent with the approach they embody was led by Norway, along with the other cosponsors: Argentina, India, Nigeria, and Russia. We began the process informally

more than a year in advance, with Norway hosting events ranging from ambassadorial dinners in Geneva to a ministerial meeting in New York, preparing the ground among governments
for the idea that the mandate's final product should be a set of
Guiding Principles, even though the Council had not specifically
requested such an instrument; and for the possibility that the
Council would endorse them, even though the use of that verb
lacked precedent. Each of the other cosponsors convened regular briefings for their respective regional groups. At the final and
decisive Council session, Ecuador, initially the one lone voice
against endorsing the GPs because they were not legally binding, joined the consensus after some back-channel work involving the capital, out of "solidarity" with the cosponsors.

VI. ACHIEVING CONVERGENCE

Unanimous endorsement by the Human Rights Council
ensured that the Guiding Principles became the authoritative
UN standard for business and human rights. But by itself this
would not necessarily mean that other relevant international
standard-setting bodies would automatically defer to the UN
and align their own standards with the GPs. Different institutions have different missions, and these often reflect the sectoral
or regional interests and concerns that are represented in them.
Therefore, achieving convergence around the GPs required an
active engagement effort.

Convergence is desirable for two reasons. First, reducing the
number of competing standards provides greater clarity and
predictability for businesses and other stakeholders alike. Thus,
it produces larger-scale change, and change that is more cumulative in its effects over time. Second, other major standard-setting

bodies active in this domain have implementation capacities the UN lacks. The OECD Guidelines involve a complaints mechanism; the IFC affects access to capital; ISO standards enjoy particularly high uptake in Asia and they feed into a sizable consulting industry that advises companies on compliance. The European Union is the world's second-largest home base of multinationals, while its central institutions have a mandate to establish common policies over a wide range of issues.

Thus, once the Protect, Respect and Remedy Framework was endorsed in 2008, I began to work with these other standard-setting bodies to see if a degree of convergence could be achieved. With success, and when coupled with the UN's own follow-up process, one could imagine the contours of a more coherent effort by these key institutions to promote essentially the same or at least complementary business and human rights standards.

The OECD was a welcoming partner. Its own Guidelines for Multinational Enterprises had come under heavy criticism from NGOs and workers' organizations—as well as from me, including in UN Human Rights Council reports—for lacking a human rights chapter; because the admissibility criteria for complaints required the existence of an "investment nexus," allowing National Contact Points at their discretion to dismiss cases involving contractual supply-chain relationships and financial intermediaries; and because negative findings by NCPs, the Guidelines' complaints mechanism, lacked any official consequences. First, the OECD Secretariat and then the Investment Committee, which comprises governments and oversees the Guidelines, invited me to address several official meetings, where I added my voice to those urging an update of the Guidelines. In 2010 the OECD Council agreed to do so, specifically noting the need to include a human rights chapter. I was invited to participate in the OECD update process as a

"Friend of the Guidelines," a group of external advisors convened by the chair of the Investment Committee. By that time
the drafting of the GPs was well advanced. Facing the possibility that the UN and the OECD might produce different and
possibly conflicting business and human rights standards, business associations began to call for convergence. For example,
the U.S. Council for International Business, the trade association of U.S. multinational corporations, sent a letter to Secretary of State Hillary Clinton making their support for the
OECD update conditional:

> A top priority in the update is to add a section on business and
> human rights, which we will strongly support to the extent that
> it is consistent with and follows from the UN framework on
> business and human rights being developed by Prof. John Rug-
> gie, the UN Special Representative of the Secretary-General.[26]

The Trade Union Advisory Committee to the OECD was
equally supportive of the idea, as was OECD Watch, its civil
society counterpart. My team and I worked closely with the
OECD drafters, and the updated Guidelines are fully aligned
with the GPs' corporate-responsibility-to-respect-human-rights
pillar, in many instances verbatim.

On a more informal basis, I also engaged with a similar process undertaken by the International Finance Corporation, the
World Bank's private sector arm. Here the political context was
somewhat tougher. The IFC was scheduled to update its Policy on Environmental and Social Sustainability, spelling out its
approach to these issues in the investments it makes and the
advisory services it provides, as well as the related performance
standards that clients are required to meet during a project's
life cycle. In the consultations leading up to the revision, civil

society organizations exerted pressure on the IFC to include explicit references to the corporate responsibility to respect human rights, as spelled out in the UN Framework, as I did in meetings with World Bank and IFC senior leadership. But now that emerging-market-economy and developing countries have acquired a greater voice in the World Bank, addressing human rights concerns has become tricky because some members of the Bank's board view them as a legacy of the "conditionality" requirements that Western donor governments imposed on them in the past. In this particular instance some of those governments also feared that an effective due-diligence process by a company might identify a government as posing human rights risks to the investment project. In a letter to Robert Zoellick, who was World Bank president at the time, I stressed that the corporate responsibility to respect human rights addresses the adverse human rights impacts of business itself, including those supported by IFC funding. I also listed the many developing countries that had made statements and cosponsored resolutions in support of my mandate in the Human Rights Council. Zoellick seemed to confirm my belief that such a letter might be useful for internal Bank purposes when he responded to my last point by saying: "Your letter gives me assurance that the global consensus you are building includes views of public and private stakeholders from the global south. This is very important for the World Bank Group."[27]

A protracted political process ultimately reached the compromise that the corporate responsibility to respect human rights would be referenced in the revised IFC policy, where it is closely aligned with all corresponding elements in the GPs. This allows the IFC to assess project-related human rights risks in its preinvestment environmental and social due diligence. Human rights do not feature as a separate performance standard for clients.

But several performance standards were strengthened, including those on indigenous peoples' rights; Performance Standard 1 requires the client to assess the project's social and environmental risks and to maintain an effective environmental and social management system; and the introduction to that standard notes that conducting due diligence using the performance standards "will enable the client to address many human rights issues in its project."[28]

ISO is the international association of national standard-setting bodies in 162 countries—for example, the American National Standards Institute in the case of the United States. Best known for having developed certifiable management systems for firms (ISO 9000 for quality management, ISO 14000 for environmental management), it moved into the social responsibility field in 2002 when it announced its intention to establish a social responsibility standard (ISO 26000), although actual work did not begin until 2005. Unusually, this standard is aimed at all organizations, not only firms, but arguably ISO was drawn into the field by the perceived opportunity to leverage its past successes with corporate management systems, its reputation for technical professionalism, and its vast networks of users—100,000 strong for the quality management standard—to capture significant market share in the highly fragmented CSR domain.[29] The ISO decision-making rules require internal consensus among all stakeholder groups in each national standards body. I assigned a team member to keep track of the human rights elements of the standard being negotiated, and after the adoption of the UN Framework to try to ensure ISO's alignment with it.

Two participants in the ISO process have posted short accounts of the impact of my mandate on ISO 26000: Sandra Atler, who represented a Swedish NGO, and Alan Fine, representing South African business. According to Atler:

[T]he UN Framework helped decisively to establish in ISO 26000 the baseline responsibility to respect human rights; to introduce the elements of human rights due diligence as the appropriate means for organizations to know and show that they respect rights; and in clarifying the concepts of complicity and sphere of influence. Moreover, the support for the Framework helped resolve a number of differences among participants in the ISO 26000 process, and increased their overall level of support for the human rights component of the standard.[30]

Fine notes that there was initially strong resistance within the business group and some states to setting a "floor" of behavior below which practices would be considered not socially responsible.[31] They argued that no single set of standards could be universally agreed upon. But the Framework's formulation of the corporate responsibility to respect human rights, meaning to not infringe on the rights of others and to conduct adequate human rights due diligence, carried the day and was accepted as an "international norm of behavior." There had been equally strong resistance to any reference to "corporate complicity," and although the language was hard-fought, ISO ultimately accepted my 2008 report on this subject as being an authoritative source. Perhaps the most difficult issue concerned the concept of "sphere of influence," which successive ISO drafts used as the basis for defining the scope of the social responsibility of all actors. If that stood, ISO 26000 would end up contradicting the UN Framework and GPs on a critical foundational issue: whether the attribution of corporate responsibility should be impact-based or influence-based. Seeing little movement, I sent a note to the ISO leadership explaining why I found the "sphere of influence" formula unworkable—much the same arguments I made in earlier chapters of this book. But NGOs in particular did not want to let go of the sphere-of-influence concept in the belief that it provided a stronger moral basis for social responsibility than the impact-based formula. In the end, I prevailed in the human rights section of ISO 26000, but traces of "sphere of influence" can be found elsewhere in the document.[32] The new standard was adopted by 93 percent of ISO member bodies, including China.

Turning to the European Union, I addressed a committee of the European Parliament in April 2009, promoting the Framework and also politely but firmly criticizing the rigid distinction between voluntary and mandatory measures that had paralyzed the CSR debate within the EU for years. Later that year, the Swedish presidency of the EU convened an EU-wide conference on the mandate at which I first tried out my conceptual deconstruction of extraterritorial jurisdiction. Subsequently, a member of my team was invited to participate in an EU project on this subject. And in the fall of 2011, the European Commission issued a new EU CSR strategy for the period 2011 to 2014. It includes a specific action item on "Implementing the UN Guiding Principles on Business and Human Rights," stating that the Commission "[e]xpects all European enterprises to meet the corporate responsibility to respect human rights, as defined in the UN Guiding Principles" and "[i]nvites EU Member States to develop by the end of 2012 national plans for the implementation of the UN Guiding Principles."[33]

Finally, in 2009, ASEAN, the Association of Southeast Asian Nations, established an Intergovernmental Commission on Human Rights. It is charged with, among other tasks, drafting an ASEAN Declaration of Human Rights. In early 2011 the Commission announced that it would also conduct a baseline study on CSR and human rights in the ASEAN region. Members of my team briefed the Commission twice, once during its visit to Washington and the second time in the region. According to a subsequent statement by one Commission representative:

> The target for this thematic study is an ASEAN Guideline that is fully compliant with the UN frameworks, especially the Protect, Respect and Remedy Framework for Business and Human Rights and the Guiding Principles for Business and Human Rights which were endorsed by the UN Human Rights Council on 16 June 2011.[34]

For these reasons, an end-of-year blog on the Web site of London's *Guardian* newspaper called 2011 "a landmark year for business and human rights"[35]—although I am the first to insist that much more remains to be done.

VII. CONCLUSION

So where are we now, along the trajectory of establishing the Guiding Principles as international norms of behavior? We are, as I stated previously, at the end of the beginning.

The views of two very different stakeholder groups illustrate that an important phase has ended—one group at the forefront of business and human rights advocacy, the other a business association in a conservative industry sector. The International Corporate Accountability Roundtable is a new coalition of leading human rights organizations that include Amnesty International, EarthRights International, Global Witness, Human Rights First, and Human Rights Watch. They held their first annual meeting in September 2011 to assess the current state of play in business and human rights, and to develop a common approach to "building a movement for corporate accountability." Under the heading of "Concluding Themes" in a report summarizing the discussions, one participant (speakers were not identified by name) observed:

> Ruggie's Guiding Principles will likely be the template for an international human rights framework for the next decade. There is a need for more discussion of these principles and for debate regarding the expectations of companies in high-risk industries to use these principles. The principles have substantive merit and campaigning utility, however, which was lacking before.[36]

Two months later IPIECA, the global oil and gas industry association for environmental and social issues, announced that it had convened its first workshop "furthering collaborative learning around due diligence and grievance mechanisms. Dedicated teams have been formed to design and execute multiyear work programs in both areas."[37] This followed a statement when the GPs were issued that expressed the hope that any UN follow-up to the mandate would "help facilitate implementation of the Protect, Respect and Remedy framework and adoption of the due diligence recommendations."[38] It is fair to say that these two groups do not agree on much. But both expect that the UN Guiding Principles will constitute the foundation for the next phase of work in business and human rights—thereby acknowledging that we now do have such a common foundation.

That there is much more to be done can be illustrated through a simple heuristic model of the life cycle of norms. Scholars who study how norms emerge, spread, and become embedded in practice have identified three phases. They call the first "norm emergence." Its main driver is said to be efforts at persuasion by so-called norm entrepreneurs. In global governance contexts, these are individuals with organizational platforms who use information and expertise, formulate organizational priorities, and engage in public advocacy to promote a particular norm or a set of norms. "The construction of cognitive frames is an essential component of norm entrepreneurs' political strategies, since when they are successful the new frames resonate with broader public understandings and are adopted as new ways of talking about and understanding issues."[39] The second phase is described as "norm cascade." This occurs when states and international institutions embrace the emerging norm. Here norm entrepreneurs and supporters persuade the relevant rule-makers of the norm's appropriateness and effectiveness to their respective organizations' mission and even legitimacy. The third phase is termed "norm internalization." This occurs when a norm begins to take on a "taken-for-granted quality" and gets incorporated into organizational routines. Professions—in the business and human rights context, lawyers and consultants, for example—often serve as important bridging agents by translating norms into action plans, implementation tools, and performance indicators.

This life-cycle model is not predictive in the sense of being able to tell which norms are likely to complete the path and which will fail to take off or get sidetracked along the way. Nor can it possibly be fully descriptive of the many diverse ways in which norms evolve in specific contexts. One reason is that "new norms never enter a normative vacuum but instead emerge in a highly contested normative space where they must compete with other norms and perceptions of interest."[40] There is no ex ante way of determining if and how this contestation will be resolved. But the model does provide us with benchmarks.

Among the main international standard-setting bodies involved in business and human rights, the corporate responsibility to respect human rights—its definition, substantive content, scope, and what companies must do to meet it—has "emerged" and in large measure "cascaded." It remains to be seen how effectively it gets "internalized" and implemented. In the world of multi-national corporations it has gone through the first two phases among many leading companies, but internalization has just begun. I suspect that the majority of multinationals and the larger universe of small and medium-sized enterprises knows little if anything yet about the Guiding Principles. Getting governments to accept the full implications of their duty to protect human rights against abuses by business enterprises remains a signifi-cant challenge—including in relation to the ever-more-prominent role of state-owned enterprises. And access to judicial remedy remains most problematic where it is most needed.

The concluding chapter picks up from this assessment and offers some reflections on next steps.

Chapter Five

NEXT STEPS

The most difficult part of any journey is often the beginning. That was certainly true in the case of my mandate. I had an impressive title: "Special Representative of the United Nations Secretary-General on the issue of human rights and transnational corporations and other business enterprises." But as I recounted in the Introduction, that was largely it. My task initially was limited to identifying and clarifying things, and I had no budget or staff. Gradually, the material constraints became less pressing and the scope of the mandate was expanded. But even then the sheer intellectual challenge remained daunting. Adapting the international human rights regime to encompass business conduct runs smack into some of the most prominent features of the current world polity and economy: national sovereignty; competition among states for markets, investments, and access to resources; the emergence of new global powers with their own views about both business and human rights; weak or corrupt governments in many countries; the corporate-law principle of legal separation between parent company and affiliates, asymmetries of capacity and influence between large companies and many governments;

large swaths of conflict zones; few and highly contested bases of extraterritorial jurisdiction—the list goes on.

How does one frame an agenda that recognizes these constraints and yet avoids being overwhelmed by them? In this already difficult context, two illusions had added to the challenge of providing more effective protection to individuals and communities against corporate-related human rights harm: that this objective is best achieved by seeking to subject the entire bundle of business and human rights issues to a binding international legal instrument; or that the combination of voluntary initiatives, new management tools, and the dissemination of best practices on its own will generate enough momentum for companies themselves to truly move markets. But neither can do what it promises: the first because it expects too much from the system of international public governance, and the second because it permits too little.

The previous chapters of this book describe and explain the more heterodox approach I developed. It combines in one single template the three distinct governance systems that shape corporate conduct in the global sphere: public, corporate, and civil. The Protect, Respect and Remedy Framework addresses *what* should be done: the state duty to protect against human rights abuses by third parties, including business enterprises, through appropriate policies, regulation, and adjudication; an independent corporate responsibility to respect human rights, which means that business enterprises should act with due diligence to avoid infringing on the rights of others and address adverse impacts with which they are involved; and the need for greater access by affected individuals and communities to effective remedy, both judicial and nonjudicial. The Guiding Principles stipulate *how* these things should be done, laying out the necessary policies and practices, including the engagement of affected people in due-diligence processes and grievance mechanisms as well as in monitoring the performance of the other two main actors against the benchmarks the Guiding Principles provide.

The three pillars are intended to be mutually reinforcing. Starting with businesses, their own responsibilities include due diligence to identify, prevent, mitigate, and account for how they address their adverse impacts on human rights; and participation in processes that enable the remediation of any adverse human rights impact they cause or contribute to. Even if no other pillar were added, this formulation of the corporate responsibility to respect human rights spells out in greater detail than ever before how companies should meet that baseline responsibility. But the corporate responsibility to respect is not a freestanding pillar. It is reinforced by the state duty to protect on one side, and judicial as well as nonjudicial remedy on the other. Finally, in this construction states and businesses are joined by actors from the sphere of civil governance. The GPs also differ from other efforts to provide guidance for business and human rights: their endorsement by a unanimous UN Human Rights Council and the adoption of core elements by other international standard-setting bodies make it, in the words of UN Secretary-General Ban Ki-moon, "the authoritative global standard for preventing and addressing adverse impacts on human rights arising from business-related activity."[1]

Only time will tell if the Guiding Principles actually generate their intended regulatory dynamic. This final chapter reports some of the steps that are already being taken in that direction, as well as further steps that I believe should be taken, for the journey to continue.

I. IMPLEMENTATION

The first "next" step is for the various standard-setting bodies and other entities that have adopted or otherwise incorporated the GPs to begin implementing their commitments. This section briefly surveys some of the ongoing activity, beginning with the UN itself.

The UN Human Rights Council has established a five-person inter-regional working group of experts to follow up on the mandate. The group issued its work plan in April 2012.[2] Its main tasks are to promote the GPs' implementation and dissemination, identify and exchange good practices, help build the institutional capacity of developing countries as well as small and medium-sized enterprises, and provide further recommendations to the Council. The working group will conduct two official country visits a year, and also convene an annual global forum on business and human rights to examine overall trends and address challenges encountered in implementing the GPs. Along with the Office of the High Commissioner for Human Rights, the working group is also expected to play a role as the GPs' guardian, tracking how they are being interpreted by various actors. The working group, like the mandate before it, has adopted a multistakeholder approach and plans to work with diverse partners in different regions of the world. Beyond the scope of the working group, Secretary-General Ban Ki-moon has issued a detailed report with recommendations on how the UN system as a whole can contribute to the GPs' dissemination and implementation.[3]

The European Commission has called on all European Union member states to submit national action plans on the implementation of the GPs by the end of 2012; at the time of writing, national consultations had taken place in Denmark, Germany, the Netherlands, and the United Kingdom. The EU has also launched work to further elaborate the GPs specifically for three different industry sectors, and for small and medium-sized enterprises. The first sector selected comprises employment and recruitment agencies, an industry that has undergone exponential growth in recent years. Adverse human rights impacts that have been identified in this sector include human trafficking, slavery, and forced or bonded labor; denial of just and favorable conditions of work; and risks to freedom of association and collective bargaining. The second sector comprises information and communication technology companies. Here the focus is on freedom of expression and privacy, as well as workplace standards in supply chains. The third sector is the oil and gas industry. The main issues to be addressed include land rights; adverse impacts on health, clean water and food; on freedom of expression and assembly; and on the physical security of the person. "The guidance developed through this project will be based on the UN Guiding Principles on Business and Human Rights."[4] The results are intended to inform future EU policy and possibly legislation on business and human rights, and corporate social responsibility more broadly.

Recall that the update of the OECD Guidelines for Multinational Enterprises included a human rights chapter for the first time, which draws on and is fully aligned with the GPs' provisions on the corporate responsibility to respect human rights. Several important developments are under way here. First, the OECD has selected the financial services sector for the development of more detailed guidance. Previously, the Guidelines required that an "investment nexus" exist in order for a complaint against a company to fall within their scope and be considered by an OECD National Contact Point (NCP)—the official complaints mechanisms in each of the forty-two adhering governments. That requirement was loosened in 2011. Now lending institutions and other types of financial intermediaries will have some due-diligence requirements under the Guidelines, which this exercise will help specify.[5]

Second, complaints are beginning to be submitted to NCPs under the Guidelines' new human rights chapter. One that was resolved quickly was brought against a Dutch agricultural multinational, Nidera Holdings, by a group of Argentine and Dutch NGOs, regarding the treatment of temporary agricultural workers in Argentine corn fields. The company agreed to upgrade its human rights policy, to adopt human rights due diligence procedures, and to permit the NGOs to monitor the particular operation by means of site visits.[6] Through such NCP deliberations, the functional equivalent of "jurisprudence" in human rights cases will emerge across the forty-two adhering governments—official interpretations of the meaning of the OECD Guidelines' requirements for the corporate responsibility to respect human rights in specific contexts, fleshing out the higher-level guidance the GPs provide. New rules also require NCPs to make public the results of every case they consider.[7] The combination of these two measures will enhance peer learning, and social learning more broadly. The OECD is also making efforts to reach beyond the current states adhering to its Guidelines; for example, China, India, Indonesia, the Russian Federation, Saudi Arabia, and South Africa were invited to participate in their update.

What still needs to happen here is for governments to agree that lack of cooperation by a company in an NCP process, either by failing to engage in it or ignoring its negative findings, will have official consequences—including the withdrawal of such public support as export credit and investment insurance, until the company can demonstrate compliance. Indeed, this reflects a more general shortcoming in the system through which governments provide this type of support to companies: it does not uniformly include due-diligence requirements even when the proposed project is destined for an area known to pose high human rights risks. I had urged the OECD Export Credit Group, which develops minimum standards among the national agencies, to adopt such requirements. It appears that the Group will endorse modest steps in this direction. A forthcoming version of the Group's "Common Approaches Recommendation" is expected to reference the corporate responsibility to respect human rights as stipulated in the GPs and to include some form of impact assessment.[8] Of course, individual national export credit agencies are free to move forward on their own to include such requirements. Non-OECD members, including China, should develop parallel policies.

As discussed in earlier chapters, ISO 26000 also includes a human rights chapter that is closely aligned with the GPs. It is officially designated a social responsibility "guidance," not a certifiable standard like ISO 14000 on environmental management systems. But apparently the marketing opportunities for a certifiable standard were too great to resist. Swiss-based IQNet, an association of more than thirty-five national certification bodies, has launched its own version of ISO 26000, calling it IQNet SR 10. According to IQNet, this standard "establishes the requirements of social responsibility management systems," enabling companies and other organizations to "gain credibility through global certification."[9]

It is too soon to see changes resulting from the International Finance Corporation's new sustainability policy and performance standards, given the lead time required for major investment projects. However, the IFC's growing collaboration with private equity firms has brought an entirely new set of actors into the arena that until recently had exhibited little concern with social, environmental, and governance issues. Several such firms, including the Carlyle Group, one of the largest, are establishing significant investment funds for emerging markets in which they lack prior experience and therefore look to IFC involvement as much for its institutional knowledge and relationships as for financing. But in return these firms are required to comply with IFC standards—including carrying out social- and environmental-impact assessments.

It is difficult to keep track of individual country and company initiatives, there being no global registry of such things. Companies tend not to announce major developments, such as adopting a new human rights policy, until they already have the main elements in place, including training their personnel. Experience suggests that it may take as long as two years for a large corporation to implement such shifts. Changes in government policies can take longer. From the available information, it seems that individual governments are still mostly in the planning stage, organizing workshops and parliamentary hearings on what the GPs mean for them and for their businesses.

Major corporations are moving more rapidly, focused in particular on how to put effective due-diligence processes into place, and in some sectors (mining, in particular) developing site-level grievance mechanisms. In February 2012, the global audit and advisory firm, Mazars, surveyed mining companies listed on eight different stock exchanges; among its findings was that "65% of respondents were actively working towards compliance with the [Guiding] Principles."[10] Numerous companies with complex supply chains are assessing the adequacy of their due-diligence systems for addressing multitiered supplier challenges. In addition, the information technology sector has become more engaged than in the past, no doubt due to user backlash when companies met demands from some governments, including during the Arab spring, to turn over user information or censor their services. The first-ever Silicon Valley Human Rights Conference was held in October 2011 sponsored by Google, Facebook, Yahoo, Mozilla, and Skype, among others. It adopted the "Silicon Valley Standard," which includes a human rights commitment: "In both policy and practice, technology companies should apply human rights frameworks in developing best practices and standard operating procedures. This includes adhering to John Ruggie's Protect, Respect and Remedy framework outlined in the UN Guiding Principles on Business and Human Rights."[11]

The International Organisation of Employers, the world's largest representative business association, with national chapters in 143 countries, has issued an "Employers' Guide" to the GPs.[12] The International Trade Union Confederation has done the same for unionists.[13] Both describe in some detail how their respective constituent member organizations can use the GPs. As reported by the UN working group, civil society organizations "are actively working to promote enhanced accountability of States and business enterprises for the human rights impact of business activity, with numerous examples referencing the 'Protect, Respect and Remedy' Framework and Guiding Principles."[14] Other international initiatives are building on, or otherwise referencing, the Framework and the GPs, ranging from UNICEF's "Children's Rights and Business Principles" to the "International Code of Conduct for Private Security Providers," orchestrated by the Swiss government and the International Committee of the Red Cross.[15] For its part, the UN Global Compact has stated officially that the GPs "provide further conceptual and operational clarity" for the human rights commitments it champions, and it convenes workshops and provides tools to promote their understanding.[16]

The process of further implementing and disseminating the GPs will take time. But they are already being called upon in more immediate situations as well. One important instance concerns Myanmar/Burma. Recent political developments, symbolized by the election to parliament of Aung San Suu Kyi, have led to the suspension of economic sanctions imposed on that country. The EU was the first to do so. On April 26, 2012, the EU foreign ministers issued a statement that included the following paragraph:

> The EU recognizes the vital contribution the private sector has to make to the development of Myanmar/Burma and would welcome European companies exploring trade and investment opportunities. This should be done by promoting the practice of the highest standards of integrity and corporate social responsibility. These are laid out in the OECD Guidelines for Multinational Enterprises, UN guiding principles on business and human rights and the EU's own CSR strategy 2011–2014. The EU will work with the authorities, the private sector and the people of Myanmar/Burma to create the best possible regulatory environment.[17]

When the United States followed suit, expressing similar expectations regarding corporate responsibility, the government went a step further and imposed a reporting requirement on U.S. entities investing in Burma, which includes a human rights component that specifically references the Guiding Principles.[18]

Myanmar poses a particular challenge for business and human rights. It is rich in natural resources, yet poverty persists. Concerns over corruption remain high, as can be seen in the Transparency International Corruption Perception Index, which ranks the country third from the bottom in the world. The rule of law is weak and the judiciary is far from independent. The government and local businesses have been closely intertwined. The military has a significant stake in many sectors of the economy, and human rights groups have shown conclusively that abusive practices such as forced labor are still widespread. In such an environment international investors will need to undertake enhanced due diligence, including exercising caution about whom they obtain access to land from, how they gain that access, and how they conduct consultations with affected communities. It also means ensuring that workers are able to form unions, are paid a fair, legal, living wage, and that no force is used in hiring workers or in their conditions at work. Companies will also have to take concrete steps to see to it that their partners, local or regional, adhere to international standards and are not implicated in any past conduct that may expose investors to complicity risks, and that they take effective steps to conduct activities without discrimination, particularly while operating in regions riven by ethnic tension and conflict.

To achieve real progress in Myanmar, governments, businesses, and civil society will need to work together to find a responsible way forward; that means companies consulting with local actors as well as assessing potentially adverse human rights impacts of business activities and relationships. As recommended by the GPs, the home states of foreign investors should provide them with clear guidance about the context in which companies will operate, including its human rights risks. Equally important, home governments should make export credit and investment insurance conditional upon companies undertaking such due diligence and developing mitigating steps in case of potential harm. Finally, the government of Myanmar should be encouraged to demonstrate its own commitment to more accountable governance, including by participating in multistakeholder initiatives such as the Extractive Industry Transparency Initiative, making public the payments it receives from petroleum, gas, and mining companies, as well as adhering to the Voluntary Principles on Security and Human Rights, which provide ground rules for the conduct of public and private security providers who protect company installations.

Individually, these steps would be significant; collectively, they offer the potential of making Myanmar an example of how the GPs can help businesses operate responsibly even in very challenging environments—though whether a Myanmar version of Protect, Respect and Remedy can be put in place rapidly enough to shape the oncoming investment flood remains an open question.

To sum up, the life of the GPs did not end with their adoption; in some ways it has only just begun. The implementation phase has gotten under way, and further dissemination is a primary task of the UN working group. Follow-up initiatives by governments and businesses are drilling down in specific industry sectors. Workers organizations and civil society actors are using the GPs as a benchmark for advocacy and assessment in relation to both. Moreover, while the GPs in themselves do not establish new international law norms, by adopting them the governments endorsed the proposition that if a company cannot know and show that it respects human rights, its claim that it does remains only that—a claim, not a fact. This soft-law formula coupled with their own business rationales is helping to drive leading companies to develop human rights due-diligence systems. In short, we are witnessing an expanding set of efforts at embedding the GPs, reflecting the different characteristics of sectors, regions, and scale of operations but based upon a common normative platform and policy guidance.

II. BUILDING ON THE GPS

During the course of my UN mandate I addressed several areas of law and policy that directly shape business practices but operate in isolation from human rights, and are largely uninformed by their implications for them. Among the most important are international investment agreements and corporate law. The prevailing understanding of their human rights linkages was too underdeveloped, however, and the diversity of policies and practices across states too great, for me to have put forward specific recommendations. But both are areas that should be targeted for further policy development building on the GPs.

Investment Agreements

Bilateral investment treaties (BITs) are concluded between governments. Nearly 3,000 BITs are in place today, following an exponential increase in the 1990s reflecting that decade's wave of globalization and privatization. Under the terms of these treaties the capital-importing country provides enforceable guarantees to investors from the capital-exporting country. The guarantees include standards of treatment to be applied to investors, and provisions for compensation in case of expropriation. These agreements are necessary to protect foreign investors from arbitrary treatment by host governments. But, as discussed in earlier chapters, they also have features that can constrain host governments' regulatory space in other, less desirable ways. José

Alvarez is a leading professor of international law who served as an investment treaty negotiator in the Reagan administration. He explains that the principal aim of U.S. BITs at the time was "to entrench . . . the underlying private law legal regimes necessary to support market transactions—and enable international law to become a force to dismantle public law regulations inimical to the market."[19] In case of an investment dispute between the host state and a foreign investor, typically a BIT permits the investor to initiate compulsory international arbitration claims against the state. The arbitration process draws its rules and practitioners largely from the world of commercial arbitration, and yet in many cases they are required to determine matters of profound public interest. Over time, what Alvarez called "inimical" regulations has been construed to include labor standards, environmental improvements, and human rights protections. In addition, unlike the field of trade law, there is no appellate procedure for arbitral rulings; inconsistent or even contradictory rulings simply are allowed to stand. According to one expert study, because few if any institutionalized checks and balances exist in investment dispute settlement there is a far higher degree of speculative forms of litigation in this area—of investors trying to push the envelope in their favor—than in the World Trade Organization.[20]

Professor Thomas Walde, an investment law and arbitration expert, chided me in his response to a speech I gave in London in 2007, in which I raised the need for states to be able to meet their human rights commitments without fear of running afoul of their investment treaty obligations. He followed up in an email:

The problem with many of the human rights claims now made is that investment tribunals have to operate with the "law appli-

cable." That is defined by the [bilateral investment] treaty. . . .
If arbitrators apply something outside the clear jurisdiction/
mandate of the treaty because they sympathize, they'll exceed
their jurisdiction, risk annulment/setting-aside and their reputation. It is law they have to apply not airy-fairy wishy-washy
concepts of desirability with a vague soft-law claim.[21]

But in the already-mentioned case brought against South
Africa by European investors who claimed that certain provisions of the Black Economic Empowerment Act were unfair,
inequitable, and tantamount to expropriation, the government
was not defending "wishy-washy" or "airy-fairy" concepts, but
its own constitution and legislative acts that sought to establish restorative justice after decades of apartheid rule. Argentina
may have botched its water privatization program, but there is
nothing "vague" about the need of its people to have access to
clean and affordable drinking water. Protecting the rights of
indigenous peoples when a mining company wishes to expand
into ancestral burial grounds is not a "soft-law" issue to them
or to the host government with which the indigenous group
may have a long-standing treaty. In short, the rules and tools of
BITs and arbitration procedures may inappropriately constrain
or punish governments for taking bona fide public interest measures, including meeting their human rights obligations, and
even where the measures affect foreign and domestic investors
equally. Nevertheless, Walde is absolutely correct: better crafted
treaties are necessary. But until recently they have been in short
supply, in part due to a lack of knowledge, in part to the power
asymmetries between the parties involved.

This situation is beginning to change as a result of several factors: emerging economies, including China and Bra-

zil, refuse to accept restrictive provisions of this sort; Western countries, including the United States, are becoming more frequent targets of suits by foreign investors; and the recognition is setting in more widely that governments require adequate domestic policy space to manage competing policy objectives and legal obligations in an ever-more-interconnected global economy.[22] A 2007 Norwegian draft model BIT signaled the change. The commentary noted that certain features of BITs pose potential risks to Norway's own highly developed system of regulations and protection, including environmental and social policies. It also stressed the vulnerability of developing countries to agreements "that tie up political freedom of action and the exercise of authority." Accordingly, the draft sought to "ensure that the State's right to make legitimate regulations of the actions of investors is not restricted by an investment agreement. However, the right to regulate must be balanced against the investors' wish for predictability, legal safeguards, minimum requirements regarding the actions of the State, and compensation in the event of expropriation."[23] In April 2012 the United States issued its new model BIT. As in all such treaties, the language is complex. But I found it interesting that the State Department's "fact sheet" describing it chose to highlight "its carefully calibrated balance between providing strong investor protections and preserving the government's ability to regulate in the public interest"; the obligation on parties to not "waive or derogate from" domestic labor and environmental laws as a lure to foreign investment, and to "effectively enforce" such laws; new provisions whereby the parties "reaffirm and recognize international commitments" under the ILO core rights at work; and the possibility of a future multilateral appellate procedure.[24] But even this latest model agreement does not explicitly address business-related human rights challenges beyond the confines of the workplace.

Corresponding changes are required in host government agreements—the contracts governments and companies enter into for specific projects. These contracts generally are not made public, but the ninety or so that I saw on a confidential basis exhibited little awareness of the fact that major projects can pose significant human rights risks. Therefore, they include few if any provisions for how those risks should be managed when they arise. Above all, contracts fail to delineate the respective roles and obligations of governments and companies for situations when things go wrong. That's not good for people or companies because it can lead to confusion and lack of direction in times of crisis, especially if military units untrained in community policing are called upon to control large-scale demonstrations. Moreover, because companies are subject to community pressures even where governments are not, in the absence of a clear ex ante specification of roles, those pressures can push companies into providing what are essentially public goods and services, for which companies are ill equipped, which is unsustainable once companies leave, and which diminishes the incentives for governments to do their job.

Moreover, as with BITs, some of the regulatory stabilization provisions that companies insist on including in investor-state contracts unduly constrain governments even when they act on bona fide public interest grounds and in a nondiscriminatory manner. Relative bargaining power can be as much in play as financial risk in determining the scope of stabilization provisions—or whether they're in a contract at all. Just as in the case of BITs, governments need to be able to construct a proper nondiscriminatory regulatory framework without fear of being sued by foreign investors.

Finally, physical harm to people in communities—including loss of life—at the hands of security providers remains a major challenge for the extractive industry. Therefore, when such companies operate in difficult environments, it is imperative that investor-state contracts include more explicit references to the need for public and private security providers to be subject to international human rights standards. This can be done, for example, by incorporating the Voluntary Principles on Security and Human Rights into contract provisions—holding both the state and the company responsible for ensuring that adequate vetting and training of security providers as well as honest incident reporting takes place.

There is no central location in the international community from which these changes can be driven. The new generation of bilateral investment treaties is being hammered out in national capitals and bilateral negotiations, under competing political pressures. And investor-state contracts are generated by individual government agencies, companies, and large numbers of law firms scattered across the world. Continued advocacy and support for more balanced approaches are necessary. UN agencies should do more to provide negotiation training and skills building for governments that have limited capacity. These concerns also need to be raised with law firms, which have been urged to support and promote the Guiding Principles by both the American and the International bar associations—and which, as businesses, have their own responsibilities to respect human rights.[25] The international and regional follow-up processes to my mandate also provide visible venues from which to expand awareness about the human rights dimensions of international investment agreements.

Corporate Law

At the very foundation of modern corporate law lies the principle of legal separation between a company's owners (the shareholders) and the company itself, coupled with its correlative principle of limited liability, under which shareholders are held financially liable only to the extent of the value of their ownership shares. This model of the joint stock company was invented when only people—"natural persons"—were owners, and it was intended to facilitate the formation of capital among them for investment purposes. Today, the model has been stretched to apply to multinational corporate groups with subsidiaries, joint ventures, contractors, and other types of affiliates in up to two hundred states and territories around the world, each of which is legally construed as a separate and independent entity even where the parent company is the sole shareholder. This raises a fundamental question for business and human rights: how do we get a multinational corporation to assume the responsibility to respect human rights for the entire corporate group, not atomize it down to its various constituent units?[26]

The attempt by the UN Sub-Commission on Human Rights to impose binding Norms on multinational corporations, which preceded my mandate, aimed a silver bullet at the problem. But it turned out to be a dud. Larry Catá Backer, a legal scholar who has written extensively on this subject, observed at the time:

The Norms internationalize and adopt an enterprise liability model as the basis for determining the scope of liability for groups of related companies. This approach does, in a very simple way, eliminate one of the great complaints about globalization through large webs of interconnected but legally independent corporations forming one large economic enterprise. The problem, of course, is that, as a matter of domestic law in most states, the autonomous legal personality of a corporation matters. Most states have developed very strong public policies in favor of legal autonomy.[27]

Indeed, my survey of the relationship between corporate law and human rights in thirty-nine jurisdictions around the world indicated that some form of legal separation and limited liability exists in all of them. Some exceptions are made in different jurisdictions, though few with extraterritorial reach. Reform of corporate and securities law and policy is under consideration in many countries as a result of the 2008 financial sector meltdown and its impact on the real economy. But the abandonment of the foundational tenets of modern corporate law is not on the agenda. Dealing with the constraints they impose in the global business and human rights context will remain a more complex affair.

Under the corporate-responsibility-to-respect-human-rights pillar, I did not set out to establish a global enterprise legal liability model. That would have been a purely theoretical exercise. My aim was to prescribe practical ways of integrating human rights concerns within enterprise risk-management systems. Multinational corporations routinely assess and address enterprise-wide risks, in addition to the risks faced by local operating units. And when they do so, they aggregate, not atomize, risks across the corporate group and functions. Separate legal personality is rarely invoked in relation to enterprise risk management. But there had been no authoritative guidance for how to manage the risks of adverse human rights impacts. The concept and component elements of human rights due diligence provide that guidance. Ongoing efforts at reforming corporate law can help build on the GPs' foundation. [28] I suggest two broad approaches, one relating to the internal dimension of corporate governance, the second to its external dimension.

We learned from our pilot projects that integrating systems for conducting human rights due diligence and managing the resulting information flows constitute complex challenges for businesses, especially for large and far-flung companies. One problem is that the individual or team responsible for assessing human rights impacts on the ground often sits apart from those conducting and overseeing the activities and relationships that generate negative impacts. So those assessing the impacts do not directly control the decisions and actions that can prevent, mitigate, or remediate impacts. And yet the speed and ease with which an enterprise can respond to its potential human rights impacts can be decisive for the effectiveness of managing those risks. Therefore, companies need to institute fully linked-up chains of responsibility across the appropriate levels and functions within the business, and budget allocations as well as incentive structures need to reinforce that responsibility chain. Among the ways that corporate law and policy can support this integration is by recognizing the concept of "corporate culture"—in this instance, a corporate culture respectful of human rights. There are precedents in domestic law that can be drawn on. For example, under the Australian criminal code a firm itself may be held liable when its corporate culture directed, encouraged, tolerated, or led to noncompliance with the relevant provisions. But only the individual who committed the illegal act may be prosecuted if the company has in place effective systems of control and supervision.[29] The U.S. Federal Sentencing Guidelines require judicial consideration of whether a corporation has an "organizational culture that encourages ethical conduct and a commitment to compliance with the law" in assessing criminal penalties.[30] Analogous provisions could be constructed in corporate and securities law, incentivizing companies to institute more integrated corporate cultures directed toward ethical conduct, which in turn would facilitate more coherent approaches to respecting human rights across a company.

A second development in corporate law and policy that would reinforce and build on this dimension of the GPs concerns corporate boards. The GPs provide that companies should undertake meaningful consultations with stakeholders when conducting human rights impact assessments, evaluating the effectiveness of mitigation measures, and constructing and operating grievance mechanisms. This would be strengthened by corporate law provisions that explicitly permit company directors, in fulfilling their fiduciary responsibility to the company, to consider its impact on other stakeholders and on society as a whole. That could encourage boards to establish more extensive oversight of company programs intended to manage social risks, including human rights, while also protecting directors from possible shareholder claims that they are breaching their duty to the company by straying too far from short-term profit maximization. Examples exist in several jurisdictions, as noted in earlier chapters. In the United States directors are given discretion to determine what is in the best interest of the company under the so-called business judgment rule, but its scope is not defined. An important next step would be to make it explicit that taking into account a company's impact on society is in keeping with directors' duties to their companies. This has been variously described as the "enlightened shareholder" or "enlightened management" approach, permitting "consideration of stakeholder interests as being broadly aligned with long-term shareholder interests, without risking legal liability for breach of duty."[31]

As is the case with investment agreements, reforms in corporate law and policy are largely domestic affairs—and regional in the case of the European Union. Therefore, similar kinds of research, capacity building, and advocacy from human rights platforms can help advance the agenda. In addition, the types of reforms discussed in this section should be a high priority of institutional investors, which have their own fiduciary responsibility to ensure long-term sustainable returns.

III. BEYOND THE GPS

I have explained at some length throughout this book why I thought it illusory to aim at establishing some single, overarching international legal framework for the entire bundle of business and human rights issues, while at the same time believing that specific legal instruments would and should be developed that address some of its specific dimensions. I have also acknowledged the tactical judgment I made that proposing any new international law norms as part of the GPs might risk their endorsement as a whole. Nevertheless, in a separate note sent to all UN member states on follow-up steps to my mandate, I recommended that they consider drafting an international legal instrument to address one specific challenge. It was not acted upon, so I reiterate that proposal here, drawing on recent developments in U.S. courts to illustrate why it is essential.

On February 28, 2012, the United States Supreme Court heard oral arguments in *Kiobel v. Royal Dutch Petroleum Co.* (Shell), brought under the Alien Tort Statute (ATS). The case was similar to the *Wiwa* case discussed in chapter 1 but involved different plaintiffs. These plaintiffs also charged that Shell aided and abetted egregious human rights abuses conducted by the

Nigerian military in the early 1990s, including a systematic campaign of torture, extrajudicial executions, prolonged arbitrary detention, and indiscriminate killings that constituted crimes against humanity, in an effort to violently suppress the Movement for the Survival of the Ogoni People.[32] Shell and the plaintiffs had agreed to settle *Wiwa*. But this time a sharply divided 2nd Circuit Court of Appeals held that the ATS does not apply to corporations, as legal persons, only to natural persons. With other circuit courts having reached the opposite conclusion, the Supreme Court agreed to hear the case. Recall that the ATS was enacted in 1789. It simply says, "The district courts shall have original jurisdiction of any civil action by an alien for a tort only, committed in violation of the law of nations or a treaty of the United States."[33] The statute was intended to establish federal jurisdiction for civil redress against violations of customary international law norms, such as acts of piracy, mistreatment of ambassadors, and violation of safe conducts. It lay largely dormant until human rights lawyers discovered it in the 1980s as a means for foreign plaintiffs to bring civil suit in U.S. federal courts against individuals of any nationality, if they are present in the United States, for certain egregious human rights abuses they committed abroad and, a decade later, for such suits against corporations.

The issue before the Supreme Court in *Kiobel* was whether the ATS applies to corporations.[34] The arguments on this point hinged on an arcane but fundamental point: does international law need to state specifically that prohibitions of egregious human rights violations extend to particular types of actors, such as corporations? The argument on the plaintiffs' side, presented by veteran human rights lawyer Paul Hoffman, was that international law frequently goes no further than to proscribe acts without specifying the actors to which the prohibition is intended to apply, leaving that question to be decided by individual national jurisdictions. According to this view, one looks to international law only to determine the content of the international law norm that is alleged to have been violated, while in this instance U.S. federal common law provides the appropriate basis for attributing liability to corporations. On Shell's side, the counterargument, made by Kathleen Sullivan, former Stanford Law School dean and highly regarded constitutional lawyer, was that the ATS requires international law not only to proscribe the acts but also to specify the actor that can be held liable for the violation. There is no international law, she contended, "that holds corporations liable for the human rights offenses alleged here," only natural persons. In the course of making that case in her oral argument, Sullivan mischaracterized a conclusion I had reached in one of my official UN reports surveying this subject and used it to support Shell's position that there is no corporate liability under international law.[35]

A number of justices seemed unconvinced by Hoffman's argument that where international law is silent on the subject of which actors can be held liable for conduct prohibited under international law one looks to domestic law to govern liability—although several justices did see it that way, as did the Obama administration, which filed an amicus brief in support of the plaintiffs.[36] In any event, the skeptical justices quickly moved on to the broader question of extraterritorial jurisdiction. Hoffman had only just finished the second sentence of his oral argument when Justice Anthony M. Kennedy interrupted him. Quoting from an amicus brief in support of Shell submitted on behalf of several U.S. companies, Kennedy questioned whether any other jurisdiction in the world "permits its courts to exercise universal civil jurisdiction over alleged extraterritorial human rights abuses to which the nation has no connection." Justice Samuel

A. Alito, Jr., added "there's no particular connection between the events here and the United States. . . . What business does a case like that have in the courts of the United States?" Chief Justice John G. Roberts pushed this line of questioning to its limits: "If there is no other country where this suit could have been brought, regardless of what American domestic law provides, isn't it a legitimate concern that the suit itself contravenes international law?"[37]

But extraterritoriality was not the issue before the Court; corporate liability was. Extraterritoriality had not been briefed. Thus, shortly after the hearing the Court issued an order directing the parties to reargue the case during its 2012–13 term, and to file supplemental briefs on this question: "Whether and under what circumstances the Alien Tort Statute allows courts to recognize a cause of action for violations of the law of nations occurring within the territory of a sovereign other than the United States." I took that opportunity to submit an amicus brief to the Court setting the record straight on the official UN mandate findings regarding corporate liability under international law as well as extraterritorial jurisdiction: that domestic courts may hold companies liable for human rights violations that rise to the level of international crimes, and that states are generally neither required to, nor prohibited from, exercising extraterritorial jurisdiction over corporations domiciled in their territory and/or jurisdiction provided that there is a recognized jurisdictional basis.[38] Shell's supplemental brief arguing against extraterritoriality is far-reaching. It seeks not only to dismiss the claims against it but also to negate the entire statutory basis making it possible to use U.S. courts as a forum to adjudicate civil liability for gross human rights violations committed abroad—even when those violations are committed by U.S. nationals, and even if the Americans are natural persons. It contends that the ATS does not apply to corporations, including U.S. firms; that as it currently stands, the ATS violates international law because it adjudicates conduct in other jurisdictions; and that, therefore, even for natural persons its reach should be pulled back to cover only violations committed within the jurisdiction of the United States and "possibly" on the high seas.[39] If these arguments were to prevail, there would be little if anything left of the ATS, which for many victims of human rights abuses, ranging from Burmese peasants to Holocaust survivors, has been a critically important means of gaining access to judicial remedy. This led me to pose several fundamental questions about the relationship between corporate social responsibility and corporate litigation in a widely distributed Internet posting:

> [W]hat would the corporate responsibility to respect human rights involve in a case like *Kiobel*? What would it imply for a corporation that proclaims and aspires to socially responsible conduct? My professional encounters with Shell suggest that it has such commitments and takes them seriously. Of course, the company must be free to argue, in the courts and elsewhere, that it met both the law and its wider responsibilities to respect human rights whenever it believes that to be the case. Yet questions remain. Should the corporate responsibility to respect human rights remain entirely divorced from litigation strategy and tactics, particularly where the company has choices about the grounds on which to defend itself? Should the litigation strategy aim to destroy an entire juridical edifice for redressing gross violations of human rights, particularly where other legal grounds exist to protect the company's interests? Or would the commitment to socially responsible conduct include an obligation by the company to instruct its attorneys to avoid such far-reaching consequences where that is possible? And

what about the responsibilities of the company's legal representatives? Would they encompass laying out for their client the entire range of risks entailed by the litigation strategy and tactics, including concern for their client's commitments, reputation, and the collateral damage to a wide range of third parties?

I don't know what the correct answers to these questions are, but because the stakes are so high *Kiobel* may be the ideal case for starting the conversation.[40]

There is no telling at the time of writing what the outcome in this case will be. Human rights litigants and corporate lawyers around the world are watching closely to see how this Supreme Court, which has expanded corporate rights substantially, will rule on corporate liability. It could effectively shut down ATS jurisprudence altogether. It could decide that the statute does not apply to corporations but remains available for use against individual corporate officers, which is how the 2nd Circuit Court of Appeals ruled. Moreover, it is not out of the question that a closely divided Supreme Court might restrict, but not eliminate, the ATS's extraterritorial application by requiring a closer nexus between defendants, including corporations, and the United States—nationality being an established jurisdictional basis in several other areas of the law, as we have seen. That would likely mean a short-term loss for business and human rights, but possibly also produce a longer-term gain. Let me explain.

The ATS has been a significant factor driving the global business and human rights agenda. As in the case of *Kiobel*, charges under the statute have been brought against companies based in other countries as well as U.S. firms. And the ATS's effects have been felt well beyond the strictly legal realm. It has more broadly reinforced the necessity for companies everywhere to develop effective systems to manage the actual and potential adverse human rights impacts of their operations and business relationships. The geographical scope of this particular driving factor would be reduced by restricting the ATS's application to U.S. nationals.

At the same time, on several occasions during the course of my mandate I expressed concern about having so large a fraction of the world's court cases against multinational corporations for involvement in human rights abuses abroad hinge on so quirky—and, as the Supreme Court hearing demonstrated, so poorly understood—a statute in one single country. No other country has a statute like it. All along it has been vulnerable to being repealed by Congress, as the business community has repeatedly urged; or restricted and even thrown out by the Supreme Court, as is now under consideration. Also, because the ATS is subject to so many procedural obstacles, such cases are also extremely costly, especially for plaintiffs in developing countries. Moreover, it also caught my attention that even progressive countries on human rights, such as Canada, the Netherlands, and the United Kingdom, have undertaken only limited efforts to hold their own multinationals liable for such overseas violations in their domestic jurisdictions. This raised the question in my mind whether the ATS's expansive jurisdictional provision, encompassing the overseas conduct of non-American corporations, has made it easier for such governments to resist domestic political pressure to take more robust measures themselves—while at the same time giving them the opportunity to file amicus briefs in ATS cases involving their companies in which they object to the fact that U.S. courts are deciding the cases so they get to have it both ways. A Supreme Court's requirement of a closer nationality link for corporate defendants might alter that political dynamic.

Some American companies and business associations like the U.S. Chamber of Commerce might protest that a ruling requiring a closer nationality link would put U.S. business at a competitive disadvantage vis-à-vis competitors based elsewhere—although it might be difficult for them to manage the optics of doing so in relation to acts that rise to the level of crimes against humanity. In any event, there is a precedent of U.S. law in a related area creating such an asymmetry, and it tells an interesting story.[41] Congress adopted the Foreign Corrupt Practices Act (FCPA) in 1977, making it a criminal offense for American citizens and firms to bribe officials in foreign countries. The U.S. business community sought to have the FCPA repealed but failed. Subsequently, companies and business associations gradually became advocates for the adoption of a multilateral convention that would create a level playing field. It took time, but in 1997 the OECD adopted the "Convention on Combating Bribery of Foreign Public Officials in International Business Transactions," and the United Nations followed suit in 2003 with the "UN Convention Against Corruption." Because not all countries recognize criminal responsibility of corporations, the conventions also provide for comparable noncriminal sanctions.

As my UN mandate drew to a close, governments invited me to make recommendations regarding priority issues for any follow-up process. In February 2011, a year before the Supreme Court *Kiobel* hearing, I submitted a memorandum to all UN member states and posted it on my Web site, outlining two main bundles of issues. One was "embedding the Guiding Principles"—focused on dissemination, implementation, and capacity building, which the UN working group that has succeeded my mandate is tasked with. The other I called "clarifying certain international legal standards."[42] The following was becoming clear, I reported:

National jurisdictions have divergent interpretations of the applicability to business enterprises of international standards prohibiting gross human rights abuses, potentially amounting to international crimes. These typically arise in areas where the human rights regime cannot be expected to function as intended, such as armed conflict or other areas of heightened risk. . . . Greater legal clarity is needed for victims and business enterprises alike.

One way to resolve the issue of divergent interpretations, I suggested, is through an international legal instrument modeled on the UN Convention Against Corruption.

Any such effort should help clarify standards relating to appropriate investigation, punishment and redress where business enterprises cause or contribute to such abuses, as well as what constitutes effective, proportionate and dissuasive sanctions. It would also address when the extension of jurisdiction abroad may be appropriate, and the acceptable bases for the exercise of such jurisdiction.

The UN working group that has succeeded my mandate is empowered to "make recommendations at the national, regional and international levels for enhancing access to effective remedies available to those whose human rights are affected by corporate activities, including those in conflict areas."[43] In my view, irrespective of how the U.S. Supreme Court rules in *Kiobel,* proposing that governments consider negotiating a carefully crafted legal instrument that clarifies the steps that need to be taken when international law prohibitions of the worst human rights abuses are violated by legal persons should be a leading candidate. The international community no longer regards state sovereignty as a legitimate shield behind which such abuses can take place with impunity; the same surely must be true of the corporate form.

IV. CONCLUSION

Business is a primary source of investment and job creation, and markets can be highly efficient means for allocating scarce resources. They constitute powerful forces capable of generating economic growth, reducing poverty, and increasing demand for the rule of law, thereby contributing to the realization of a broad spectrum of human rights. But markets work optimally only if they are embedded within broader social and legal norms, rules, and institutional practices. Markets themselves require these to survive and thrive, while society needs them to manage the adverse effects of market dynamics and produce the public goods that markets undersupply. Indeed, history teaches us that markets pose the greatest risks—to society and to business itself—when their scope and power far exceed the reach of the institutional underpinnings that allow them to function smoothly and ensure their political sustainability. Ours is such a time, and how to adapt the human rights regime to provide more effective protection to individuals and communities against corporate-related human rights harm is one of our core governance challenges.

Multinational corporations operate globally. Political authority remains fragmented and anchored in territorial states. International organizations cannot adequately compensate for the resulting governance gaps because they simultaneously lack the global reach of markets, firms, and civil society actors on one side, while remaining tightly constrained by territorial states on the other side. Thus, the elements of any solution must involve not only states and cooperation among them but also draw upon the interests, capacities, and engagement of market actors, civil society, and the intrinsic power of the idea of human rights itself. The UN Guiding Principles on Business and Human Rights, at one and the same time, express the potential of this "polycentric" approach to addressing business and human rights governance gaps, and constitute a normative platform and policy guidance for driving it into the policies of states, corporations, and other social actors.

My mandate ended on June 16, 2011, when the UN Human Rights Council endorsed the Guiding Principles. The fact that other standard-setting bodies, national and international, have also adopted core elements of the Guiding Principles, and that each is proceeding with its own implementation process, has added to the prospects for positive and cumulative change. Equally important has been the uptake by those who are directly involved with these challenges on a daily basis: affected individuals, communities, companies, civil society organizations, and governments. In this final chapter, I have suggested additional steps to build on, and in some instances take us beyond, the Guiding Principles. My working hypothesis when I set out on this journey was that it might be possible for such a UN mandate to generate an unfolding dynamic that would lead to greater protection against corporate-related human rights harm and contribute, thereby, to a socially sustainable globalization. I cannot foresee how transformative these efforts will be in the long run. But looking back now a little more than a year after the Human Rights Council decision, that possibility seems considerably less hypothetical than even I had dared imagine.

NOTES

Introduction: Why Business and Human Rights?

1 I borrow this phrase from Thomas Risse, "The Power of Norms versus the Norms of Power: Transnational Civil Society and Human Rights," in Ann M. Florini, ed., *The Third Force: The Rise of Transnational Civil Society* (Washington, DC: Carnegie Endowment, 2000).

2 Tagi Sagafi-nejad, *The UN and Transnational Corporations: From Code of Conduct to Global Compact* (Bloomington: Indiana University Press, 2008).

3 "Draft Norms on the Responsibilities of Transnational Corporations and Other Business Enterprises with Regard to Human Rights," UN Document E/CN.4/Sub.2/2003/12/Rev. 2 (2003).

4 "Doing the Wrong Thing: Human-Rights Activists Fall out Over How to Deal with Companies," *The Economist*, October 27, 2007.

5 Statement on file with the author.

6 "The FIDH welcomes the dialogue with the Special Representative of the Secretary General on human rights and transnational corporations," September 15, 2005 (letter on file with author).

7 Guy Sebban and Antonio Penalosa, "Initial IOE-ICC Views on the Mandate of the UN Special Representative on 'Business and Human Rights,'" October 14, 2005 (letter on file with author).

8 UNCTAD, *World Investment Report 2002* (New York: UNCTAD, 2002), p. 7.

9 The London-Based Business and Human Rights Resource Centre keeps track of companies' human rights policies. http://www.business-humanrights.org/.

10 http://www.un.org/en/documents/udhr/.

11 http://www.hrweb.org/legal/cpr.html.

12 http://www2.ohchr.org/english/law/cescr.htm.

13 http://www.ilo.org/declaration/thedeclaration/textdeclaration/lang
    --en/index.htm.

14 For an extensive empirical study, see L. T. Wells and Rafiq Ahmed,
    Making Foreign Investment Safe (New York: Oxford University Press,
    2007).

15 Liezel Hill, "Canadian Lawmakers Vote Down Controversial Bill
    C-300," http://www.miningweekly.com/article/canadian-mps-vote-
    against-bill-c-300-2010-10-28.

16 Amartya Sen, "Human Rights and the Limits of the Law," *Cardozo
    Law Review* 27, no. 6 (2006).

17 Amartya Sen, *The Idea of Justice* (Cambridge, MA: Harvard Univer-
    sity Press, 2009), pp. 357–58.

18 Amartya Sen, "Elements of a Theory of Human Rights," *Philosophy
    and Public Affairs*, 32 (Autumn 2004), p. 319.

19 Jane Perlez and Lowell Bergman, "Tangled Strands in Fight over
    Peru Gold Mine," *New York Times*, October 25, 2005.

20 http://www.infomine.com/minesite/minesite.asp?site=yanacocha.

21 Omar Mariluz, "Peru Protesters Dig in Heels After Newmont Mine
    Halted," http://www.reuters.com/article/2011/11/30/peru-newmont
    -conga-idUSL4E7MU10820111130, story filed on November 30,
    2011.

22 http://www.pbs.org/frontlineworld/stories/peru404/.

23 "Peru Prime Minister: Stalled Conga Mine's Review to Focus on
    Water," *Dow Jones Newswires,* January 24, 2012.

24 CAO Exit Report: "Regarding Two Complains Filed with the CAO
    in Relation to Minera Yanacocha, Cajamarca, Peru," Office of the
    Compliance Advisor/Ombudsman, International Finance Corpora-
    tion, Multilateral Investment Agency, p. 3.

25 Angel Paez, "UN Mission Probes Private Security," IPS News, Feb-
    ruary 7, 2007, http://ipsnews.net/news.asp?idnews=36478.

26 *Interim Report of the Special Representative of the Secretary-General on the
    Issue of Human Rights and Transnational Corporations and Other Business
    Enterprises*, UN Document E/CN.4/2006/97 (February 22, 2006).

27 Samuel Moyn, *The Last Utopia: Human Rights in History* (Cambridge,
    MA: Belknap Press, 2010), p. 9.

28 For discussions relevant to our concerns here, see Larry Catá Backer,

"From Institutional Misalignments to Socially Sustainable Governance: The Guiding Principles for the Implementation of the United Nations' 'Protect, Respect and Remedy' Framework and the Construction of Inter-Systemic Governance," electronic copy available at http://ssrn.com/abstract=1922953; and Kenneth W. Abbott and Duncan Snidal, "Strengthening International Regulation Through Transnational New Governance: Overcoming the Orchestration Deficit," *Vanderbilt Journal of Transnational Law* 42 (March 2009). Also see John Gerard Ruggie, "Reconstituting the Global Public Domain: Issues, Actors, and Processes," *European Journal of International Relations* 10 (December 2004).

29 John Gerard Ruggie, "Business and Human Rights: The Evolving International Agenda," *American Journal of International Law* 101 (October 2007).

30 Joseph S. Nye, *The Future of Power* (New York: Perseus Books, 2011).

Chapter 1: The Challenge

1 David Barboza, "After Suicides, Scrutiny of China's Grim Factories," *New York Times,* June 6, 2010.

2 Charles Duhigg and Keith Bradsher, "How the U.S. Lost Out on iPhone Work," *New York Times,* January 21, 2012.

3 Simon Zadek, "The Path to Corporate Responsibility," *Harvard Business Review* 82 (December 2004).

4 Jennifer Burns and Debora Spar, "Hitting the Wall: Nike and International Labor Practices," *HBS Case 9-700-047* (Boston: Harvard Business Publishing, 2002).

5 Ibid.; and CBS Street Stories, "Just Do it; Nike Cheap-Labor Factories in Indonesia," *CBS News Transcripts,* July 2, 1993.

6 Sydney Schanberg and Marie Dorigny, "Six Cents an Hour," *Life,* June 1996.

7 Burns and Spar, "Hitting the Wall."

8 The following, based on news accounts, is not an exhaustive rendering.

9 Klein cleverly called Nike "unswooshworthy." Naomi Klein, *No Logo* (New York: Picador, 2002), p. 203.

10 John Cushman, "Nike Pledges to End Child Labor and Apply U.S. Rules Abroad," *New York Times,* May 13, 1998.

11 http://www.business-humanrights.org/Categories/Lawlawsuits/

Lawsuitsregulatoryaction/LawsuitsSelectedcases/Nikelawsuit KaskyvNikeredenialoflabourabuses?&batch_start=51.

12 Nike not only became a pioneer in supply-chain monitoring, but it also turned over its own internal monitoring data to Professor Richard Locke of the MIT Sloan School of Management for analysis and publication, which has deepened our understanding of the process and its limits. See Richard Locke, Fei Qin, and Alberto Brause, "Does Monitoring Improve Labor Standards? Lessons from Nike," http://www.reports-and-materials.org/Does-Monitoring-Improve -Labor-Standards-July-2006.pdf.

13 Mark Whitaker, "It Was Like Breathing Fire," *Newsweek*, December 17, 1984.

14 http://bhopal.net/.

15 Sanjoy Hazarika, "Bhopal Details Remain Unresolved," *New York Times*, February 16, 1989.

16 Bhopal Information Center (Union Carbide Web site), "Chronology," www.bhopal.com/chrono.htm.

17 Ajoy Bose, "Gas Leak Starts Criminal Action: US Company Union Carbide Faces Legal Action over Gas Leak at Bhopal, India," *The Guardian* (London), December 7, 1984.

18 William Claiborne, "American Lawyers Flock to Bhopal: 'Get Union Carbide' is their Slogan," *Washington Post*, December 12, 1984.

19 Julia Khou and Debora Spar, "Union Carbide's Bhopal Plant," *HBS Case, 9-796-035* (Boston: Harvard Business Publishing, 1996).

20 *In re Union Carbide* 634 F.Supp 842 (1986), 866.

21 U.S. Court of Appeals, case 809F.2d 195 (2nd Cir. 1987).

22 "Bhopal Trial: Eight Convicted over India Gas Disaster," BBC News, http://news.bbc.co.uk/2/hi/south_asia/8725140.stm. Warren Anderson, the American then-chairman of the U.S. parent company, has been the subject of an Indian arrest warrant since shortly after the disaster struck.

23 The seminal work was Terry Lynn Karl, *The Paradox of Plenty: Oil Booms and Petro-States* (Berkeley: University of California Press, 1997); see also Karl, "Understanding the Resource Curse," in *Covering Oil: A Reporter's Guide to Energy and Development* (New York: Open Society Institute, 2005), available at http://www.soros.org/sites/ default/files/osicoveringoil_20050803.pdf.

24 See, for example, two recent reports from the respected International Crisis Group (ICG): "Nigeria: Ogoni Land After Shell," Africa Briefing No. 54 (September 18, 2008), and "Nigeria: Seizing the Moment

in the Niger Delta," Africa Briefing no. 60 (April 30, 2009); also Lynn Sharp Paine and Mihnea C. Moldoveanu, "Royal Dutch/Shell in Nigeria (A)," *HBS Case No. 9-399-126* (Boston: Harvard Business Publishing, 2000).

25 *"Chop Fine": The Human Rights Impact of Local Government Corruption and Mismanagement in Rivers State, Nigeria*, Human Rights Watch, January 31, 2007.

26 http://web.worldbank.org/WBSITE/EXTERNAL/COUNTRIES/ AFRICAEXT/NIGERIAEXTN/0,,menuPK:368906~pagePK :141132~piPK:141107~theSitePK:368896,00.html.

27 ICG, Africa Briefing no. 54.

28 Ibid.

29 Ibid.

30 Luc Zandvliet and Mary B. Anderson, *Getting It Right: Making Corporate-Community Relations Work* (Sheffield, UK: Greenleaf, 2009).

31 http://www.waado.org/nigerdelta/RightsDeclaration/Ogoni.html.

32 ICG, Africa Briefing no. 54.

33 Quoted in ibid, p. 6.

34 See my "Clarifying the Concepts of 'Sphere of Influence' and 'Complicity'," *Report of the Special Representative of the Secretary-General on the Issue of Human Rights and Transnational Corporations and Other Business Enterprises, John Ruggie*, UN Document A/HRC/8/16, May 15, 2008.

35 Matthew Green and Michael Peel, "Shell Faces Saro-Wiwa Death Claim," *Financial Times*, April 3, 2009.

36 The Statute reads in full: "The district courts shall have original jurisdiction of any civil action by an alien for a tort only, committed in violation of the law of nations or a treaty of the United States." (U.S. Code, Title 28, Section 1350.)

37 Most have been dismissed on various procedural grounds, which in many cases are under appeal. Several have been settled. In the only major corporate case to go to a jury trial thus far, *Bowoto v. Chevron*, the company won.

38 Paul Lewis, "Blood and Oil: After Nigeria Represses, Shell Defends Its Record," *New York Times*, February 13, 1996; Chris McGreal, "A Tainted Hero," *The Guardian* (London), March 23, 1996; Steve Kretzman, "Hired Guns: Shelling Out for Murder," *In These Times* 21, no. 6 (February 3–16, 1997).

39 "Nigeria: Delta Blues," *The Economist*, February 13, 1999; Kretzman, "Hired Guns"; ICG, Africa Briefing no. 54.

40 McGreal, "A Tainted Hero."

41 SPDC Press Statement, October 31, 1995, quoted in Bronwen Manby, *The Price of Oil: Corporate Responsibility and Human Rights Violations in Nigeria's Oil Producing Communities* (New York: Human Rights Watch, 1999).

42 Several former Shell and BP executives had already formed the Amnesty International UK Business Group, but according to the group's founder, "Shell's experience in Nigeria and, later, BP's in Colombia provided us with a platform and breakthrough." See Sir Geoffrey Chandler, "The Amnesty International UK Business Group: Putting Human Rights on the Corporate Agenda," *Journal of Corporate Citizenship* 33 (Spring 2009), p. 31.

43 Michael D. Goldhaber, "A Win for Wiwa, a Win for Shell, a Win for Corporate Human Rights," *American Lawyer*, June 11, 2009.

44 For a mapping of countries and tools, see "Internet Censorship Worldwide," available at http://opennet.net.

45 Mure Dickie, "China Traps Online Dissent," *Financial Times*, November 12, 2007.

46 Rebecca MacKinnon, "Asia's Fight for Web Rights," *Far Eastern Economic Review*, April 2008, available at http://www.feer.com/essays /2008/april/asias-fight-for-web-rights.

47 Quoted in ibid.

48 "U.S. Rebukes Yahoo over China Case," http://news.bbc.co.uk/1/hi/ technology/7081458.stm.

49 Summarized in Rebecca MacKinnon, *Consent of the Networked: The Worldwide Struggle for Internet Freedom* (New York: Perseus, 2012).

50 http://www.globalnetworkinitiative.org/.

51 For example, Yahoo was convicted and fined in a Belgian court—a country in which it has no physical presence, unlike in China— for refusing to release user information to Belgian authorities in connection with a criminal investigation into credit card fraud using Yahoo email accounts. The ruling could set a precedent for any country demanding the release of user identity of anyone, anywhere. The case is on appeal. http://www.techcrunch .com/2009/03/02/yahoo-fined-by-belgian-court-for-refusing-to-give- up-e-mail-account-info/.

52 David Barboza and Miguel Helft, "A Compromise Allows Both China and Google to Claim a Victory," *New York Times*, July 10, 2010; Loretta Chao and Amir Efrati, "China Renews Google's License," *Wall Street Journal*, July 11, 2010.

53 *Wall Street Journal*, January 12, 2012.

54 MacKinnon, *Consent of the Networked.*

55 Timothy Williams, "China Oil Deal Is New Source of Iraqi Strife,"
    New York Times, September 6, 2009. See also Mary Fitzgerald, "Zam-
    bia Becomes Shorthand for What Can Go Wrong," *Irish Times*,
    August 25, 2008; Ian Evans, "Dockers' Protest Forces Arms Cargo
    Away from Durban port," http://www.zimbabwesituation.com/
    apr19a_2008.html. "China's African Dilemma," *The Straits Times* (Sin-
    gapore), April 28, 2007; "Revolt in the Andes," *The Economist*, Septem-
    ber 20, 2007. In an unprecedented step, the Global Compact Board
    agreed to discuss the case of PetroChina, after a protest against its
    membership by more than eighty civil society groups: "Groups Ask
    the UN Initiative to Remove PetroChina as a Participant Unless it
    Acts to Help End Human Rights Violations in Sudan," http://www
    .corporatejustice.org/Over-80-organizations-ask-Global,431.html.

56 "Concern Grows over Peruvian Protests," *E&MJ Engineering and
    Mining Journal* 22 (December 2011), available at http://www.e-mj.com/
    index.php/news/leading-developments/1478-concern-grows-over-
    peruvian-protests.html.

57 Tania Branigan and Julian Borger, "China Looks to British Experi-
    ence for African Expansion," http://www.guardian.co.uk/world/2009/
    may/21/chinese-companies-investment-africa. On the development of
    standards for Chinese companies in Africa, see Simon Zadek et al.,
    "Responsible Business in Africa: Chinese Business Leaders' Per-
    spectives on Performance and Enhancement Opportunities," *Work-
    ing Paper #54*, Corporate Social Responsibility Initiative, John F.
    Kennedy School of Government, Harvard University (November
    2009).

58 http://www.business-humanrights.org/. The Centre also hosts my
    mandate's portal.

59 For the full report, including capsule case descriptions, see "Cor-
    porations and Human Rights: A Survey of the Scope and Patterns
    of Alleged Corporate-Related Human Rights Abuse," *Report of the
    Special Representative of the Secretary-General on the Issue of Human Rights
    and Transnational Corporations and Other Business Enterprises, John Rug-
    gie*, UN Document A/HRC/8/5/Add.2, available at http://www
    .reports-and-materials.org/Ruggie-2-addendum-23-May-2008.pdf.

60 While there is no agreed definition or list of "gross" or "egregious"
    violations, there is general consensus that the category includes
    extrajudicial killings. See United Nations Basic Principles and
    Guidelines on the Right to a Remedy and Reparation for Victims of

Gross Violations of International Human Rights Law and Serious Violations of International Humanitarian Law (General Assembly Resolution 60/147).

61 "Vienna Declaration and Programme of Action," UN Document A/CONF.157/23 (July 12, 1993).

62 *Interim Report of the Special Representative of the Secretary-General on the Issue of Human Rights and Transnational Corporations and Other Business Enterprises*, UN Document E/CN.4/2006/97 (February 2006), paragraphs 24–32.

63 The index measures the extent to which people have confidence in and abide by the rules in their societies. See http://www.worldbank.org/wbi/governance/govdata/.

64 The index ranks more than 150 countries in terms of perceived levels of corruption, as determined by expert assessments and opinion surveys. See http://www.transparency.org/policy_and_research/surveys_indices/cpi.

65 See http://www.freedomhouse.org/template.cfm?page=15&year=2005.

66 ICMM, "Second Submission to the UN Secretary-General's Special Representative on Human Rights and Business," October 2006, http://www.icmm.com/document/216.

67 Chiquita disclosed these payments to the government.

68 Michael Evans, " 'Para-Politics' Goes Bananas," *The Nation*, April 4, 2007.

69 Quoted in Gary Marx, "Colombian Official Seeks US Papers on Chiquita," *Chicago Tribune*, March 22, 2007.

70 A suit has also been brought against Chiquita by the survivors of men killed by one of the guerilla groups, the Revolutionary Armed Forces of Colombia (FARC).

71 Talisman held a 25 percent share in the Greater Nile Petroleum Company, which also included the China National Petroleum Company, Petronas of Malaysia, and the Sudan National Petroleum Corporation.

72 Ian Fischer, "Oil Flowing in Sudan, Raising the Stakes in its Civil War," *New York Times*, October 17, 1999.

73 "Human Security in Sudan: The Report of a Canadian Assessment Mission." Prepared for the Minister of Foreign Affairs, January 2000, available at http://www.reliefweb.int/library/documents/can sudan2.pdf. Talisman's operation, which included the airstrip, was a joint venture with Sudan.

74 The case was *Presbyterian Church of Sudan v. Talisman Energy, Inc.*, No.

07-0016, decided October 2, 2009. In an address to the International Commission of Jurists "Access to Justice Workshop" in Johannesburg, South Africa (October 29, 2009), I noted that this test "went against the weight of international legal opinion," and added: "As long as an I.G. Farben intended only to make money, not to exterminate Jews, [the *Talisman* standard] would make it permissible for such a company to keep supplying a government with massive amounts of Zyklon B. poison gas knowing precisely what it is used for." http://www.business-humanrights.org/SpecialRepPortal/Home/Speechesinterviews/2009.

75 UN Document S/PRST/2000/20, June 2, 2000.

76 UN Document S/2003/1027, October 23, 2003, paragraph 10.

77 Ibid., paragraph 9.

78 S/2001/357, paragraph 15.

79 See, for example, the comments to this effect by Patrick Mazimhaka, special envoy of Rwandan President Paul Kagame, quoted in Charles Cobb, Jr., "Congo-Kinshasa: Dispute over UN Congo Report Clouds Peace Effort," *allAfrica.com*, May 4, 2001, available at http://allafrica.com/stories/200105040437.html.

Chapter 2: No Silver Bullet

1 Elliott Schrage, now a senior executive at Facebook, speaking at the 2005 Annual Conference of Business for Social Responsibility.

2 UN Document E/CN.4/Sub.2/2003/12/Rev.2, August 26, 2003.

3 Louis Henkin, "The Universal Declaration at 50 and the Challenge of Global Markets," *Brooklyn Journal of International Law* 17 (April 1999), p. 25.

4 "State Responsibilities to Regulate and Adjudicate Corporate Activities Under the United Nations Core Human Rights Treaties: An Overview of Treaty Body Commentaries," *Report of the Special Representative of the Secretary-General on the Issue of Human Rights and Transnational Corporations and Other Business Enterprises,* UN Document A/HRC/4/35/Add.1 (February 13, 2007).

5 CESCR, General Comment 18, paragraph 52.

6 HRC, General Comment 31, paragraph 8.

7 "Basic Principles and Guidelines on the Right to a Remedy and Reparation for Victims of Gross Violations of International Human

Rights Law and Serious Violations of International Humanitarian Law," A/RES/60/147, March 21, 2006. "Gross" and "egregious" mean the same thing; in U.S. courts the term "atrocities" or "heinous" is often used to refer to the same category of acts.

8 *Kiobel v. Royal Dutch Petroleum Co.*, United States Court of Appeals for the 2nd Circuit, 05-4800-cv, 04-4876-cv, decided September 17, 2010.

9 Anita Ramasastry and Robert C. Thompson, *Commerce, Crime, and Conflict: Legal Remedies for Private Sector Liability for Grave Breaches of International Law* (Oslo: Fafo, 2006).

10 I commissioned a comparative study of extraterritoriality in different areas of law (see Jennifer A. Zerk, "Extraterritorial Jurisdiction: Lessons for the Business and Human Rights Sphere from Six Regulatory Areas," available at http://www.hks.harvard.edu/m-rcbg/ CSRI/publications/workingpaper_59_zerk.pdf) and convened two international expert consultations on the subject.

11 See, for example, General Comment 15, paragraph 33.

12 David Weissbrodt and Muria Kruger, "Norms on the Responsibilities of Transnational Corporations and Other Business Enterprises with Regard to Human Rights," *American Journal of International Law* 97 (October 2003), p. 901.

13 David Kinley and Junko Tadaki, *From Talk to Walk: The Emergence of Human Rights Responsibilities for Corporations at International Law*, 44 Va. J. Int'l L. 931 (2004).

14 Philip Alston, "'Core Labor Standards' and the Transformation of the International Labour Rights Regime," *European Journal of International Law* 15, no. 3 (2004), rejecting even the ILO's core labor standards on these grounds.

15 "Draft Norms," paragraph 1.

16 Office of the High Commissioner for Human Rights, *The Global Compact and Human Rights: Understanding Sphere of Influence and Complicity* (Geneva: OHCHR, 2004).

17 Philip Alston, "The 'Not-a-Cat' Syndrome: Can the International Human Rights Regime Accommodate Non-State Actors?" in Alston, ed., *Non-State Actors and Human Rights* (New York: Oxford University Press, 2005) 3, 13–14.

18 Ibid.

19 David Weissbrodt and Muria Kruger, "Human Rights Responsibilities of Businesses as Non-State Actors," in Alston, *Non-State Actors*, p. 340.

20 John H. Knox, "The Ruggie Rules: Applying Human Rights Law to Corporations," in Radu Mares, ed., *The UN Guiding Principles on Business and Human Rights: Foundations and Implementation* (Leiden: Martinus Nijhoff, 2010), p. 54.

21 Unlike other NGO statements I quote, this email was not made public by its author. Therefore, I have deleted the name of the organization after the first "we." The email was dated January 17, 2006.

22 *Interim Report of the Special Representative*, paragraphs 59 and 69.

23 "'Principled Pragmatism' or Mere Antagonism? How Professor Ruggie's Censure of the Norms on TNCs has Affected the Stakeholder Initiative," *Human Rights Features*, September 18–24, 2006.

24 Letter to author, dated April 27, 2006.

25 "Interview: Louise Arbour," *Financial Times*, January 8, 2008.

26 For a detailed history of the failed attempt to negotiate a code of conduct on transnational corporations, which began in 1977 and was suspended in 1992, see Tagi Sagafi-nejad, *The UN and Transnational Corporations: From Code of Conduct to Global Compact* (Bloomington: Indiana University Press, 2008).

27 South Africa, Department of Trade and Industry, "Bilateral Investment Treaty Policy Framework Review," June 2009, p. 5.

28 See, among others, Thomas Risse, Stephen C. Ropp, and Kathryn Sikkink, *The Power of Human Rights* (New York: Cambridge University Press, 1999); Oona Hathaway, "Do Human Rights Treaties Make a Difference?" *Yale Law Journal* 111 (June 2002); Emilie Hafner-Burton and James R. Ron, "Seeing Double: Human Rights Impact Through Qualitative and Quantitative Eyes," *World Politics* 61 (April 2009); and Beth Simmons, *Mobilizing for Human Rights* (New York: Cambridge University Press, 2009).

29 Thomas Risse and Stephen Ropp, Introduction to a forthcoming book, *From Commitment to Compliance: The Persistent Power of Human Rights*, ed. Thomas Risse, Stephen Ropp, and Kathryn Sikkink, manuscript, p. 7.

30 International Law Commission, "Fragmentation of International Law: Difficulties Arising from the Diversification and Expansion of International Law," UN Document A/CN.4/L.682 (April 13, 2006).

31 http://italaw.com/documents/SuezVivendiAWGDecisiononLiability.pdf, paragraph 262.

32 Article 53 of the Vienna Convention on the Law of Treaties, UN Treaty Series 1155, 331.

33 Andreas L. Paulus, "From Territoriality to Functionality? Towards a Legal Methodology of Globalization," in Ige F. Dekker and Wouter G. Werner, *Governance and International Legal Theory* (Leiden: Martinus Nijhoff, 2004), p. 73. The same is true of the overlapping category of *erga omnes* obligations, which states are said to owe to the international community as a whole.

34 Andreas Fischer-Lescano and Gunther Teubner, "Regime-Collisions: The Vain Search for Legal Unity in the Fragmentation of Global Law," *Michigan Journal of International Law* 25 (2003–4), p. 1004.

35 See C. K. Prahalad and Stuart L. Hart, *The Fortune at the Bottom of the Pyramid: Eradicating Poverty Through Profits* (Upper Saddle River, NJ: Prentice Hall, 2005); and Beth Jenkins and Eriko Ishikawa, *Scaling Up Inclusive Business: Advancing the Knowledge and Action Agenda* (International Finance Corporation and Harvard Kennedy School of Government Working Paper, April 2010), http://www.hks.harvard .edu/m-rcbg/CSRI/publications/other_scaling_up_inclusive_ business_4-10.pdf.

36 Michael E. Porter and Mark R. Kramer, "Creating Shared Value," *Harvard Business Review* 89 (January-February 2011).

37 These are posted at http://www.business-humanrights.org/Special RepPortal/Home.

38 This is the subject of a nonbinding declaration adopted by the UN General Assembly, article 1 of which states: "The right to development is an inalienable human right by virtue of which every human person and all peoples are entitled to participate in, contribute to, and enjoy economic, social, cultural and political development, in which all human rights and fundamental freedoms can be fully realized." A/RES/41/128 (December 4, 1986).

39 "Protect, Respect and Remedy: A Framework for Business and Human Rights," *Report of the Special Representative of the Secretary-General on the Issue of Human Rights and Transnational Corporations and Other Business Enterprises, John Ruggie,* UN document A/HRC/8/5 (April 7, 2008), paragraph 7.

Chapter 3: Protect, Respect and Remedy

1 For example, the International Covenant on Civil and Political Rights and the Convention on the Rights of the Child use "respect

and ensure," with "respect" in the state context meaning that the state must refrain from violating the rights. The Convention on the Rights of Persons with Disabilities requires states parties to "ensure and promote," and to take appropriate measures to "eliminate" abuse by private "enterprises." The International Convention on the Elimination of All Forms of Racial Discrimination requires that each state party "shall prohibit and bring to an end . . . racial discrimination by any persons, group or organization." The Convention on the Elimination of All Forms of Discrimination Against Women requires states parties "to take all appropriate measures to eliminate discrimination against women by any person, organization or enterprise." In the International Covenant on Economic, Social, and Cultural Rights, states parties undertake "to take steps . . . achieving progressively the full realization of rights," while its rights-specific provisions, such as those dealing with labor, refer to states "ensuring" those rights.

2 "Protect, Respect and Remedy: A Framework for Business and Human Rights," *Report of the Special Representative of the Secretary-General on the Issue of Human Rights and Transnational Corporations and Other Business Enterprises, John Ruggie,* UN Document A/HRC/8/5 (April 7, 2008), paragraph 27.

3 http://www.ifc.org/ifcext/enviro.nsf/AttachmentsByTitle/p_ StabilizationClausesandHumanRights/$FILE/Stabilization+Paper .pdf.

4 Surya P. Subedi, *International Investment Law: Reconciling Policy and Principle* (Oxford: Hart, 2008) p. 60.

5 See letter from Daniel Bethlehem, QC, Legal Adviser, UK Foreign and Commonwealth Office, and my response to Bethlehem, both available at http://www.business-humanrights.org/Search/Search Results?SearchableText=daniel+bethlehem.

6 In phone calls from Office of the Legal Adviser, U.S. Department of State.

7 K. D. Opp, "Norms," in *International Encyclopedia of the Social and Behavioral Sciences,* vol. 10, ed. Neil J. Smelser and Paul B. Baltes (Amsterdam: Elsevier, 2001).

8 International Organization of Employers, International Chamber of Commerce, Business and Industry Advisory Committee to the OECD, "Business and Human Rights: The Role of Business in Weak Governance Zones," December 2006, paragraph 15, available

at http://www.ioe-emp.org/fileadmin/user_upload/documents_pdf/policy_area/esr/csr_eng_governancezones.pdf.

9 *New York Times*, December 18, 2008, p. A35.

10 "Concern Grows over Peruvian Protests," *E&MJ Engineering and Mining Journal* 22 (December 2011), available at http://www.e-mj.com/index.php/news/leading-developments/1478-concern-grows-over-peruvian-protests.html.

11 Business Leaders Initiative on Human Rights, "A Guide for Integrating Human Rights into Business Management," http://www.integrating-humanrights.org/.

12 "Clarifying the Concepts of 'Sphere of influence' and 'Complicity,'" *Report of the Special Representative of the Secretary-General on the Issue of Human Rights and Transnational Corporations and other Business Enterprises, John Ruggie*, UN Document A/HRC/8/16 (May 15, 2008).

13 http://www.ohchr.org/EN/NewsEvents/Pages/AMilestoneforBusinessandHumanRights.aspx.

14 http://www.regjeringen.no/en/dep/ud/press/News/2009/social_responsibility_abroad.html?id=543620, p. 78.

15 http://www.biac.org/statements/investment/08-05_IOE-ICC-BIAC_letter_on_Human_Rights.pdf.

16 http://www.reports-and-materials.org/BLIHR-statement-Ruggie-report-2008.pdf.

17 http://www.hrw.org/en/news/2008/05/19/joint-ngo-statement-eighth-session-human-rights-council.

18 http://ebookbrowse.com/amnesty-submission-to-ruggie-jul-2008-doc-d11711003.

19 Final Statement by UK National Contact Point for the OECD Guidelines for Multinational Enterprises: Afrimex (UK) Ltd., August 28, 2008, paragraphs 41, 64, 77, http://www.berr.gov.uk/files/file47555.doc.

20 Martha Finnemore and Kathryn Sikkink, "International Norm Dynamics and Political Change," *International Organization* 52 (Autumn 1998), p. 913.

21 Available at http://www.ohchr.org/Documents/Issues/Business/2010GA65Remarks.pdf.

22 The Commentary on supply-chain issues is more complex—it takes additional factors into account, including the severity of the abuse and the human rights impact of terminating the relationship. A fuller exposition may be found in an interpretive guide produced by my team, *The Corporate Responsibility to Respect Human Rights*

(Geneva: Office of the High Commissioner for Human Rights, 2011).

23 For an example of the latter, see Mark B. Taylor, Robert C. Thompson, and Anita Ramasastry, "Overcoming Obstacles to Justice," the report of a workshop cosponsored by Amnesty International, Fafo (Norwegian Institute for Applied International Studies), and the Norwegian Peacebuilding Centre, available at http://www.fafo.no/pub/rapp/20165/20165.pdf; and The Corporate Responsibility Coalition (CORE), "The Reality of Rights, Barriers to Accessing Remedies When Business Operates Beyond Borders," http://corporate-responsibility.org/wp/wp-content/uploads/2009/08/reality_of_rights.pdf.

24 Recommendations on follow-up to the mandate," http://www.business-humanrights.org/media/documents/ruggie/ruggie-special-mandate-follow-up-11-feb-2011.pdf.

25 All of the comments quoted below are available at http://www.business-humanrights.org/SpecialRepPortal/Home/Protect-Respect-Remedy-Framework/GuidingPrinciples.

26 http://www.state.gov/r/pa/prs/ps/2011/05/164453.htm.

27 "International Finance Corporation's Policy on Environmental and Social Sustainability," http://www.ifc.org/ifcext/policyreview.nsf/AttachmentsByTitle/Updated_IFC_SFCompounded_August1-2011/$FILE/Updated_IFC_SustainabilityFramework Compounded_August1-2011.pdf.

28 "Communication from the Commission to the European Parliament, The Council, the European Economic, and Social Committee, and the Committee of the Regions," http://ec.europa.eu/enterprise/newsroom/cf/_getdocument.cfm?doc_id=7010.

29 http://www.corporatejustice.org/IMG/pdf/EP_April_2009Ruggie.pdf.

30 Mark Taylor, "The Ruggie Framework: Polycentric Regulation and the Implications for Corporate Social Responsibility," *Nordic Journal of Applied Ethics* 5, no. 1 (2011), http://tapir.pdc.no/pdf/EIP/2011/2011-01-2.pdf.

31 Ibid., p. 24.

32 John Gerard Ruggie, "Business and Human Rights: The Evolving International Agenda," *American Journal of International Law* 101 (October 2007), p. 839.

33 http://www.ohchr.org/Documents/Issues/TransCorporations/HRC%202011_Remarks_Final_JR.pdf.

Chapter 4: Strategic Paths

1 Martha Finnemore and Kathryn Sikkink, "International Norm Dynamics and Political Change," *International Organization* 52 (Autumn 1998).

2 All papers are posted at http://www.business-humanrights.org/ SpecialRepPortal/Home/BriefingDiscussionReferencepapers.

3 http://amlawdaily.typepad.com/amlawdaily/files/wachtell_lipton_ memo_on_global_business_human_rights.pdf.

4 http://amlawdaily.typepad.com/amlawdaily/files/weil_gotshal_ response_to_un_report_on_human_rights_and_business_final.pdf.

5 http://www.reports-and-materials.org/Ruggie-corporate-law-project -Jul-2010.pdf.

6 "Stabilization Clauses and Human Rights," *Report of Research Conducted for the IFC and the United Nations Special Representative to the Secretary-General on Business and Human Rights*, March 11, 2008, http://www.ifc.org/ifcext/enviro.nsf/AttachmentsByTitle/p_ StabilizationClausesandHumanRights/$FILE/Stabilization+Paper.pdf.

7 "Principles for Responsible Contracts: Integrating the Management of Human Rights Risks into State-Investor Contract Negotiations: Guidance for Negotiators," UN Document A/HRC/17/31/Add.3 (May 25, 2011).

8 World Resources Institute, "Development Without Conflict: The Business Case for Community Consent," available at http://pdf.wri .org/development_without_conflict_fpic.pdf.

9 Goldman Sachs Global Investment Research, "Top 190 Projects to Change the World," April 25, 2008.

10 Some of this research is reported in Rachel Davis and Daniel M. Franks, "The Costs of Conflict with Communities," http://www .csrandthelaw.com/uploads/file/Costs%20of%20Conflict.pdf.

11 "Business and Human Rights: Further Steps Toward the Operationalization of the 'Protect, Respect and Remedy' Framework," *Report of the Special Representative of the Secretary-General on the Issue of Human Rights and Transnational Corporations and Other Business Enterprises, John Ruggie*, UN Document A/HRC/14/27 (April 9, 2010), paragraph 47.

12 Jennifer A. Zerk, "Extraterritorial Jurisdiction: Lessons for the Business and Human Rights Sphere from Six Regulatory Areas," available at http://www.hks.harvard.edu/m-rcbg/CSRI/publications/ workingpaper_59_zerk.pdf.

13 Karin Buhman, "The Development of the 'UN Framework': A Pragmatic Process Towards a Pragmatic Output," in Radu Mares, ed., *The UN Guiding Principles on Business and Human Rights: Foundations and Implementation* (Leiden: Martinus Nijhoff, 2012).

14 A/HRC/Res.8/7 (15 June 2008), paragraph 3.

15 Buhman, "The Development of the 'UN Framework,'" p. 86.

16 The term originated with Thomas Franck, *The Power of Legitimacy Among Nations* (New York: Oxford University Press, 1990).

17 http://www.business-humanrights.org/SpecialRepPortal/Home.

18 The group included Kofi Annan (Ghana), former Secretary-General of the United Nations; Souhayr Belhassen (Tunisia), President, Fédération Internationale des Ligues des Droits de l'Homme; John Browne (UK), Managing Director of Riverstone Holdings LLC, former Group Chief Executive of BP plc; Maria Livanos Cattaui (Switzerland), member of the Board of Directors, Petroplus Holdings AG, former Secretary General of the International Chamber of Commerce; Stuart Eizenstat (USA), Partner, Covington & Burling LLP, former U.S. Deputy Secretary of the Treasury, Under Secretary of State, Under Secretary of Commerce, Ambassador to the European Union; Luis Gallegos (Ecuador), Ambassador of Ecuador to the United States, former Vice-Chair, UN Commission on Human Rights; Member of the UN Committee Against Torture; Neville Isdell (USA), Chairman of the Board of Directors, The Coca-Cola Company; Hina Jilani (Pakistan), Member of the Council, Pakistan Human Rights Commission, former UN Secretary-General's Special Representative on Human Rights Defenders; Kishore Mahbubani (Singapore), Dean, Lee Kuan Yew School of Public Policy, National University of Singapore, former Ambassador of Singapore to the United Nations; Narayana Murthy (India), Chairman, Infosys Technologies Limited; Sonia Picado (Costa Rica), Chair, Inter-American Institute of Human Rights, former Judge and Vice-Chair of the Inter-American Court of Human Rights; Cyril Ramaphosa (South Africa), Executive Chairman, Shanduka Group, former Secretary General of the African National Congress; Mary Robinson (Ireland), Chair, Realizing Rights: The Ethical Globalization Initiative, former President of Ireland and United Nations High Commissioner for Human Rights; Guy Ryder (UK), General Secretary of the International Trade Union Confederation; and Marjorie Yang (China), Chairman of Esquel Group.

19 http://www.mineafrica.com/documents/A3%20-%20Macleod%20 Dixon1.pdf.

20 http://www.abanow.org/2012/01/2012mm109/.

21 Global Compact Network Netherlands, "How to Conduct Business with Respect for Human Rights," p. 12, available at http://www .unglobalcompact.org/docs/issues_doc/human_rights/Resources/ how_to_business_with_respect_for_human_rights_gcn_netherlands _june2010.pdf.

22 Available at http://www.ihrb.org/pdf/The_State_of_Play_of_Human _Rights_Due_Diligence.pdf.

23 See Caroline Rees and David Vermijs, "Mapping Grievance Mechanisms in the Business and Human Rights Arena," *Corporate Social Responsibility Initiative Report #28*, Kennedy School of Government, Harvard University (January 2008), available at http://www.hks .harvard.edu/m-rcbg/CSRI/publications/Report_28_Mapping.pdf.

24 "Piloting Principles for Effective Company/Stakeholder Grievance Mechanisms: A Report of Lessons Learned," *Report of the Special Representative of the Secretary-General on the Issue of Human Rights and Transnational Corporations and Other Business Enterprises, John Ruggie*, UN Document A/HRC/17/31/Add.1 (May 24, 2011).

25 www.baseswiki.org.

26 http://www.state.gov/secretary/rm/2011/05/164340.htm.

27 Letter on file with author.

28 http://www1.ifc.org/wps/wcm/connect/115482804a0255db96fbffd1a 5d13d27/PS_English_2012_Full-Document.pdf?MOD= AJPERES.

29 Craig N. Murphy and JoAnne Yates, *The International Organization for Standardization (ISO): Global Governance Through Voluntary Consensus* (New York: Routledge, 2009).

30 Sandra Atler, "The Impact of the United Nations Secretary-General's Special Representative and the Framework on the Development of Human Rights Components of ISO 26000," available at http:// www.business-humanrights.org/media/documents/impact-un-special -representative-on-iso-26000-sandra-atler-24-may-2011.pdf.

31 Alan Fine, "Impact of the Work of the UNSG's Special Representative on Business and Human Rights on Deliberations in the Industry Stakeholder Group in ISO's Working Group on Social Responsibility," available at http://www.business-humanrights.org/ media/documents/impact-un-special-representative-on-iso-26000 -alan-fine-24-may-2011.doc.

32 http://www.iso.org/iso/iso_catalogue/management_standards/social_ responsibility.htm.

33 "Communication from the Commission to the European Parliament, the Council, the European Economic and Social Committee, and the Committee of the Regions," http://ec.europa.eu/enterprise/ newsroom/cf/_getdocument.cfm?doc_id=7010.

34 Remarks by Rafendi Djamin, Indonesian Representative to ASEAN Intergovernmental Commission on Human Rights, at Asia Pacific Forum of National Human Rights Institutions Regional Conference on Business and Human Rights, October 11–13, 2011, Seoul, South Korea. Also, the African Union is developing a plan of action called African Mining Vision 2050. It will be based on a preparatory report that states: "The UN Protect, Respect and Remedy Framework offers a useful and comprehensive set of principles which can be applied to the duties of states and the responsibilities of mining firms in respect of the human rights impacts of mineral operations." http://www.au.int/en/sites/default/files/Overview%20of%20the%20 ISG%20Report.pdf

35 Alison Braybrooks, "Why 2011 Was a Landmark Year for Business and Human Rights," (December 16, 2011), available at www.guardian .co.uk/sustainable-business/human-rights-business.

36 ICAR, "Building a Movement for Corporate Accountability," First Annual International Corporate Accountability Roundtable Meeting, Washington, D.C., September 8–9, 2011.

37 http://www.ipieca.org/news/20111114/business-and-human-rights -collaborative-learning-projects-underway.

38 http://www.ipieca.org/news/20110131/ipieca-provides-input-professor -ruggies-draft-final-report-un-human-rights-council.

39 Finnemore and Sikkink, "International Norm Dynamics," p. 897.

40 Ibid.

Chapter 5: Next Steps

1 "Draft Report of the Secretary-General on How the United Nations System as a Whole Can Contribute to the Advancement of the Business and Human Rights Agenda and the Dissemination and Implementation of the Guiding Principles," p. 3.

2 http://www.ohchr.org/EN/Issues/Business/Pages/WGHRand transnationalcorporationsandotherbusiness.aspx.

3 "Draft Report of the Secretary-General."

4 http://ec.europa.eu/enterprise/newsroom/cf/itemdetail.cfm?item_id=5752&lang=en.

5 OECD, "Draft Terms of Reference for Future Work on Due Diligence in the Financial Sector," Note by the Chair of the Working Party of the Investment Committee, DAF/INV/WP/RD(2012)1.

6 "Agreement Between Nidera Holdings B.V. and CEDHA, SOMO, Oxfam Novib, and INCASUR, http://wp.cedha.net/wp-content/uploads/2012/03/CEDHA-et-al-vs-Nidera-joint-public-agreement-25112011.pdf.

7 OECD, "Implementation of the 2011 Update of the OECD Guidelines for Multinational Enterprises," Note by the Chair of the Working Party of the Investment Committee, DAF/INV/WP(2012)4.

8 Based on interviews with participants in March 2012.

9 http://www.iqnet-certification.com/.

10 http://www.mazars.co.uk/Home/News/Latest-news/Survey-Results-Mining-companies-UN-Human-Rights.

11 http://www.rightscon.org/2011/10/silicon-valley-human-rights-standards/.

12 International Organization of Employers, "Guiding Principles on Business and Human Rights: Employers' Guide," http://bclc.uschamber.com/article/employers-guide-un-guiding-principles-business-and-human-rights.

13 International Trade Union Confederation, "The United Nations 'Protect, Respect, Remedy' Framework for Business and Human Rights and the United Nations Guiding Principles for Business and Human Rights: Briefing Note for trade unionists," http://www.ituc-csi.org/IMG/pdf/12-04-12_ruggie_briefing_note.pdf.

14 *Report of the Working Group on the Issue of Human Rights and Transnational Corporations and Other Business Enterprises*, UN Document A/HRC/20/29 (April 10, 2012).

15 See, respectively, http://www.unicef.org.uk/Documents/Publications/PRINCIPLES_23%2002%2012_FINAL.pdf; and http://www.icoc-psp.org/uploads/INTERNATIONAL_CODE_OF_CONDUCT_Final_without_Company_Names.pdf.

16 http://www.unglobalcompact.org/docs/issues_doc/human_rights/Resources/GPs_GC%20note.pdf.

17 http://www.consilium.europa.eu/uedocs/cms_data/docs/pressdata/EN/foraff/129739.pdf.

18 http://www.state.gov/secretary/rm/2012/05/190260.htm.

19 J. E. Alvarez, "The Evolving BIT," *Transnational Dispute Management* (June 2009).

20 Jürgen Kurtz, "The Use and Abuse of WTO Law in Investor-State Arbitration: Competition and Its Discontents," *European Journal of International Law* 20 no. 3 (2009).

21 Email from Thomas Walde to the author, May 21, 2008. Subject line: International human rights treaties justiciable-relevant-applicable in investment disputes. On file with the author. The email was also posted on the OGEMID (oil gas energy infrastructure and investment disputes) internet-based discussion group, which Prof. Walde moderated, so it was not considered private.

22 On this last point, see Dani Rodrik, *The Globalization Paradox* (New York: W. W. Norton, 2011).

23 "Comments on the Model for Future Investment Agreements (English Translation)," December 19, 2007 (copy on file with the author), p. 27.

24 http://www.state.gov/r/pa/prs/ps/2012/04/188199.htm. The full text of the model treaty is available at http://www.state.gov/e/eb/ifd/bit/index.htm.

25 See Advocates for International Development, "Law Firms' Implementation of the Guiding Principles on Business and Human Rights," available at http://www.shiftproject.org/publication/law-firms-implementation-guiding-principles-business-and-human-rights.

26 The presumption of atomization drives the analysis of Radu Mares, "Responsibility to Respect: Why the Core Company Should Act When Affiliates Infringe Human Rights," in Mares, ed., *The UN Guiding Principles on Business and Human Rights: Foundations and Implementation* (Leiden: Martinus Nijhoff, 2011).

27 Larry Catá Backer, "Multinational Corporations, Transnational Law: The United Nations' Norms on the Responsibilities of Transnational Corporations as a Harbinger of Corporate Social Responsibility in International Law," *Columbia Human Rights Review* 37, no. 2 (2005), pp. 169–70.

28 Peter Muchlinski explores potential long-term implications of the GPs for corporate law, in "Implementing the New UN Corporate Human Rights Framework: Implications for Corporate Law, Governance and Regulation, *Journal of Business Ethics,* 22 (January 2012).

29 Section 12.3 of Australia's Criminal Code Act 1995; http://www
.comlaw.gov.au/Series/C2004A04868.

30 Chapter 8 of the U.S. *2006 Federal Sentencing Guidelines Manual*,
§8C2.5(b)(1).

31 Muchlinksi, "Implementing."

32 http://www.americanbar.org/content/dam/aba/publications/
supreme_court_preview/briefs/10-1491_petitioner.authcheckdam
.pdf.

33 28 U.S.C. § 1350.

34 For the transcript of the entire hearing, see http://www.supreme
court.gov/oral_arguments/argument_transcripts/10-1491.pdf.

35 As discussed in earlier chapters, in 2007 I produced a report mapping international human rights standards applicable to companies. I
stressed that "the most consequential legal development" in business
and human rights is "the gradual extension of liability to companies
for international crimes, under domestic jurisdiction but reflecting
international standards." Here is what Sullivan said about this in her
oral argument: "We cite the U.N. special representative, saying 'I
have looked at the international human rights instruments that are
out there, and I find no basis for corporate liability.' That's the U.N.
[speaking], not Congress." Technically the statement is not incorrect.
But one would never know from it that my use of the term "instruments" referred specifically to UN human rights treaties, which
hardly comprise the entirety of relevant international law, and that I
did identify a basis for corporate liability in other areas of law. Shell's
written brief contains the same claim. (For Sullivan's statement,
see "Transcript of Oral Argument," p. 49, available at http://www
.supremecourt.gov/oral_arguments/argument_transcripts/10-1491
.pdf/.)

36 *Kiobel v. Royal Dutch Petroleum*, No. 10-1491 (U.S. Supreme Court),
"Brief for the United Sates as Amicus Curiae Supporting Petition-
ers," December 2011.

37 See "Transcript of Oral Argument."

38 *Kiobel v. Royal Dutch Petroleum*, No. 10-1491 (U.S. Supreme Court),
"Brief *Amici Curiae* of Former UN Special Representative for Business and Human Rights, Professor John Ruggie; Professor Philip
Alston; and the Global Justice Clinic at NYU School of Law in Support of Neither Party," June 12, 2012.

39 *Kiobel v. Royal Dutch Petroleum*, No. 10-1491 (U.S. Supreme Court), "Supplemental Brief for Respondents," August 1, 2012.

40 "Kiobel and Corporate Social Responsibility," Issues Brief, Harvard Kennedy School of Government, September 4, 2012, available at http://www.business-humanrights.org/media/documents/ruggie -kiobel-and-corp-social-resonsibility-sep-2012.pdf.

41 The story is well told by Kenneth W. Abbott and Duncan Snidal, "Values and Interests: International Legalization in the Fight Against Corruption," *Journal of Legal Studies* 31 (January 2002).

42 http://harvardhumanrights.files.wordpress.com/2011/02/mandate -follow-up-final.pdf.

43 A/HRC/RES/17/4, paragraph 6 (e).

INDEX

Page numbers in *italics* refer to figures and tables.